TWAYNE'S WORLD LEADERS SERIES

Max Scheler

TWLS 55

Max Scheler

MAX SCHELER

By EUGENE KELLY

*Manhattan Community College of the
City University of New York*

TWAYNE PUBLISHERS

A DIVISION OF G. K. HALL & CO., BOSTON

Library of Congress Cataloging in Publication Data

Kelly, Eugene, 1941–
   Max Scheler.

   (Twayne's world leaders series ; TWLS 55)
   Bibliography: p. 197–200.
   Includes index.
   1.   Scheler, Max Ferdinand, 1874–1928. I.   Title.
B3329.S484K44   193   76–16774
ISBN   0–8057–7707–5

To Zuzana

Contents

About the Author

Eugene Kelly is a native of New York City, where he attended Queens College. After graduation, he spent three years abroad, first traveling in the Far East and India, later as an exchange student and research fellow in philosophy and comparative literature at the Free University of Berlin and the University of Cologne in Germany. He did most of his graduate work at New York University, where he received the Ph.D. in 1971. Dr. Kelly has worked as a teacher and coordinator of the division of history and philosophy of the CAPP (police department) program of the New York Institute of Technology. He is presently Assistant Professsor in the Social Science Department of the Borough of Manhattan Community College, CUNY.

Foreword

For someone who came into philosophy in the 1930s and matured in the following two decades, the present situation in philosophy, particularly in ethics, presents some very striking changes. My generation shied away from substantive questions of ethics. Under the powerful influence of Positivism, value judgements were looked on as pseudo-statements, disguised emotive expressions of one form or another, and the job of the philosopher was to rip off the disguise. So far as ethics remained a legitimate discipline, its role lay in the logical analysis of value statements, never in the attempt to sort out and judge specific values themselves. Meta-ethics replaced ethics; and if concrete judgements of value appeared at all, they were only by way of illustration, and usually the more trivial they were the better they suited their author's purposes. "The steaks at Barney's are good," for some reason is one of the refrains that haunts me from that period. A whole generation of philosophers failed to deal with the substantive questions of ethics — such was part of the legacy of Positivism. Ideas do have consequences, and not always for the best.

The pendulum has now swung to the opposite extreme: the substantive issues of ethics are what agitate the younger philosophers. Questions of social justice, civil rights, women's rights, abortion, euthanasia, gay liberation, and so on and forth — the more concrete the question the more it engages these philosophers. All this is to the good. It is good for philosophy to get back into the arena; if you are going to deal with ethics at all, your thinking should at least bear upon the material issues that are troublesome in our actual life, rather than box itself into the formalism of logic from which there is never any exit. Better to muddle with the questions of the good life than refine them out of existence.

Still, there is something a little disquieting about this new outburst of material ethics. Its curiosity about philosophic principles seems to be minimal; on the whole it takes the form of a headlong rush back into the old and simple framework of Utilitarianism. And for the most part this framework is accepted so unconsciously, so without question, that the younger people seem to be unaware that there might be any other point of view from which to attack the questions of ethics. One would think that after our long interregnum from substantive ethics, we could take just a little more time now to look around, begin at the beginning again and build from the ground up. Before we embark on a new utilitarian calculus for the quantitative distribution of values in society, we ought to be a little more inquisitive about the nature of value itself: how values arise from, and are grounded in the human condition; and, above all, what intrinsic rank or hierarchy of values, if any, can be established within experience. The time is ripe for a new look at ethical foundations; and it would be regrettable if immediate social issues, however admirable our concern with them may be, should distract us altogether from this search.

All of which is by way of calling attention to Max Scheler as a figure apposite to our time. Scheler, of course, is a figure worth restoring in his own right. He was one of the three major philosophers — Husserl and Heidegger are the other two — of the great period of pre-Hitler Germany, which looms more than ever as one of the vanished high points of modern culture. If his name has lapsed in relation to those two of his contemporaries, part of the reason is that his thought, constantly searching, never left a system that could easily recruit followers. Yet he remains one of the seminal thinkers of the century. I remember the late Hannah Arendt telling me in conversation of the powerful impact Scheler had on the philosophic youth of Germany in the 1920s. And if we turn to him now, I think we shall find that he still retains this extraordinary power of stimulation.

Dr. Eugene Kelly has written an excellent and useful introduction to Scheler's thought, which should be of especial value in our present transitional philosophical situation. He presents his subject in the round, but at sufficient depth so that we can gauge clearly what Scheler is about at the various stages of his thought. The matter of ethics here is not exclusive, but it remains central; for even when Scheler is speculating metaphysically, the speculation is still concerned with our human condition. Dr. Kelly's study is particularly helpful in locating Scheler within the broad spectrum of existential and phenomenological thought that has now become an established part of American philosophy. This book will be welcome both to students of philosophy, who may be led by it to further study of

Foreword

Scheler, and to those general readers who are interested in fresh and stimulating insights on the perennial questions of human life. My hope for it is that it wins the wide public it deserves.

WILLIAM BARRETT

New York University

Preface

Max Scheler has yet to be awarded a place in the history of philosophy. For a time regarded as the leading personality in German philosophy, his star fell as quickly as it rose, and despite efforts to revive his works after 1945, postwar German thought appears to be developing without the frequent references to his name enjoyed by Husserl, Weber, Heidegger, and, of course, Karl Marx. How this came to pass is not hard to understand if we consider how antipathetic Scheler was toward these modes of thought, characterizing the present-day scene as they did his own age: the revival of Marxism, to which Scheler opposes intellectual elitism and a mode of social criticism based upon the ideals of early Christian brotherhood; antimetaphysical schools of positivism and pragmatism, to which he opposes metaphysical constructivism and existential commitment; cultural nihilism, to which he opposes Christian belief and the hope in the development of a world culture. Even during his own times — especially during the post–World War I years — Scheler's thought stood apart from the prevailing intellectual trends, except in matters of method. Once intellectually mature, he never belonged to a philosophical school — hence we must be careful not to read him as a representative even of the phenomenological school. The following he had among students is due at least in part to the attractiveness of his powerful personality and to the fact that he was a man speaking for a high ideal in a time of defeatism and nihilism.

Scheler was born near Munich in 1874. He was of mixed parentage: his father was Protestant and his mother Jewish. It appears that he was raised in, or was converted to, the Catholic faith at an early age, only to leave the Church before the end of his student years. He was educated at Munich and Berlin, and finally at the University of Jena, where his mentor was Rudolf Eucken, a member of the neo-Kantian school, who was later to be a recipient of a Nobel prize for literature. Under his guidance, Scheler prepared a dissertation on the compatibility of the transcendental imperatives of logic and those of ethics. The direction of Scheler's later interests is already visible in this rather difficult little work, which is written in a neo-Kantian jargon that has now largely gone out of fashion. Scheler is raising here the question of man's existence and is discovering in him a divided soul, a cleavage in his essence, such as he was to posit on the basis of different considerations toward the end of his life in *Die Stellung des Menschen im Kosmos*. The anthropological question, posed in the dissertation with urgency, is answered there without despair; he sets himself the task of bringing the parts of man's essential constitution into harmony with one another. But because the division is built into man's nature, any harmonizing will have to be tenuous, and brought about by contingent means. Any treaty between man's warring parts will thus not be without risk, and only possible after long negotiations. Yet throughout Scheler's work, beginning with this dissertation, there is the element of hope in a future in which the balance will be struck, and the spiritual and moral reconstruction of the individual achieved.

Scheler's thought developed rapidly during the years at Jena, where he was retained as a teacher after his *Promotion* in 1889, and his ideas were soon no longer to be contained within the boundaries established by the transcendental method of neo-Kantianism. A work written for the *Habilitation* at Jena two years after the dissertation still defends the transcendental method of philosophy, however, while it rejects the method of psychologism that, Scheler believed, implied the subjugation of the spirit to psychological laws. Yet if the transcendental method could still guarantee for Scheler the autonomy of the human spirit, it was not capable of the wide application his imaginative mind demanded of a philosophical method. Moreover, it seemed not able to grant the certainty that he believed must be the province of philosophy as opposed to the positive sciences. It appears to be not entirely clear what was Scheler's reaction to his first meeting with Husserl in 1901 and to his reading of the latter's *Logische Untersuchungen* after its publication in 1900–01. Yet from this time forth, we observe Scheler philosophizing in a phenomenological key. The transcendental method is subjected to a critique from the point of view of the new method, and Scheler begins to adapt Husserl's method to his own thought.

Scheler's preoccupation with the new method induced him to leave Jena, and in 1907 he requested Husserl to recommend him for a post in Munich. There he joined a circle of people who were attempting to do philosophy along the lines laid down in the

Logische Untersuchungen. He quickly established a reputation for extemporaneous brilliance, which some criticized for a lack of discipline. He wrote little during his years in Munich, concerning himself chiefly with his lectures and discussion with his colleagues.[1] His collected works list no publications for the years between 1901 and 1911. The people who knew him at this time remarked on his vitality and intensity, the range of his interests, and the spellbinding quality of his personality in conversation and in lectures. His tenure at the University of Munich was broken in 1910. He submitted his resignation, Staude tells us, because of the public outcry against an incident relating to his private life.[2]

After leaving Munich, Scheler began to write. He gave a few public lectures and occupied himself mainly with students. This period, which lasted until the outbreak of World War I, was a time of intense philosophical activity. He worked out a rigorous theory of phenomenological method and applied it to an analysis of ethical concepts in what is his most ambitious and probably his greatest work, *Der Formalismus in der Ethik und die materiale Wertethik* (Part I, 1913; Part II, 1916), as well as in a shorter but no less systematic work, *Zur Phänomenologie und Theorie der Sypathiege-fühle und von Liebe und Hass,* which was later expanded to become the better-known *Wesen und Formen der Sympathie.* Both works assert the capacity of the spirit to attain objective and certain truths about value and essence. They contain no speculative metaphysics. These works are occupied with theoretical and methodological problems, for the most part; the divisions in the human spirit that were first attacked in the dissertation and the urgent and concrete problems resulting from these divisions are less evident here. Scheler appears to have embraced various social and political movements with great fervor at this time, but he does not yet place the weight of philosophical analysis behind any specific ideology. Nevertheless, we find essays on specific social and political problems dating from this time: essays on the "rehabilitation of virtue," the women's movement, and the spirit of capitalism and bourgeois values were assembled by the author for publication in 1915.

This patient and composed analysis of abstract philosophical problems and their relevance to the spirit of the times did not survive the outbreak of war. Scheler, a professor without a chair, occupied himself for a time with the German foreign service in Switzerland, but he devoted himself mainly to public lectures and impassioned essays on the German cause and on the political and cultural outlook for Europe. Viewed in general and from some distance in time, these essays are a reaction against the Protestant bourgeois liberalism to which he was exposed as a young man. He was not alone in his reaction; Simmel and Weber on the one hand, active Socialists and Communists on the other, rejected the then-dominant bourgeois materialism and its neo-Kantian ethics erected upon the concept of duty. If Scheler was at one time an enthusiastic frequenter of Ibsen's and Hauptmann's plays, then the intellectual-elitist republicanism he espoused after the Great War represents a certain estrangement from the social values represented by the two great playwrights. Scheler wished to return to precapitalistic values, not "advance" to the values of a broader-based democracy. The reasons for this estrangement lie in his high cultural idealism and his belief in spiritual discipline as a necessary condition of social amelioration. Leadership must be provided by a cultural elite such as the German university system traditionally attempts to produce; it will not be obtained simply by extending democracy to the un-educable masses. As Staude notes, the Junker aristocracy, criticized as a system by more liberal-minded men, is attacked by Scheler only for its failure to live up to its noble traditions and ideals — for becoming, in effect, a titled, nonintellectual bourgeoisie.[3] Scheler's political conservatism makes an interesting contrast with the radically experimental speculative metaphysics toward which *Die Stellung des Menschen im Kosmos* directs us.

The postwar period witnessed fundamental changes in Scheler's world view. Appalled by the destruction and apparent senselessness of the war, he reacted in two ways. On a social and political level, he repudiated his "nationalistic" works; he then began to direct his energies toward the production of a world culture and the reconciliation of national differences, which he believed would be consequent upon its establishment. His goal was not a united world in which *institutional* differences between the nations would be eliminated. Rather, he sought a world in which the peaceful coexistence and the mutual understanding, even the mutual love, of the nations and traditions would be attained. This hope is parallel with his faith in an eventual integration of the warring elements in man's constitution. Indeed, men must integrate themselves as individuals before they can hope for an end to war among the nations.

On the level of Scheler's theory, we can take as an illustration of his faith that the reconciliation of nations and cultures and classes is both possible and necessary, the reawakening in him of his former commitment to the Catholic religion. In 1916 he returned to the Church. Spiegelberg notes that his renewal of membership did not bring about participation in the Sacraments, and we have it from his own writings that it did not imply an adherence to the Thomistic philosophy.[4] Nevertheless, his conversion helped him to obtain a professorship at the University of Cologne, and 1921 saw the publication of *Vom Ewigen im Menschen,* a series of essays that had been written after 1917. Its phenomenological and philosophical analyses reveal a strong Augustinianism, a philosophy of personal engagement, and a faith in the power of Christian love as a means to knowledge of essence and personal salvation. Scheler undoubtedly saw in the practice of the Christian virtues and beliefs the only hope for a Europe in ashes. His essay on repentance and rebirth in *Vom Ewigen im Menschen* is directed as much toward the "spiritual personalities" he attributes to the nations of the world as toward the souls of individual persons.

Scheler, as always a man of crises, underwent his last crisis in the years 1922–24. Seeing the futility of his demand for a Catholicism without Thomism, and having lost, as a result of his researches, his belief in theism, he broke with the Catholic Church. This final period of his work is characterized not only by an increasing interest in speculative metaphysics but also by an attempt to develop a comprehensive philosophy of man on the basis of his earlier phenomenological studies and the contributions of the natural sciences, insofar as the latter are relevant to the special problems he encountered here. The changes in his outlook begun here are incomplete: he died before he was able to complete the systematic works on metaphysics and philosophical anthropology to which he makes frequent reference in his last works. These last works are essays of varying length in which his old problem of the unity of man, so long submerged by abstract philosophy and Christian hope, reappears in his theory of the dualism of vital and spiritual principles, which he discovers in the Ground of Being and thus in man conceived as a microcosm.[5] Sadly, these few works contain all of what we now possess of his metaphysics. He warns us, however, with an insistence expressed by his use of italics for the entire sentence, that "one will only understand the metaphysics of the author when one has read this work"[6] — that is, the never-written first volume of his metaphysics. He undoubtedly wrote more on these topics before his death in 1928, shortly after having begun an appointment at the University of Frankfurt. However, the manuscripts he left have not yet been published.[7]

Scheler's intellectual history can be arranged, on the basis of the foregoing biographical sketch, into three major periods: the "neo-Kantian," the "phenomenological," and the "metaphysical." In each case, he occupies himself with similar problems from different points of view. The themes and problems he took up were not infrequently determined by the intellectual, social, and political climate of his day; for in Scheler we find a balance of the theoretical and the practical that is the essence of philosophy. Thus, as a force for ethical absolutism and philosophical objectivism, Scheler stood practically alone in his age, which had passed through a period characterized by the breakdown of metaphysical and ethical systems and had arrived at the antimetaphysical stance of ethical relativism and pragmatism. Positivism in various forms had replaced the neo-Hegelianism that had for so long dominated thought in the schools and universities of Europe. From its scientific outlook, molded by the enormous influence of Darwin, had emerged a picture of man whose spirit was a function of his biology and whose values were a by-product of his vital interests. The school of neo-Kantianism, on the other hand, to which Scheler at first belonged by virtue of his training under Eucken, represented the Protestant cultural liberalism that had been so severely criticized by Nietzsche, and the breakdown of its systems of values had been heralded by new and revolutionary modes of thought. There seemed to be two possible alternatives to this philosophical picture. One was the maintenance of the older systems of thought, despite the growing destructive criticism; the other was to seek refuge in one of the various forms of irrationalism and intuitionism that were being developed at this time.

For this reason, the writings of Edmund Husserl had a pronounced effect upon those thinkers in Germany who had been touched by the positivist critique of previous philosophers. Husserl's early writings, while officially antimetaphysical, nevertheless provided a framework and a method for attaining absolutely certain knowledge concerning the essential nature of objects of consciousness. Scheler followed Husserl's lead in the investigations he conducted into ethics, sociology, theology, and the philosophy of man, regions of thought that had been most fundamentally shaken by the relativistic tendencies of the critical thinkers.

Eventually, however, Scheler was not to remain content with purely phenomenological inquiries, nor even with practical attacks in public lectures against the ethical relativism he identified with cultural decadence. He went over into the realm of speculative metaphysics in the search for a basis for philosophical and social-political assertions. His epistemological realism, his belief that a phenomenological description of moral and nonmoral values can be employed as a norm for ethical decision making, as well as his later sketch of a metaphysical system, are symptoms of this effort, and we will have to consider whether these attempts constitute a misuse of the phenomenological method he had adopted. Insofar as ethical relativism and nihilism are in part psychological phenomena and in part philosophical positions, it may seem fitting to reply with a counterideology. Yet the very failure of Scheler's metaphysics to live up to its absolutist pretensions perhaps ultimately contributed to skepticism, nihilism, and relativism, despite its acknowledged positive effect upon the youth of the Weimar Republic.

Yet the real vitality of Scheler's attacks on the mental and political climate of his times lies not in his metaphysics or his political ideals but rather in his attempts at a philosophical analysis of the concepts that underlay that climate: thus his analysis of the concept of "relative knowledge" itself; his descriptions of various types and levels of relativity and objectivity; his posing of the question of just what the relativist believes all knowledge to be relative *to;* and finally, his development of the logic of a correct usage of the term. And this task involves, for Scheler, the development of a concept of phenomenological method and its application. For that reason, we begin our study of his philosophy with this method. But in no case do we find in Scheler an attempt to counter relativistic philosophies simply by positing an intellectual intuition or other special source of knowledge that would enable him to justify arguments in favor of epistemological objectivism. It is in the spirit of his phenomenological approach, rather than in the spirit of his counterideologies, that we shall read him in the following pages.

Now this approach seems to indicate that Scheler's "place" in the history of philosophy is as a phenomenologist. On this interpretation, Scheler appears as a "test case" for Husserl's method: if Scheler has shown that Husserl has provided a unique standpoint for intuiting the essential structures of consciousness and of the essences encountered in the world, and if he has, in addition, employed the method to provide us with new insights into the areas he has studied, then we have grounds for the belief that phenomenology has the promise as a tool of philosophical analysis that Husserl insisted upon. And in fact we are going to develop Scheler's concept of method, and then trace its applications to the areas of ethics, sociology, and philosophy of religion.

Whether a later history will judge that this is where Scheler's greatest significance lies, whether others will employ the results of his thought in their own investigations, and in this way carry on his work, one cannot tell. Certainly, thinkers in various fields are today carrying on inquiries whose methodological framework is similar to that established by Scheler. In his own times, however, the picture we get of Scheler's significance as a philosopher is quite different. To his contemporaries, Scheler appeared as a brilliant inspiration, a philosophical gadfly, whose works were read avidly, whose lectures were well attended, but whose beliefs and doctrines seem to have had little effect outside a small circle of colleagues. Gustav René Hocke, in an essay composed upon the one-hundredth birthday of Scheler, compares him to a Socrates, who composed his works in cafés over a glass of wine, undisturbed by the revelry around him, who enjoyed conversations with people from all walks of life, whose extemporaneous philosophizing dazzled students, and who possessed a manly virility and charm.[8]

Our own generation might, of course, continue to read Scheler in this way: as an inspiration and a challenge, promising us that the harmony of men and peoples with each other and of persons within themselves is attainable, but warning us of the difficulties that lie along the way. And it is difficult to read him and not share his excitement and his optimism: he is a great teacher. We might read him to take part in his wide range of interests, from the study of ancient modes of religious belief to the attempt to assimilate the most recent advances in biology and psychology of his day to a broad philosophical outlook. Or we might come back to him as a philosophical maverick and gadfly to whom we turn for impassioned defenses of unpopular positions such as we mentioned on page 11: ethical absolutism (emen a claim that we can discover apodictic evidence for ordering values according to their relative worth, a program he attempted to carry out in part); political conservativism; support of the possibility of natural theology and metaphysics; criticism of the scientific world view — directions of Scheler's thought that we shall examine in their proper place. Indeed, his thought seems to stand outside the mainstream of scientific rationalism and the existentialist reaction to it; yet he works from within that mainstream as both its critic and its admirer.

If, now, we are asked to pick out some concrete elements in Scheler's thought that constitute his unique legacy to the future, and then attempt to "place" him within twentieth-century thought in terms of this accomplishment, we would turn back, as we have already indicated, to the method of philosophical analysis that he developed and to the rather original epistemological framework in which it operates. Since this method is similar in important respects to that developed by Edmund Husserl, we will refer to the method as "phenomenological," although Scheler's concept of method and the use he makes of this method are broader than Husserl had anticipated. For that reason, our study of Scheler begins with a consideration of his concept of phenomenological method. But are there, then, thinkers after Scheler who continue to employ his method or the results of his method in their own work? Or, as with Sartre and Heidegger, have his works had an effect upon tendencies in art or literature, or do they help us understand later trends in art and literature? For both these questions, I believe, the answer would have to be a guarded "no." Scheler certainly cannot be thought of as an "existentialist," if only because he retains a faith in the ideal of reason and does not share the existentialist concern with despair, anxiety, and loss of meaning. Yet his insistence upon the indefinability of the concept of Person might well inspire an existentialist opposition to the "objectification" of the human person, although few existentialists seem to have studied the long analysis of the concept of "person" in the second half of *Der Formalismus in der Ethik und die materiale Wertethik*. And also, where an existentialist — let us take Sartre — will see the operation of bad faith structuring our relationships with others, Scheler sees the community as founded in love.

Nor has Scheler provided us with an aesthetics, or even with categories adequate to the analysis of trends in modern art. Yet in such a book as Richard Bernheimer's *The Nature of Representation: A*

Phenomenological Study, although no reference is made to Scheler, one can feel the painstaking procedure that Scheler outlined in his writings and, in his best moments, applied to the phenomena we will be considering in this book in the author's laborious attempts to develop a theory of representation by "exhibiting" the phenomenon of representation in art by means of distinguishing other representation phenomena, by citing dozens of carefully chosen examples, and by pointing to accepted linguistic usages of the term.[9]

Nor does it appear that Scheler has had much influence upon developments in religion or theology in our time, although his professed aims were to provide an alternative to traditional modes of religious faith and to provide a phenomenological basis for the study of religion.[10] And yet again, with respect to the latter, we can surely see the parallel with Scheler's "Die Wesensphänomenologie der Religion" (Essential Phenomenology of Religion) and the sections on religion in *Probleme einer Soziologie des Wissens* (Problems of a Sociology of Knowledge) in the procedures adopted for the study of religion in Ninian Smart's *The Science of Religion and the Sociology of Knowledge: Some Methodological Questions,*[11] though once more, Scheler's name is not mentioned. And further cases of Scheler's unspoken presence in more recent twentieth-century philosophy might be cited.

One might object that it is useless to judge the merits of a philosopher solely in terms of his influence upon the future; it would be enough that he engage our interest, that he illuminate our own studies, that he inspire us to rethink our beliefs. The task of the philosopher, William James once said, is to provide us with alternatives; that is, to suggest new ways of approaching familiar themes, new modes of thought that rouse us from our satisfaction with more familiar categories. Anyone who desires this sort of challenge will find Scheler to be a worthwhile companion. But in return, we must be discriminating, and not allow him to dazzle us with his suggestiveness, his enthusiasm, his overabundance of thought. And this again is a reason why we will seize upon the systematic aspects of his thought as the foundation of our presentation and our critique. Our procedure will be critical in that we are not simply going to present doctrines. We intend to demand of Scheler the evidence by which his doctrines are asserted, and we expect to find that this evidence is of a type that corresponds to his definition of what phenomenological evidence is.

Thus, the first four chapters of this study will be concerned with an investigation of his doctrine of method. It will be our contention that despite certain logical inconsistencies on Scheler's part, the method, as he presents it, is sound. Chapters five through eight will then be dedicated to tracing out the applications he makes of his method to the central areas of his philosophical concern. Our contention will be that despite the promise of his procedure, and the inherent interest of the specific doctrines he advances as based upon the phenomenological method, he is rewarded with only occasional success, when one judges his thought with reference to his own claims to rigorously systematic phenomenological investigation. To anticipate the outcome of our study a bit, the reasons for this lack of success are to be sought in the following places.

First, it can be shown that Scheler suffers from a lack of the philosophical discipline required by his method. This lack of dedication, which results in the confusion of phenomenological evidence with other kinds of evidence, is undoubtedly due to the fact that Scheler was a political man with a special ax to grind. But of course the problem goes deeper than this. Julius Kraft, who views Scheler's entire philosophy as a failure, points out that it is Scheler's attempts to plead the case for Christianity that led his vision away from those problems of religion where phenomenology might have been capable of making a real contribution.[12] There is some justice in this view, but not, it seems to this reader, for the reasons that Kraft adduces: he holds that Scheler could never become more than an apologist for whatever cause he set his heart upon, because he makes the application of the phenomenological method dependent upon a concept of reduction that involves the fulfillment of moral conditions by the practitioner (e.g., that the investigator must be a "believer"). I believe it can be shown that the truth of what is attained by phenomenological investigation is in no way logically dependent upon the performance of the Schelerian reduction. Nevertheless, it is true that Scheler was unable to view phenomenology as the *whole* of philosophy and as the provider of a rigorous basis for inquiry in the empirical sciences, as did Husserl, but, in addition to its use in philosophical analysis, considered phenomenology to be a means for providing evidence for those metaphysical and social ideologies he hoped would bring about the *Ausgleich,* the reconciliation of material and spiritual conflicts that was so desperately needed by the Germans and the European community of Scheler's time.

It is also true that Scheler is suffering from the same bifurcation that he discovers to be the essence of man. His desire for metaphysical knowledge, his need for moral perfection, and his hopes to bring spiritual enlightenment and moral renewal to men could not be brought in harmony with the strict systematic method he adopts. He might have been either an evangelist, basing his pronouncements upon the free speculations of his imagination — such as he believes to be of the essence of metaphysical creativity — or he might have been a phenomenological researcher into the essences given to the metaphysical, ethical, and social standpoints. The point is that he often tries to do both of these at the same time, and this attempt leads him to grief. He is a tender-minded philosopher who adopted a tough-minded method.

Moreover, there are logical difficulties involved in his conception of an applied phenomenological science. Specifically, these problems are tied to his notion of apodictic evidence and the vagueness of his concept of truth. These difficulties will be analyzed during the course of our discussion, and we will not outline them here, for their elaboration is dependent upon an understanding of Scheler's theory of knowledge.

Finally, a general critical observation: Husserl's hope that phenomenology would be systematically applied by communities of scholars working together to refine and describe their intuitions of essences and thereby attain a unified body of knowledge embracing all the sciences was, and remains, a dream. The reason lies perhaps neither in the fundamentals of its theory nor in the obscurity of its subject matter, but rather in its dependence upon individuals of genius for its fruitfulness. Scheler perhaps saw this, and for that reason did not follow Husserl in the latter's identification of phenomenology as the most rigorous of the descriptive sciences. Insofar as phenomenology is, as we shall show, a "prelinguistic" discipline, possessing no criteria of truth and falsity other than truth itself, it requires practitioners who are seers, and able to make other men see. There are borderline areas, of course, places where vision comes more easily, places where the essences given in phenomenological reflection are more easily expressed in language than others. The very fluidity of the phenomenological quest, then, would seem to demand great care in application as well as vision;

but Scheler, with the *hubris* of a Faust, recognized in the end no limits to what might be accomplished on a phenomenological foundation, and ultimately arrived at a picture of the world that is itself rather Faustian, with its notion of man the microcosm, its glorification of Spirit and Nature, and a belief in the power of love as the means of bursting the limits of one's own being.

But does it make sense for *philosophers* to talk about, and speculate upon, the nature of love and hate, of spiritual rebirth, of the "group spirit" of communities and nations, as Scheler does? Or should such matters be the province of psychology, religion, and sociology or poetry? The premise of all Scheler's work is that it does make sense, if one prepares oneself with a strict method, coupled with a "reverence for all being and essence," and that one may discover truths that the psychologist, religious believer, sociologist and poet glimpse without understanding. Our purpose in this book is to prepare an affirmative case for this belief.

Chronology

1874 Max Scheler born on August 12, in Munich.

1893 Enrolls at the medical faculty of the University of Munich.

1894 Enrolls at the philosophical faculty of the University of Berlin.

1895 Marries Amelie von Dewitz. Enters the University of Jena.

1897 Doctoral dissertation: *Beiträge zur Feststellung der Beziehung zwischen den logischen und ethischen Prinzipien.*

1899 Scheler retained as an instructor at the University of Jena. Habilitation: *Die transzendentale und die psychologische Methode.*

1900 First meeting with Husserl.

1900– Husserl's *Logische Untersuchungen* published.
1901

1907 Obtains a professorship at the University of Munich.

1910 Separated from Amelie. Submits resignation at Munich, returns to private life in Göttingen.

1911 Marries Maerit Furtwaengler.

1913 *Der Formalismus in der Ethik und die materiale Wertethik,* Part I, published.

1914 Attempts to enlist in the German army but is rejected for reasons of age.

1916 *Der Formalismus,* Part II, published. Scheler is reaccepted as a Catholic.

1917– Works for the German Foreign Service in Switzerland.
1918

1919 Appointment to a professorship in Cologne.

1917– Writes the essays published under the title *Vom Ewigen im*
1921 *Menschen* in 1921.

1922 Breaks with the Catholic Church.

1923 Divorced from Maerit.

1924 Marries Maria Scheu.

1926 *Die Wissensformen und die Gesellschaft* published.

1927 *Die Stellung des Menschen im Kosmos* published.

1928   Accepts an appointment at the University of Frankfurt. Dies
       of a heart attack on May 19.

For details on Scheler's personal life we are indebted to John
Raphael Staude, who, in preparation for his *Max Scheler,
1874–1928: An Intellectual Portrait,* conducted extensive interviews
with people who had known Scheler personally. He tells us that
Scheler's widow, Maria, lost all of Scheler's correspondence and
other personal papers during World War II.

CHAPTER 1

From the Natural Standpoint to Phenomenological Intuition

I *Husserl and the Problem of Phenomenology*

P HENOMENOLOGY is a method for conducting philosophical analyses; that is, it is expected to provide us with a clarification of those same problems of description that begin with Socrates' questions to the Athenians: "What is justice? What is piety? What do we *mean* by these terms, what is their essential nature?" The tool that modern phenomenological analysis employs in its investigations into the nature of phenomena is intuition, an intellectual reflection upon the meanings involved in our cognition of the objects we encounter in the world.

This word "intuition," which we encounter so often in discussions of the phenomenological method, has definite historical associations. The notion of an intellectual intuition, that is, a mode of insight that gives us direct knowledge of the essence of its object apart from its sensible apprehension, had been rejected by Kant, and was in disrepute among the members of the philosophical schools in which Husserl and Scheler had been trained. The philosophy of mind then in fashion in Germany denied that the mind possessed a faculty that enabled it to transcend the "laws of mental operation," which were imposed upon it from without, so to speak, and to attain knowledge of the "really real." The best that philosophical activity could do, in this view, was to discover the laws of thought that determine scientific and everyday cognition. Often it was hoped that a reduction of the mathematical thinking that forms the basis of theoretical physics to the *a priori* laws of logic contributed by the mind could be effected. In this way, knowledge claims were to be justified by reference to abstract theoretical laws assumed to be *a priori*. A second view that both Scheler and Husserl learned in school was referred to as *psychologism*. This theory held that the laws of thought that determined cognition and to which knowledge could be reduced were psychological, and thus discoverable in principle by the methods of empirical psychology. Against these views, Husserl and Scheler would raise the following objections.

First, both views deny an *immediate* relationship between knowing and being known. What is known is said by these theories to be known only mediately, through the medium of psychological or transcendental laws. Such a view leads of necessity to skepticism concerning the possibility of our grasping the essence of what is given in everyday experience, that which Husserl was to call experience on the "natural standpoint." Again, the discovery of these laws itself presents a problem of knowing. Such laws that regulate everyday experience cannot, on the letter of the theory, be *given to* experience; they are either objects of speculation, at best, or simple abstractions from the "natural experience" they are supposed to regulate or determine, at worst. Both doctrines are self-defeating; they rest on presuppositions whose unverifiability in principle is implied by the theory itself. Such views led, in general, either to pragmatic theories of fictions, such as we find in Hans Vaihinger's well-known *Philosophie des Als-Ob,* or to positivism. Phenomenology, on the other hand, was founded on the belief, which took different forms in Scheler and Husserl, that what is central to reality is given directly to the experiencing mind. The question of philosophical knowledge is then not to discover the *laws* by which we cognize the given, but to perfect those techniques in which that which is cognized in everyday experience may be distinctly and unambiguously given to consciousness. This "new beginning" thus requires a method of expanding our consciousness of the world.

Second, both Scheler and Husserl believed that psychologism and neo-Kantianism lead to the *prejudicing* of inquiry into what is immediately given on the natural standpoint. After all, these doctrines assume that what is immediately given is determined by a *single* set of psychological or aprioristic laws. In the early writings of Husserl, this critical objection was closely related to his official rejection of metaphysics; later, his notion of a phenomenological reduction was intended to eliminate the possibility of affirming anything not given to transcendental consciousness in a single act of reflective intuition. In this way, he hoped to avoid the development of such expectations as that all knowing is a function of a single set of laws of mental operation. Such expectations are founded upon metaphysical hypotheses concerning the nature of knowledge, and can only cloud the issue of what is in fact given to intuition. Only in the case of the immediately given, Husserl claimed, was absolutely certain knowledge possible. Speculations concerning the ultimate nature of the mind were not to be made, nor was the metaphysical question of the ultimate nature of reality to be raised.

Scheler was not to follow Husserl entirely in the rejection of metaphysics, but he would insist as strongly as Husserl that it is always the intention of phenomenological inquiry to establish knowledge independently of hypotheses; that "philosophy may not presume the truth of acquisitions either of history (including the history of philosophy) or of 'science' in general or of any individual science, or revelation, or of the 'common sense' attitude and its observations."[1] The philosophical attitude demands that each philosopher seek out by himself the intuitions upon which a knowledge claim is based: "The man who strives for an outlook founded on philosophy must dare to stand on his *own* reason. He must tentatively doubt all inherited opinions and must accept nothing that he cannot *clearly see* and prove."[2] Again and again, throughout his phenomenological analyses, Scheler pleads: "I beg him [who holds a given view] to direct himself back from such questionable hypotheses to the phenomenological facts of the case."[3] The discovery of the "phenomenological facts of the case" presupposes the development of a method for going directly to the seat of the knowing process and clearly and distinctly "seeing" what is given to consciousness. Husserl's famous cry of "to the things themselves" is a call to reject speculations concerning *how* things are given and to direct one's attention to what is in fact given. This very objection points toward the new starting point of philosophical analysis: the natural, "everyday" world of lived experience, in which we encounter "things," a world that must be re-experienced phenomenologically, not so that we may go "beyond" things to their noumenal basis, but so that they may be experienced more *adequately.*

Now we must ask for a definition of "phenomenological experience." What is "given" in a phenomenological experience? What are these "essences" or meanings, the "what" of experience, that the phenomenologist — in this case, Scheler — is directing his attention toward? Why, moreover, should whatever is given in such experience have priority with respect to truth over all other modes of apprehension? We will begin our analysis of Scheler's adaptation of Husserl's method by discussing the nature of the given in everyday experience, that is, the experience from the so-called natural standpoint, for this is the starting point of all phenomenological analyses.

II *The Natural Standpoint*

"The task of philosophy," Scheler writes in "Die Lehre von den drei Tatsachen," "is a *cleansing* of the contents of intuition [*Anschauungen*] from the physical sensations that accompany them."[4] This is to say that philosophers are to be responsible for disengaging the essential contents of everyday perceptions from their physical basis, and that "intuitions" — or what Scheler calls more generally an act of perception — are to be viewed as a mixture of two elements: the data given to the senses that serve as the "sign" for the physical thing perceived, and the meaning of the thing, or, that which we perceive it *as*.[5] Thus the notion of perceiving an object may never be understood merely as conscious awareness of the object; perception refers to the act of understanding the object *as* the object that it is: in other words, as carrying essence, as *meaning* something. Perception is the understanding awareness of a sensibly given object *as* something or other. It is this "as," this meaning and its constituents, that the phenomenologist is after.

Implied in the above quotation from Scheler is a criticism of a view, familiar to students of British empiricism, that he believed would deny the possibility from the outset of totally disengaging the essential content of perceptions from physical sensations. He attacked this doctrine under the name of "sensualism"; it is generally referred to in the United States as "psychological atomism." Scheler identified this doctrine as the epistemological basis of positivism and traced it back historically through Kant to David Hume. It holds that consciousness is constituted in time out of the stream of atomic sense data — Hume called the constituents of this stream "impressions" — and that all thought and meaning — everything on the level of what Hume calls "ideas" — are derived from, hence reducible to, the impressions given to the mind through the senses. Scheler denies this doctrine of reducibility and holds that while every perception has internal or external stimuli as a necessary condition, still each contains an element of meaning given *with* the sense impression. The object of phenomenology is hence to disengage the meaning element from the accompanying sense data, and then submit the former to analysis.

Let us begin our attempt to understand this difficult thought by considering a concrete example of this analysis that Scheler himself uses in *Der Formalismus in der Ethik und die materiale Wertethik*:[6]

When one asks, e.g., what is given in the perception of a physical cube, the answer of sensualism, that what is given is a perspective, a side view, or even the "content given through the senses," is fundamentally incorrect. What is given is the cube as a whole physical thing, as a definite, spatially unified form. A whole succession of acts of natural perception is required to attain that which the sensualistic epistemologist naively takes as a point of departure.... In the "seeing" of, e.g., a facade, the fact is always also given [*mitgegeben*] that it has another side, although that other side is not "sensed."

The "sensualist" might reply to this objection to his theory that the knowledge that the cube whose one side we "sense" has another side can be explained as the addition of habit to the perceived one side, and that in any case the perception of a cube as a cube is possible only upon granting the basis in sense experience. Scheler would answer this rebuttal with two observations that reflect his phenomenological procedure.

The first of these observations is that that which is in question for a philosopher is *what* is given, and not what are the *causal conditions* of that thing's being given; the latter is a question for the psychologist and perhaps also the neurologist. The further question of *how it is possible* for something to be given at all is perhaps legitimate, but (1) it involves the metaphysical question of the mind-body relationship, and (2) the question arises only on the basis of the presupposition that something has in fact been given. Phenomenology, for Scheler and Husserl — and also later for Heidegger — pretends to be the most fundamental of disciplines because it begins its investigation with the bare fact that something is given and seeks to describe what the thing is given *as,* that is, how it is cognized.

Second, an unprejudiced examination of what is actually given when one looks at a cube will reveal that the cube is *first* apprehended as a cube. From this original or "primordial" perception of the cube as a whole we may, if we wish, abstract what we call a "side view" of the cube. Thus, in Scheler's view, what would correspond to the classic English notion of a sense datum (*Empfindungsinhalte:* colors, a tone, etc.) is *never immediately given* but is rather a construction out of what is given to a human subject from the natural standpoint — a construction, Scheler would go on to point out, that is usually intended to fulfill the purposes of scientific theories. The correctness of Scheler's observation will be obvious to anyone who attempts to "see" a cube *as* a white, square or foreshortened facade upon a background of a certain color, and so forth. Such "sense data" are never the immediate objects of external perception; we see objects. This is of course not to say that the cube as a whole can ever be given in perception without the sense data, which are, after all, the causal condition of the appearance. But the notion that things are primordially given in the lived experience of everyday perception as meaningful wholes requires further analysis.

Let us first take one of the difficulties involved in Scheler's doctrine that the cube is *originally* or *primordially* given as a meaningful whole rather than as a side view in perspective. The expression "primordially given [*originär gegeben*] from the natural standpoint" is taken from Husserl. Primordial experience is for Husserl perception, which may be divided into inner and outer. Husserl, like Scheler, conceived the task of phenomenology to be the isolation and disengagement of levels of meaning and sense involved as "moments" in everyday perception. What is primordially given from the natural standpoint thus contains disparate elements of sense and meaning out of which the thing given is constituted in and by the act of consciousness that intends it. Where Scheler distinguishes his view from Husserl's in this matter is in his expansion of the notion of a primordially given perception. For the Husserl of the *Ideas* (*Ideen*), what is given to consciousness in everyday external perception is to be sought not only in the things themselves but in the acts of consciousness that constitute them. Acts of the Husserlian transcendental conciousness "animate" the side views, that is, the sense data, of the thing. The meaning elements, through which the thing is given as a unity, are thus contributed by consciousness. Thus for Husserl what is primordially given on the side of the object are simply perspectival views — much as Scheler finds in the "sensualists," although Husserl, by virtue of his doctrine of constitutionality, of course denies that perception can be reduced to what he calls the "hyletic data" given through the senses.

In opposition to this view, Scheler holds that the "place" of meaning is the object, not the subject; meaning is given *to* consciousness *with* the sense-data "sign": or, as he sometimes puts it, essences are "carried by" objects; they present themselves as that which they are in reality. Similarly, whereas what for Husserl is primordially given in internal perception is "ourselves and our states of consciousness," but never the states of consciousness of other men,[7] Scheler holds, as we see in *Wesen und Formen der Sympathie,* that other men are primordially given *as* "being happy," "in deep sorrow," and so forth. By adopting the view that essences are real and not constituted by consciousness, Scheler avoided Husserl's later difficulties in distinguishing the act of consciousness from the object intended, and in avoiding solipsism, which Husserl sees approaching him in the *Cartesian Meditations.* Of course, Scheler, too, is involving himself here in a metaphysical assumption, which his method warns him to avoid; we will observe the consequences of this later.

The import of Scheler's interpretation of the nature of perception is clear, however: primordially given in external perception are the things themselves, and not their mere "appearance." Moreover, perception is expanded by Scheler to include the "unsensed" sides of physical objects, and the positive and negative *values* that are given with physical objects, acts, and events. Even other minds are said to be immediately given: in acts of sympathy, one is *directly* aware of the feelings of other men, not indirectly, as via an inference from observed behavior to an unobserved foreign emotional state. Further, Scheler claims that we directly perceive action-reaction processes: the notion of a causal relation, understood as consisting of a series of atomic perceptions of changes in states of affairs plus a psychologically or transcendentally conditioned projection of necessity, is as much the construction of a metaphysical scientism as is the concept of a sense datum. In fact, he holds, we directly perceive the effectiveness (*Wirksamkeit*) of a stone in breaking a glass.

Scheler's phenomenological analyses of the phenomena of sym-

pathy and causality will be discussed in their proper place. Let us
return to the thought with which we began this section: that what is
given in everyday perceptual experience appears to be constituted
out of two elements, the sensible and the cognitive. Scheler has the
task of providing us with a method that will enable us to distinguish
these two elements — to "reduce" the concrete perception to its
cognitive content — and to make this cognitive content and its constituents the theme of descriptive analysis. Thus a central subject of
phenomenological analysis — although not the only subject — is
the "cognitive content of perceptions" — the essences and their
modes and relations that Scheler claims we refer to implicitly when
we grasp a sensibly given object *as* a chair, a tree, or a flea.

III   *Phenomenological Facts*

Pure facts, or more generally, essences, which constitute the
meaning elements given in or implied by a perception, are said by
Scheler to be capable of being self-given, or what is the same, non-
mediately or directly (*unmittelbar*) given. In phenomenological
reflection, according to him, the attempt is made to "reduce" natural perceptions to their essential components and to bring these
essential components to self-givenness. This reduction involves the
effort to "see" in intuition the objects we encounter in everyday
awareness as examples of essential states of affairs. These are the
basic tenets of Schelerian phenomenology. Let us try to understand
the key concept of immediacy by asking ourselves what is meant
when a thing can be said to be *not* self-given or mediately given, as
Scheler believes is always the case in perceptual experience, that is,
experience upon Husserl's "natural standpoint."

Let us note first of all that nonphenomenological facts are never
given in *one intentional act* of apprehension but contain a plurality
of components, or "moments." Take the example of a cube, which
we mentioned earlier. What we intend when we perceive the cube
from the natural standpoint is the cube *as* a whole material thing in
space. It has sides and an interior that are not sensibly given, but
that are nonetheless intended in the perceptual act. In addition, the
cube is perceived as having a significance for us as well; we ask,
"What is that cube doing here!" insofar as it is primordially perceived *as* possibly possessing a value of some sort.

Thus we see that the perception of the cube is made up of various meaning and value components. In addition, there are the sense data, which Scheler calls the causal conditions of the perception. The sense data give us the existing thing on which the meaning and value elements are given. Insofar as these elements of meaning and value are thought of in terms of the physical object, they are not given directly, but mediately, or through the medium of sense data. Thus the essence "cubeness" is given *by means of* the physical appearance. Scheler implies by this that the phenomenological facts or essences can never be given to the natural standpoint, for the natural standpoint is constituted in part by inner or outer sense perception. Thus again, investigation of the cognitive element in perception requires a special, a phenomenological, standpoint. From this standpoint, Scheler holds, essences can be given directly, without the mediation of sense data, pictures, or symbols, to intuitive reflection; the things thus given are pure facts, phenomena, meanings, *essences* apart from their being instanced by an existing, sensibly perceived intentional object.

When he defines a pure fact in this way, Scheler has before his critical eye what he calls the "pragmatic" doctrine of facts. The "pragmatic" fact is not simply given but contains elements contributed by the human intellect, whose operations are understood by the "pragmatist" to be exclusively a function of its vitally directed efforts to master its environment. Language as well as facts, in this view, are constructs, weapons in the struggle; facts are simply details picked out of the chaos of flowing human experience as having significance within this struggle. Essences, in Scheler's sense, contrast with the "pragmatic" fact by containing no elements contributed by the human mind, however understood; they are simply given to an intuition purged of all sensible and conceptual elements.[8]

Now in order to ensure the apodicticity of our knowledge of them, phenomenological facts must possess the additional characteristic of *simplicity;* that is, they must be capable of being given in a single intentional act. This necessity presents Scheler with a problem, for the meaning content of a single perceptual act may be quite complex; it may contain various components, as we have seen. The perception of something as a cube implies, of course, that we come to the cube with a concept — a prior understanding — of cubicness. But now the understanding of the concept of cubicness in turn implies the givenness of essences that are logically prior to that of cubicness itself, such as spatiality and thingness. How do we go about distinguishing these *essential* constituents of perceptions? Scheler refers to this notion of logical priority as the "order of foundation," and it is the subject of a special analysis. Let us take a moment for a preliminary analysis of this central concept, for it will help us make clear the distinction between pure facts and essences, as well as Scheler's concept of the *a priori* element in perception, which we will study in Chapter 2.

If the main themes of phenomenological reflection are essences and essential relationships, still a description of these is not the only result that Scheler hopes to obtain from such studies. We have already mentioned in passing that all acts of understanding on the natural level and most intuitions of essences on the phenomenological level (all except those that intend pure facts) are "founded" upon "prior" understanding of other essences. To pick a new example, we note that in order that a knowing subject correctly identify a given object as a tree, he must have some prior knowledge of "life"; otherwise we would not say that he understands what a tree is. "Life" is a pure fact, according to Scheler, hence *its* understanding presupposes no other knowledge. An intuitive, pre-analytic understanding of this phenomenon is not obtained by definition or by induction; rather, it is *fundamental* to the way human beings experience the world. On the other hand, a tree is also a physical object, and its unification in a perception thus presupposes an understanding of the phenomenon of physicality. Physicality, though an essence, is not a pure fact, for *its* understanding presupposes the givenness of spatiality, a pure fact, to the subject who perceives the object as a tree. This relationship — (1) this physical object, (2) physicality, (3) spatiality — is an example of what Scheler calls an "order of foundation." Thus any given perception may be analyzed both with respect to its essential content and with respect to its order of foundation.

Now this order is clearly not a genetic order; it does not give an answer to the question of how a child learns to use language; this would be a question for an empirical psychologist. Rather, the order of foundation is a relation among essences: it asks what meanings must already have been grasped by the conscious subject before the meaning of this perception could have been grasped. The deepest meaning level is, of course, the level of pure facts; they are never founded. Thus Scheler asserts that pure facts in the narrow sense of the term appear contingent from the standpoint of pure logic;[9] whereas pure facts in the narrow sense are phenomenologically intelligible and may be perfectly self-given to intuition, they are founded in nothing else: they are the most basic facts about the world. Thus one can intuit the essence of "life," but this essence has no foundation, no deeper meaning through which we can grasp this phenomenon; for that reason the phenomenon of life seems to us to be simply a "brute fact." For this reason, also, the metaphysical attempt to reduce all phenomena to some "highest concept" is doomed to failure: that there is an essential relationship between, for instance, "value" and "vital interest," or between "matter" and "life," as some positivists maintained, is no more intuitively evident than Thales' dictum that all things are essentially related to water.[10]

On the other hand, pure facts in the wider sense include those essential relations described in pure logic. These relations are founded in the essence of "object," if Scheler is right; indeed, he refers to pure logic as *Gegenstandstheorie,* the theory of object, and holds — as an example of a foundation relation — that the essence of "object" must be understood before such propositions of logic as the principle of contradiction can be understood. Similarly, in the case of other phenomena, certain essences must be grasped, certain intellectual acts performed by the knowing subject, before it becomes possible for that subject to grasp what is given upon the natural standpoint, that is, before men can "have a world." "There is a firm *order of foundation,"* he declares, "according to which ... phenomena come to givenness, such that a phenomenon A cannot be given if a phenomenon B has not been given before it in the order of time.... So is spatiality [*Räumlichkeit*] given before and independently of shapes in space, before and independently of the place and position of any things whatever, only before and independently of qualities. Also thingness, materiality, physicality of a given physical thing [is given] before its quiddity [*Wesheit*] and its materially instanced properties *material erfüllten Eigenschaften*]."[11] Elsewhere he notes as a further example that first we must think thingness before we can think of causality, "for only things can effect and be affected."[12]

Thus we see that on each level of the order of foundation there is a task for phenomenological analysis: to reexperience fully and to bring to language the act that is the condition of a higher order act.

In this way the meaning structure of what is given upon the natural standpoint in perception through the medium of internal or external sensations or of symbols may be exhibited. Thus there are two and possibly three general themes of phenomenological analysis: the phenomenology of the intentional object, the phenomenology of intentional acts and their order of foundation, and, finally, the phenomenology of the relationship between intentional act and intentional object, which Scheler pursues occasionally, notably in his "essential phenomenology of religion."

Now we may return to our earlier problem of the *simplicity* of the phenomenological fact. In general, Scheler uses the word "essence" to refer to higher-order phenomenological facts, that is, those that are complex, such as cubicness, which, we have observed, contains a plurality of elements. Pure facts would then be those essences that are simple, and thus capable of being *self*-given, or given in one intentional act. Lower-order essences, while still possessing no elements of sensation, contain yet other elements that "found" them — that is, their understanding presupposes the prior understanding of other essences, and hence they cannot be given *entirely* in one intentional act. It is clear that despite his epistemological realism, Scheler does not hold — as Plato appears to have held — that there is a single pure fact for everything for which we have a name. The essence of many things can be grasped on the basis of other acts of understanding; there is in such cases nothing primordial, indefinable in them that can be given in one intentional act and only in one. Scheler notes in this context that there is no pure fact of "treeness," for example.[13] A thing can be grasped as a tree on the basis of one's having grasped other meaning elements, although these other meaning elements may only have been grasped on the basis of a primordial intuition. On the other hand, he holds the essence of "life" to be a pure fact, indefinable because intuitable in one intentional act. Thus we see that our phenomenological study of a given perceived object may involve a long series of intuitive reflections upon the contents of perceptual acts before we reach the simple essences that "found" the perception and are themselves unfounded.[14]

Furthermore, a pure fact is said to be self-given where there is established a congruence of what is intended with what is given *(Gemeintes und Gegebenes kommen zur Deckung).*[15] This definition again implies that the content of a pure phenomenological intuition must be simple, for only where the mind has fastened itself upon a single simple object can we speak of such congruence. Thus clarity and distinctness are understood in terms of this experience of congruence of the intention with the intended, and Scheler will raise the edifice of phenomenological evidence and the claim of apodictic knowledge upon it. In sum, the content of a perceptual act is first to be reduced to its cognitive content and then to be reduced further to the simple elements that constitute it, and it is these simple elements that are said to be capable of being self-given. "Pure facts," Scheler claims, "are facts that come to givenness through the content of an immediate intuition."[16]

We have noted that Scheler claims as an epistemological characteristic of essences that they are given *before* all *inductive* experience. That is, with respect to the epistemological question of the origin of our conceptual framework, Scheler holds that concepts are *not* simple abstractions from the repeated experience of objects; rather, all induction depends upon the prior intuition of essences. This point influences Scheler's views on how we are to reexperience our system of concepts phenomenologically: our first concern has to be with the way in which concepts are originally given to us, rather than with how they function in our "everyday" perception of the world. But then it follows that the way into the realm of essences in terms of which we perceive the world cannot itself be empirical. It is true that the phenomenological intending of essence is a mental act, and as such presupposes a "perception" in Scheler's use of the term—something must be given whose essence we wish to describe—but not the type of perceptual act involved in collecting examples and comparing qualities or of noting regularities in the temporal order of succession of sense data or of physical objects. The phenomenologist may need only one example to arrive at an intuition of essence, states Scheler:

I have here and now a pain in my arm—how did it come about, and how can I get rid of it? To establish this would be the task of the positive sciences, of physiology, of psychology, of medicine. I can, however, grasp this same point in a more distant, thoughtful, contemplative attitude toward this same experience as an *"example"* of the very strange and very surprising *essential* state of affairs, that this world is *at all* sullied with pain, evil, and suffering; then I would ask a different question: Just what is *"pain itself,"* apart from the fact that I now feel pain—and how must it be with the ground of things, such that a thing such as *"pain itself"* is possible?[17]

A final remark concerning the nature of essences, the "cognitive content of perceptions": Scheler makes it clear that essences do not *exist* as do contingent, changing, particular objects. Essences are ideal entities, and perfect knowledge of them is apodictic knowledge, and is necessary and valid for all possible instances on the perceptual level. Scheler's attempt to perfect Platonic idealism is clearly stated in the following passage:

Once we have fully perceived the pure essential content of an object. . . our perception has peculiarities which fundamentally distinguish it from all knowledge of the realm of relative and contingent existence. It is definitive, thus incapable of increase or diminution—that is to say, it is strictly *self-evident*, whereas knowledge of contingency, however attained, whether by direct perception or by the drawing of inferences, never arrives at more than presumptive truth, which is certainly conditional upon the findings of later experience. . . . The intuition of essences is insight, and, as judged, is "true" *a priori* for all possible existents having the same essence.[18]

In brief conclusion, then, our description of Scheler's adaptation of the phenomenological method has discovered the following points of emphasis:

(1) The importance for phenomenology of the claim of the priority of the unified perception of an object on the natural standpoint over the analysis of that object into a temporally and spatially articulated set of sense data;

(2) the attempt to "cleanse" these naturally given objects of their externally caused, spatio-temporal components (namely, sense data) in order to facilitate the analysis of the meanings and meaning relations given with the concrete perception of the object;

(3) the attempt to differentiate these meaning components according to their priority with respect to each other—that is, the phenomenological description of the order of foundation of the essential moments of the contents of the perception;

(4) the attempt to reexperience and describe the essential nature of each of these components.

In this chapter we have attempted simply to describe, as fairly and accurately as possible, the fundamentals of Scheler's phenomenological method and the general nature of the objects he proposes to study. To destroy by criticism these fundamentals would be to rob Scheler of the underpinnings that give sense to most of the philosophical analysis he conducts in his mature works. Let us grant that the idea of intuitive reflection upon the meaning contents of perception is not misconceived—in view of the fact that the philosophical vocabulary of our own times lacks a clearly articulated concept of intuition, and that the semantics of "perception" are now assumed to be quite different from Scheler's conception. Then we may pass on to a consideration of three epistemological categories that are fundamental to Scheler's methodology —apriority, phenomenological evidence, and realism. Although he presents us with profound and original insights under each of these headings, still he is troubled with vagueness and logical inconsistency that will haunt him when it comes time to apply the method to concrete philosophical problems.

CHAPTER 2

The Doctrine of Functionalization and the Constitution of the Natural and Scientific Standpoints

SCHELER's epistemology represents an attempt, similar to those made so often in the past from the time of Plato and Aristotle, to explain where we get our concepts. Plato, at various points in the dialogues, notably in the *Phaedo,* explains that we come by our concepts before we are born; we are able before birth to gaze upon the *Wesensreich,* which our concepts vaguely intend. Only vaguely, for when we are born we are separated from this realm, and we can no longer recall with perfect adequacy the essences we saw there. Scheler denies that our concepts are inborn, but affirms at the same time that our concepts are *derived from* primordial (*originär*) intuitions of pure facts.[1] He calls the theory of this derivation "functionalization" and claims that the phenomenological method will enable us to learn the specifics of this derivation.

The problem, as he understands it, concerns the fact that the implicit and preanalytic understanding we have of essences and essential relationships is nonverbal and at first rather vague, much as the slave boy's "understanding" of the properties of squares in the *Meno* was vague, until Socrates helped him to perfect his understanding of them. Moreover, such knowledge, as essential, is extremely general; that is, it is not understood as relating to specific, concrete objects. How can such "knowledge" be applied to what is given on the natural level, that is, to specific perceived objects? This problem is parallel to the problem Kant faces in the *Critique of Pure Reason,* where he asks how the "subsumption of intuitions under pure concepts, the application of a category to appearances, is possible," in view of the fact that the "pure concepts of understanding, being quite heterogenous from empirical intuitions, and indeed from all sensible intuitions, can never be met with in an intuition."[2] In answer to this problem, Kant develops the doctrine of the schematism of the pure concepts of the Understanding.

Scheler's answer to this problem, as posed in the language of his thought, is indirect. We do not learn a theory of *how* the application of knowledge of essence to what is given through the senses is possible; rather, he makes a piecemeal attempt to exhibit phenomenologically specific instances in which objects given in the natural standpoint are cognized "according to" specific essential rules and meanings. To show this is to show how, in each specific case, knowledge of essence "functions" on the natural standpoint "behind" explicit rules and concepts, so to speak, as the ground of their possibility. Theoretically, this could be done for any given perception or judgment upon the natural standpoint. In this chapter, we will content ourselves with presenting and analyzing a few of Scheler's most interesting examples of this kind of phenomenological analysis.

Thus it appears that Scheler's doctrine of the *a priori* element involved in perception upon the natural standpoint differs considerably from that of Kant. Scheler's *a priori* is *material:* that is, it possesses an intuitable content that may be exhibited by phenomenological analysis. Scheler undertakes a direct confrontation with Kant on this issue, and we should consider what he says there before continuing our discussion of his own account.

Scheler devotes approximately fifty pages in *Der Formalismus* to distinguishing his concept of the *a priori* element in experience from that of Kant. We will not go into great detail here but simply note these two central points.

(1) Scheler rejects Kant's identification of the *a priori* with the "rational" or the "actively thought" element in cognition and its opposition to the *a posteriori* element, which is identified with the "irrational" or "sensible" element. One reason for this refusal stems from his denial that knowing consists in the application of a synthesizing function by the mind to chaotic elements presented in sensation. No, Scheler claimed, what is given in sensation *comes with* an *a priori* structure; the content of that structure is phenomenologically intuitable; and even human feeling, thought of by Kant as a chaos of pleasurable and painful sensations, has an *a priori* structure. It is this latent *ordre du coeur,* an order of prefer-

ring and rejecting, that he submits to the phenomenological analysis upon which he bases his ethics.

(2) In Kant's view, the *a priori* is a phenomenon that attaches itself to propositions as the pure form of judgments. Scheler holds, on the contrary, that the *a priori* belongs to the given, thus to the sphere of facts rather than to that of judgments; hence the *a priori* is material, not formal. "Kant is not aware," he declares, "of a phenomenological experience in which what is already present in natural and scientific experience as 'form' or as 'presupposition' is exhibited as the factual content of intuitions."[3] It is these facts, according to Scheler, that are at all times latent within the knowing subject, and to which the knowing subject has at all times access; they are there before all experience upon the natural standpoint, and serve as its foundation, by permitting us to select from what is given through the senses and to unify what is thus given in a "perception." They are therefore *a priori* with respect to experience upon the natural standpoint. Thus it is because we already possess the concept of physicality that we are able to understand the everyday phenomenon of cubicness. Scheler holds that an animal, who does not possess a concept of physicality, does not perceive figures in space *as* physical objects, but rather his relation to his environment is determined simply by his instinctual apparatus, and not by the realm of meanings to which men alone have access.[4]

Now let us return to Scheler's doctrine of functionalization. He states his position succinctly: "knowledge of essence becomes functional as a law of the simple 'application' of the understanding when it is directed toward contingent facts, which [understanding] grasps, analyzes, looks at, judges the contingent world of fact 'according to' essential relations."[5] The knowledge of essence referred to here is preanalytic but not inborn; Scheler, as we shall see, believed that the concept of inborn categories rendered knowledge static. Rather, as we noted in the first chapter, Scheler holds that there is a primordial intuiting of essences that, despite its apparent actual occurrence in time, serves as the *logical* presupposition of our bringing to givenness the objects of perception that make up our world of the natural standpoint. Something is vaguely intuited: an essence, an essential relation. This intuition may "function" as a *principle of selection* in our future experience from among the contingent facts presented to us through the senses, and thus — and in this sense only — as a "law" of possible experience. For example, Scheler points out that we are able to recognize a specific act of a specific person as "unjust" because we already have some insight into the nature of justice and injustice. This primordial insight — which we may have had on the occasion of some specific event or set of events — "leads" us in our future experience. Similarly, insight into a certain kind of essential relation may be "functionalized" and attain concretion as a law of *logic;* the laws of identity, of noncontradiction, and of excluded middle, are functionalized intuitions of very basic essential relations that structure our experience of reality.

Moreover, essences are "functionalized" on various *levels,* according to Scheler's theory; there is a scale extending from the most primordial and vague apprehension of meanings through levels in which consciousness operates more or less unreflectively according to specific essences and essential relations, up to the level upon which consciousness operates according to explicitly formulated rules (e.g., moral principles, scientific or logical rules of inference and observation). Finally, of course, the essences and essential relations themselves may be made explicit, by being brought to self-givenness in phenomenological reflection. A good example of the type of phenomenological analysis based upon the concept of functionalization is Scheler's study of the levels of *Weltanschauung;* another is Scheler's analysis of the "levels of relativity" of values, and how ethical behavior may be "guided" (or, in the language of the theory, ethical knowledge on the natural standpoint is a function of knowledge of value essences and their order of relative worth) on the one hand by ethical "rules" that are unformulated and unquestioned, and on the other hand by explicitly formulated maxims and decision rules, and in all cases by primordial insight into the values themselves. Both of these analyses will be described and analyzed in Part II of this work. They will serve us as examples of the application of this most fundamental epistemological concept to the sociology of knowledge.

Essential to this epistemological theory is the thought that the function of essences in knowledge upon the natural standpoint is not, as Kant would have it, a spontaneous synthesizing of the materials given through the senses, a constructing of objects given to the natural standpoint — for the understanding contributes nothing, according to Scheler — but rather knowledge of essence functions upon the natural standpoint when I recognize something *as* meaning something, *as* corresponding to a meaning to which I have already been exposed, which I already "know." Because each person, each cultural tradition, may possess a different set of insights into the realm of essence, and because this essential knowledge may function in a different way for each, we can justly say that the "world" of the natural standpoint is "thought of" differently for "each"; each person, each cultural tradition, thus constitute a "world" on the basis of their insights into essence and value, but they do not in any way "create" or "constitute" the objects there, although they may fail to take cognizance of them.

Now from within the context of Scheler's phenomenology, the import of this doctrine is clear: the mind of a person is structured by its openness to the sphere of essences; it is from that sphere that his concepts are derived; on the basis of knowledge of essence and the givens of sense experience, he "constitutes" a "world"; and it is the task of the phenomenologist to work his way back from the world of everyday experience in which essences function as a symbol or as a formula, or perhaps as an unexpressed and semiconscious prejudice that guides experience, into the sphere of essence itself, in order to apprehend more perfectly these principles according to which men, and only men, understand a world. We understand the world of the natural standpoint (and it is clear from the above that this "world of the natural standpoint" is no "one thing"; "my" world may differ in certain respects from "your" world, the world of an ancient Greek, etc.) primarily through the medium of symbols and rules, which are "functionalized" essences. Most frequently, we come to understand the objects of perception, not as instances of essences, but simply as the X that corresponds to a concept or rule. This procedure, in which we substitute a symbol for the object given, is even more marked when one adopts what Scheler calls the "scientific standpoint." This insight led him to embark upon an analysis of the scientific world view that pervaded his own epoch, and ours. We will study this analysis in detail in a moment.

Now we must not confuse Scheler's notion of a "leading" of thought by "intuitions of essence" functioning as concepts or rules on the natural standpoint with the leading of *attention* (*Aufmerksamkeit*). The latter is a vital or biological response to the physical environment and is thus not a function of what he calls the understanding. This biological relationship of the individual to his environment will, however, determine to some extent what portion of the *Wesensreich* is actually intuited. As the dog's attention is directed toward the scent of danger, so are men attracted toward aspects of their world that may be used for the satisfaction of their needs. We are more likely to notice things that are useful to us, and this fact *conditions* the way a man's "world" will be constituted. Indeed, this interest motive may lead to *distortions* of the primordial insight into the *Wesensreich*. It receives further analysis and exemplification in Scheler's well-known essay on the phenomenon of *ressentiment;* we will discuss the phenomenology of this concept in Chapter Seven.[6]

A more positive consequence of the theory of functionalization is that *a priori* knowledge can *grow;* it is not static (confined to twelve or any given number of categories that are common to all men), as in the philosophy of Kant. Given the proper circumstances, a given society or individual can not only increase the adequacy of its knowledge of essence but actually widen the range of this knowledge. An individual may increase his knowledge of the *Wesensreich* by contemplation, the study of the minds of other men, peoples, and cultures, and especially, Scheler claims, by the study of philosophy and the practice of the "intellectual love of essence": a concept we shall present in the next chapter as fundamental to Scheler's concept of phenomenological reduction. But apart from this theoretical consideration, Scheler was not at all shy about using this concept of the variability of *a priori* knowledge to make ideological points: his recommendation of an *Ausgleich* among the peoples of the world was grounded in part upon the fact that the relativity of certain essences to a given people makes necessary the cooperation among the peoples of the world if men are to penetrate the entire sphere of essence. It led further to an insistence upon the importance of preserving and carefully investigating the cultures of the past; for the forms of thought revealed in the works of these cultures may be founded in essential insights of which our epoch is oblivious, or to which it is no longer capable of attaining.

The theory of functionalization is clearly not without severe problems. The trouble that we experience with it concerns the fact that Scheler does not enlighten us as to how we obtain the so-called primordial knowledge of essence. His notion of priority is especially unclear, and here lies the crux of the problem: does Scheler mean that a given conscious act, the grasping of an essence, must have been *actually performed* in the history of an individual's conscious life before an act of a lower order relative to it can be performed by that individual? *In what sense* do I "presuppose" thingness before I can think of causality? In what sense must thingness "already have been given to me" before I can understand such a thing as a causal relation? The suggestion of one author that knowledge *a priori* is not prior in time but *only* in logical significance seems to overlook the fact that for Scheler this primordial "grasping" of essence is an act, and therefore must take place in time.[7] Thus if the order of foundation is a *logical* order, then Scheler's use of such terms as "already given" and "presupposed" is misleading, since no actual temporal order of even unconscious acts of grasping essences would be involved. Yet if the order he is describing is a purely logical order, then his central point, that the possibility of our actually grasping a phenomenon from the natural standpoint is contingent upon having already grasped another, would be vitiated. Scheler specifically denies that a study of the process of functionalization can be carried out on the basis of psychology; only phenomenology is equipped to do this, for we are concerned with the content of cognitions, and not with behavior.

Yet had Scheler considered the possibility that the appropriation of the *Wesensreich* to our knowledge of physical reality is a matter of *learning* — and that the seeing of certain kinds of logical relations and their possible applications to concrete situations is something we first do as children — he might have opened a fruitful path of inquiry for science. Such an inquiry would, however, no longer be a purely phenomenological inquiry, but rather a matter for empirical psychology; for then we would have to deal, not only with questions of the essences underlying behavior, but with the *acts* of applying these insights, with the laws of their "function," and with the genetic order of these acts. The development of psychology in recent decades is tending away from the behaviorism of Scheler's day toward a view of human learning in which the implicit, nonverbal understanding of grammatical, logical, and causal relationships is presupposed by explanations of the behavior of infants and small children. It is hoped that studies of the learning behavior of infants will indicate the rules and structures according to which this learning is accomplished.[8] Such psychological theories are quite compatible with Scheler's theory of functionalization, although it suggests that the notion of the *Fundierungsordnung* (i.e., the doctrine that the order in which knowledge of essence functions on the natural standpoint is a purely logical order) be supplemented by an empirical study of children in which the assumptions and structures that underlie their behavior — especially their learning behavior — be more clearly brought out. Scheler might possibly be in favor of such a study — he suggests at one point the possibility of an "empirical-phenomenological" study in sociology, for example — and this psychological study would require both the observation of infant behavior and the attempt to understand the essential meaning structures in which the possibility of such behavior is founded. As his theory now stands, the *actual process* in which the mind is structured by its openness to essence, and further, the way these structures function on the deepest level, in which a "world" is "constituted," remain something of a mystery, one that explicit knowledge of essence through phenomenological reflection cannot clarify.

The insight at the roots of the notion of functionalization is profound and persuasive if not entirely original with Scheler, however; and it is refreshing that our own age has also seen a turning away from a Humian-behavioristic interpretation of the peculiar fact that men perceive the world in terms of concepts and symbols, and are alone able to reflect upon the meaning contents of these. Recent experiments in the teaching of symbolic languages to chimpanzees do not, it appears to this observer, vitiate Scheler's claim that only human beings are able to do philosophy, that is, are able to reflect upon the *content* of the symbols they use to communicate. Whether future experiments will disclose this capability in chimpanzees is, of course, uncertain. For Scheler, this reflective capacity opens the doors of the spirit to men and makes language more than a practical, "biological" tool. The human intellect cannot be separated from concrete experience; those concepts and symbols that man evolves are founded upon his integration in his natural environment, and they cannot take us beyond what is given. The theory of functionalization is based upon the insight that man's peculiar intellectual and physical constitution permits a wide range of conceptual interpretations of what is given. Human understanding is not limited by inborn structures; how it develops and what categories it chooses to undertake an interpretation of the world will depend upon various circumstances on each level of its development and operation.

Insofar as phenomenology enables us to obtain direct and explicit knowledge of these categories, it can perform a critical function: it can *enlarge* our view onto the world, where that view is too narrow; it can point out where our beliefs and attitudes and theories have perverted the very categories on which they are founded. The theory of functionalization plays an enormous role in Scheler's attempts to criticize the world views prevelant in his own times. He was an intensely critical thinker, and one of the values of reading him is his consistent, sustained, and penetrating criticism of the way of looking at the world that is founded upon the insights of the modern scientific standpoint. Scheler's critique of that standpoint and of its *Weltanschauung* is a study of that functionalization of essence that is the "scientific way of thinking." He tries to exhibit scientific knowledge as both derived and relative to an arbitrarily selected point of view; and he goes on to criticize the metaphysics of "pragmatism" as a function of the scientific definition of knowledge. We will not occupy ourselves with Scheler's effort to crush "pragmatism" and to substitute a "phenomenological" *Weltanschauung* for it, but a study of the salient features of Scheler's attack on the notion of "scientific knowledge" will give us an excellent opportunity to illustrate the theory of functionalization and to specify further his own definition of phenomenological and nonphenomenological knowledge.

In our next chapter we will discuss the problem of establishing the validity of phenomenological knowledge claims, and we will discover that no general, universally applicable criterion of truth and falsity is available to the Schelerian phenomenologist. On the other hand, it is clear that the sciences are able to provide themselves with such criteria, and, for that reason, it is claimed that the sciences possess universal validity (*Allgemeingültigkeit*).[9] The question then arises as to how this universal validity is possible.

We have seen that for Scheler the primordial knowledge relationship is that of the individual human subject perceiving objects; the subject is given a world, and he recognizes individual objects in it as referring to some essence or essences: this is a book, this is another human being, and so on. The possibility of having an everyday world is thus founded upon the subject's openness, not just to sense qualities, but to the *Wesensreich*. For that reason, the phenomenological act of reflective intuition, in which essences are given *as* themselves, repeats the primordial act of knowing, but in a purer and more adequate manner, namely, apart from the specific sense data through which the everyday object is given.

Now whereas phenomenology attempts in this way to expand and make explicit our knowledge of the world of meanings given in natural perception, Scheler holds that science is founded upon an *artificial attenuation* of lived experience. Scheler enumerates several stages of the scientific "reduction," that is, its *abstraction* from the everyday world and its renunciation of knowledge of essence.[10] It is interesting to note that what comes out of Scheler's enumeration is not simply an objection to the failure of science to look upon its object from the point of view of the subject — that is, to examine what Husserl would call the acts of transcendental consciousness constituting the object, or what Scheler calls the order of foundation of the intentional acts in which the object is grasped. What appears to bother him most centrally is that the sciences leave out of consideration the value element that is a moment of every perception. (We will study in chapter five the role of the act of *feeling,* in which values are given, in the constitution of the natural standpoint.) The fact that he holds that the world of the natural standpoint is apprehended as possessing positive and negative values, and that the abstraction from matters of value is fundamental in the sciences, is thus a central reason for Scheler's claim that science cannot "grasp" lived experience in its fullness.

Now it is not only the value element from which the sciences abstract; abstraction is also made from the individual moment that is contained in every "world" given to a person. Here we may again refer to a later discussion in which we will examine Scheler's view that those who imagine that the only knowledge worthy of this name is intersubjectively verifiable knowledge will turn away from the individual element in knowledge, will attempt to get around it. But this, again, is only possible by abstracting from the fullness of the given, by restricting one's vision: "the world" is understood by the sciences as relative to an individual subject of knowledge thought *abstractly,* as a corporeal living being, and not as a concrete human person.[11] This produces a certain uniformity on the side of both the knower and the known: insofar as *all* men are *at least* corporeal living beings, the world given to subjects thus conceived will be the same. This world, we have just noted, Scheler believes to be the world described by mechanistic physics.

Scheler's thought here seems to be that the qualitative fullness of the world given to a knowing subject increases as we conceive the world as relative to a more concrete carrier of knowledge (i.e., as we progress from the human subject thought of as corporeal living being to the thought of him as human being in general, as European, as German, as eighteenth-century German, as Immanuel Kant), yet the number of men to whom that world is immediately given decreases. Moreover, the more concretely we conceive the knowing subject, the more difficult it is to convey, by means of a description, an exact intuition of the specific objects given to him. In order to intuit the world given to the ancient Greek, I am forced to study many aspects of Greek culture in the hope of approaching what can never be the case, namely, seeing the Greek world as an ancient Greek and not as the non-Greek that I am. What I will be trying to do, in Scheler's language, is to reperform in reflective intuition (i.e., an intuition that is no longer immediate and pre-analytic) mental acts performed by a Greek individual in his capacity as a Greek, or what Scheler calls the acts of the Greek "group spirit." He would hold that the difficulty of this sympathetic apprehension increases as the knowledge carrier becomes more concrete, more particular, less dependent upon faculties common to all men — all other things being equal, especially that the number of data I have at my disposal concerning the nature of the acts I am attempting to reperform remains equal in every case. Obviously it is easier for me to understand what is most personal about my friend than what the "typical" Etruscan is like, because I know a lot more about my friend than about the Etruscans.

In the case of the world described by mechanistic physics, this problem of sympathetic understanding vanishes; for while I am not an ancient Greek, I am a corporeal living being, and this "world" is hence as immediately accessible to me as it is to every other corporeal living being. Universally acceptable criteria of truth and falsity are possible here; exactness is possible, because the world of the natural standpoint has been reduced to a world of discrete quantities. The *cognition* of this world in terms of mechanical physics is nevertheless possible only for that kind of corporeal living being that is possessed of understanding; for mechanical physics is a symbolic representation of this world. A symbol is, of course, also derived, as is the subject of knowledge conceived as a corporeal living being; in the case of the symbol, the derivation is made on the side of the object rather than on the side of the knower.

The next stage in the argument that scientific knowledge is derived knowledge concerns the notion of transcendence. Perception from within the natural standpoint, as we recall, is for the most part perception of a thing, not as the thing itself, but rather in terms of a symbol or sign for the thing. In this way, the content of the natural perception possesses elements that transcend what is given in the intuitional apprehension of the pure fact. The pure fact is involved in the perception as its logical presupposition, yet it is apprehended, not as itself, but rather by means of a "concept" or a "picture." It is the task of phenomenology progressively to de-symbolize the natural world, to go back to the intuitions of essence in which the symbols are founded. Now the scientific fact, unlike the perceived fact, does not possess the sensible element: it is pre-sented purely by means of an *artificial* symbol, constructed with a certain theoretical purpose in mind, and defined in terms of for-mulae relating it to observable entities. Thus, Scheler observes, whereas on the natural standpoint the sense element is present in a perception — for example, one apprehends the red color among the green leaves as a sign for the cherry — the scientist abstracts from the red color in its function as the property of a thing, and thinks of the color symbolically, as a mathematical shape, and thus no longer as a sign through which we represent to ourselves the cherry as a unity of physical properties, meanings, and values.[12] This is to say that the scientific fact is founded upon the natural fact but is also transcendent of it, much as the natural fact is transcendent of the pure fact. The element present in the scientific fact that is absent from the natural fact is the artificial symbol. The sky of the astron-omer, Scheler tells us quite simply, is rather different from that given to the natural standpoint; the mathematically conceived movements and forces of the stars and planets are not contained in any sense impression (we do not see the earth traveling around the sun, rather the contrary), nor are the mathematical and theoretical concepts used in astronomy's description of the heavens directly derived, as is the case of concepts used upon the natural stand-point, from intuitions of essences, but rather from our everyday concepts. Art, as Plato maintained, is twice removed from reality; and is science not an art?

As a more concrete example of the foregoing discussion, let us analyze Scheler's critique of previous philosophical descriptions of the causal relation and attempt to indicate the direction of a phenomenological description of causality, showing how the scientific (i.e., for Scheler the Humian) notion of causality is derived from the concept of causality that functions in our everyday awareness.

The focal point of Scheler's critique of previous analyses of the phenomenon of causality was directed at the transformation of this problem by Hume and Kant into logical and metaphysical problems concerning the *nature* of the causal relation and the possible *justification* of causal ascriptions. This attack, he holds, assures us of a false start. For insofar as the question is one of either the *reality* of the causal relation or the *certainty* of general causal laws, it is unanswerable. This does not mean, however, that a certain amount of clarity about what we mean by "causal relation" and about how we come by a concept of causality is not possible. Furthermore, questions of inductive logic, or, more generally, of the logic of causal reasoning in the sciences, concern a peculiar *definition* of causality — the so-called regularity theory of causality. But is it correct to imagine, as did Kant, that the causal relation is first given to us as a regular sequence of "cause" and "effect"? Might it not be that this regularity theory is *derived* from a more immediate understanding we have of the essence of causality? And if so, should not our attempt to understand what causality is begin with the primordial givenness of this phenomenon and then proceed to an analysis of the way we use the term "causality," first in everyday language and then in scientific discourse? Thus Scheler asks how a causal relation is first given, or what knowledge of essence is presupposed by our ability to identify something on the natural standpoint as a causal relation.

His analysis begins, quite naturally, from everyday experience and attempts to look at the causal phenomenon apart from all theories of causality:

First of all, the facts show that the point of departure for the natural conception of causality does not lie in any kind of "regularity." As the first glance at a physical object does not give us an independent "appearance" which when joined to a succession of other appearances leads to the supposition of things, but rather the case is that in every appearance a physical object presents itself, so in the same way a repeated sequence of events A and B does not lead to the idea of a causal connection. Rather, this connection is already given in *every individual* case, where a thing *acts upon* another thing and through its action and through the passivity [*Leiden*] of the other thing the peculiar unity of a process [*Vorgang*] separates itself from the vague fullness of the environment.[13]

The key concepts here are *thing, activity and passivity,* and *process,* for the intentional acts in which these things are grasped are the foundation of the "natural" apprehension of the causal relation. The causal relation is first observed as taking place between things acting upon each other; and it is this act of awareness of activity in which the possibility of grasping as a unity the process that we call the "causal relation" is founded. We will not bother to go further into the phenomenological analyses of these key concepts (which would involve, of course, a description of those acts in which the possibility of grasping "thingness" and "activity" and "passivity" are founded). Rather, we will head in the other direction: what are the essential elements in the traditional scientific-philosophical analysis of causality, and how are these elements founded in the act of grasping the causal relation from within the natural standpoint?

We discovered one element in our earlier discussion of Scheler's critique of "sensualism": from the primordial perception of a thing as that thing, a series of "sense data" or appearances is derived, which, the doctrine states, must be "synthesized" by the mind operating according to laws of association, thus constituting the object. Similarly, the traditional analysis is an attempt to show that the causal relation is a questionable joining together of discrete appearances. The grasping of a thing as a pure appearance is only possible, we have tried to show by following Scheler, on the basis of the perception of *things.* Thus in the "scientific" analysis of causality the derived notion of "appearance" is put in the place of "thing." These "appearances" are understood as constituting a *Sachverhalt,* or "state of affairs" — a "redness," a "coldness," or whatever. *The scientific notion of causality is then understood as a relation holding between states of affairs.* States of affairs, unlike things, are not "perceived"; rather, they are the objects of "observation" (*Beobachtung*).

Now all perception from within the natural standpoint, we recall, occurs upon a spiritual and a vital basis; when we look around a room, for example, our attention is directed not only by our previous knowledge of the things that make up the furnishings of the room but also by our interests as vital, living beings. We come into the room "for a reason"; we are "looking for something," perhaps simply for a place to sit down; things then appear to us within the horizon of our interests and desires. In "observation," on the other hand, the attention is artificially directed, Scheler claims, "by the intention upon something that I want to observe. This something is, however, always the idea of a state of affairs: I want to see if it takes place or not, or how it looks in this situation or on that thing or other."[14] In the theoretical sciences, observation is directed toward establishing the occurrence or nonoccurrence, not of things or processes, but of changes in states of affairs, and science then constructs theoretical substances (e.g., the point mass) and laws with which to explain the occurrence or nonoccurrence of these states of affairs. What comes out of this is a notion of causality that is no longer founded upon the activity of things upon each other, but upon "the idea of an activity which no longer has its place in one of the two things, but rather takes place *between them.*"[15] This notion of activity is capable of exact symbolic representation and scientific description; indeed, a "state of affairs," as Scheler understands this term, is no more than those aspects of a thing that can be quantitatively described. Of course his point is that this quantifiability is only possible by "leaving out of consideration" those qualitative aspects of a thing that are included in our natural apprehension of the world.

But his critique goes further than this. He accuses the sciences, not only of employing symbolical representation of derived concepts, but of pretending to explain with these symbolical representations and the causal laws in which they occur the *essence* of things. "Things" are understood by "science," not as intuitable phenomena, nor even as objects of perception on the natural standpoint, but as the "carriers" of states of affairs. Thus the sciences, Scheler holds, reverse the normal direction of knowing: they attempt to understand appearances not as containing a meaning element that can be given to consciousness in reflective intuition but as the X corresponding to concepts derived from objects given to sense observation on the natural standpoint. Thus, it is said, a "scientific" chair is a mass of atomic elements in regular motion, whereas the "perceptual" chair is an illusion created by the action of our organs of vision upon the quanta of light reflected by the electromagnetic field surrounding the atomic elements. Out of this comes the view that the "essential" chair (or the "real" chair!) is the atomic chair, because our natural perception of the chair is "caused" by it.

To sum up our analysis thus far, we find that Scheler's critique of the sciences is not directed in any way upon the concrete results of scientific investigations of the physical world; specifically, his critique is not predicated on Husserl's claim that the efficiency of the sciences depends upon the prior phenomenological clarification of its key concepts. Scheler, I am sure, would have agreed that the language of science, while founded upon knowledge of essence, is autonomous. Its concepts are geared to the specific problems scientists set out to solve, and the best judge of whether a scientific concept or "theoretical term" is "clear" or "adequate" or "serves its purpose" is the scientist himself, or his helper, the logician. Rather, this critique of the sciences is directed, on the one hand, to the belief that the empirical method establishes the limits of possible knowledge (i.e., everything knowable is knowable scientifically), and on the other hand, toward the scientific "cultural *Weltanschauung*" that has attained dominance over the minds of Western men as a result of the enormous impression created by the achievements of science.

Technically, and in brief, our analysis established that scientific knowledge in no sense represents the primordial and ultimate knowledge of reality but on the contrary is a derived and artificial "function" of primordial insight into essence and essential relations. The unity of the sciences and their universal validity are possible only as a consequence of a two-sided abstraction. On the side of the subject, the "world" that is constituted by the concepts and laws of physics is a world reduced to a set of quantitative relations apprehensible in principle by all men regardless of education or historical or social situation. As opposed to this, the fundamental-phenomenological analysis of "world" reveals that the "world" given to an individual human subject on the natural standpoint is in fact a far more concrete and individual entity than that described by physics, and that the latter "world" is founded upon the former. On the side of the object, the scientific fact was shown to be a construction out of the concepts of "thing" and "process" with which we operate on the natural level. We were furthermore prepared to accept as an example of this derivation of the scientific fact from the natural fact Scheler's contention that the scientific notion of causality as the relation of regular succession between states of affairs is derived from the naturally given phenomenon of the *activity* of a thing upon another. A further discussion of Scheler's critique of the sciences would involve us in a consideration of his attack on the "scientific Weltanschauung." This attack is based upon the consideration that the scientific notion of "world" is *relative to* living corporeal beings, and not to concrete human persons; is *founded in* the phenomenological notion of world; and is *fundamental to* the scientific *Weltanschauung,* which he identifies with the philosophy of pragmatism. Since this critique is not immediately relevant to our analysis of the theory of functionalization, although fundamental to Scheler's own *Weltanschauung,* it will not be discussed here.

CHAPTER 3

The Phenomenological Reduction and the Problem of Evidence

I The "Moral Conditions" of Phenomenology

IN chapter 1, we discovered the theoretical basis of Scheler's phenomenological method in his distinction between the *essential* content of perception and the *sensible* content. The former is said to be the logical condition of perception; the latter is its causal condition. Sense data assure us of the existence of some indeterminate thing; knowledge of what that thing is depends upon our "openness" to the *Wesensreich*. In Chapter 2, we noted in passing that every perception possesses a value element; we perceive things *as* useful or worthless, dangerous or inviting, holy or evil. Values are thus given with things, as a part of their essential content; hence Scheler's contention that values are *cognized,* as opposed to the "reductionist" view that values are simply a physical response to the pleasures and pains that the representation of an object may cause in us. This point is the theoretical basis of the attempt in *Der Formalismus* to make the values themselves the objects of phenomenological scrutiny.

Now in addition to his belief that our everyday value judgments have cognitive content — that values are essences — Scheler held that value essences are *first* in the order of givenness of objects; that is, that the givenness of values "found" our knowledge of all other essences. Hence we would never attain knowledge of what things are unless things were first given as possessing a positive or negative value. This view will be submitted to critical analysis in a moment. First we want to call attention to the fact that Scheler's attempt to take account of the priority of the givenness of value

59

brought about a reinterpretation of Husserl's notion of the phenomenological reduction.

The doctrine of reduction was first developed by Husserl in answer to the question of how we detach the act center — that area of consciousness out of which intentional acts of knowing, apprehending, willing, believing, feeling, all flow — from the psychophysical sphere of the mind — that through which material is presented to consciousness by what Scheler was to call the "functions" of seeing, hearing, smelling, and so on — in order that the phenomenologist might separate in intuition the meaning element of an intentional act from the so-called contingent elements (especially the sense data, or "representation," of the thing) that, together, make up this specific intentional act. Husserl's method of reducing an intentional act to its meaning elements involved various intellectual exercises, the most central of which was suspending judgment concerning the existence of the thing perceived. Scheler agrees that judgment concerning the existence or nonexistence of the thing perceived must be suspended; he adds that judgment concerning the value of the specific, perceived object should be suspended as well. The point is that the phenomenologist is not concerned with the individuality of the object given, but with the object as a carrier of essence. However, Scheler denies that the reductive acts are purely intellectual and thus demand "scientific" neutrality on the part of the phenomenologist, as Husserl held. Rather, the act of phenomenological reflection upon essences demands the emotional and spiritual rebirth of the investigator, at least where the investigation concerns matters of the spirit. The justification of this view lies in Scheler's epistemological speculations, which, briefly, are as follows.

At the beginning of our awareness of an external world — which takes place in the experience of resistance to our will, or, in the *Stellung des Menschen im Kosmos,* to our instinctual drives — the world first presents itself to us as possessing value, and this long "before" it presents itself to us as fulfilling concepts, that is, *as* a tree, *as* possessing spatial relations, and so forth. All later intellectual apprehension thus has this primordial apprehension as its causal precondition. Scheler's attempt to discover in this genetic order the *logical* priority of value essences over all other essences exhibits his fundamental confusion concerning the order of foundation, which we criticized earlier. His statement of the doctrine of the pregivenness of value is not without interest, however:

>...And it seems to me to be a rigid law of the essential makeup of the higher "spiritual" acts just as much as of the lower "functions" which give material to the spirit, that in the order of possible givenness of the *entire objective sphere* the value qualities and value unities of this order are *given before* everything that belongs to the value-*free* level of being: such that nothing value-free can be given *originally* as the object of a perception, act of memory, expectation or, in second place, of thought or judgment whose value-quality or whose value-relation to another thing ... was not given to us already in one way or other. ... All value-free or value-indifferent things are such only by means of a more or less artificial *abstraction,* through which we leave out of consideration values that are not only always given along with it, but also constantly pre-given.[1]

What Scheler has discovered here is that when we disengage the meaning content of perceptions from their sensible conditions and submit the former to phenomenological scrutiny, we find that (1) the thing given in perception was apprehended as a carrier of a positive or negative value of some specific kind; (2) it could not have been perceived as that thing had the value component not been given along with it; (3) the act in which the value component was intended is the *highest* act logically presupposed by the act of perception; that is, had there not been an element of intentionality directed toward values contained within the unified act of perception, none of the other intentional acts coimplied within the perception could have taken place. Nothing can be given if value is not: we first and always apprehend the world and each thing in it as bearing value. All modes of awareness that appear to be value-free either are not in fact, or else are based on abstractions (e.g., scientific "observation") from the primordial mode of apprehension, that is, perception from the natural standpoint.

The discovery of this new "moment" of perception raises serious questions. Clearly, the claim that this doctrine makes is founded at least in part upon pure speculation rather than upon phenomenological evidence. Strangely enough, although fundamental for Scheler's phenomenological point of view, the objection that no experience could contradict this doctrine, at least with respect to the first and second of the three theses distinguished above, is *least* damaging. It might be said, for example, that it would always be possible to show that my apprehension of a given thing, for example, a table as a table, would not have been possible had I not at some prior time grasped the value of "usefulness," insofar as what I *mean* by "table" is, among other things, something that is useful. To leave this value element of "usefulness" out of the definition of "table" would be to falsify the meaning of "tableness." Similarly, in the definition of any given object we can, and must, in Scheler's view, take account of its possible values as an object: for any given object one can raise the question, "What is it good for?"

Yet it seems to this observer that there are insurmountable difficulties present in Scheler's efforts to establish thesis three, that the value element is the highest or absolutely first act implied in the perception of the table as a table. To show this, Scheler would have to demonstrate that the other "moments" implied in the act of apprehending the table (e.g., the act of intending its spatiality) are similarly impossible without the prior cognition of value. Certainly this is not clear upon phenomenological reflection upon the essence of spatiality, nor does our use of language justify this (for spatiality is not an object of perception, about which we could ask, "What is it good for?"), nor does Scheler's contention that all awareness of an external world begins with the apprehension of the negative value of frustration enable us to affirm that value awareness is logically prior to all subsequent intellectual acts. Here again, then, we reach an impasse; Scheler's claim in thesis three requires a phenomenological grounding that he does not supply; yet we must grant him this point of the priority of value givenness to all other intentional acts if we wish to study the epistemological horizons of his method. And with that in mind, we turn to a consideration of what we have called his concept of phenomenological reduction.

Scheler's problem, given the fact that in each perception there is an intentional act directed upon a value given with the perceived object, is to make that value essence, along with all the other essential elements, accessible to reflective intuition. This value essence must be disengaged from the other essential constituents of the perceptual act. His reply to this problem is that the phenomenologist must not go about his investigations simply as a disinterested scientist, but must engage his *whole person,* must obey Plato's "*first* rule" for philosophers, that philosophy "requires a collective act [*Gesamtakt*] of the essence of the person, such as is not found upon the natural standpoint and in the quest for knowledge founded in it, just in order to bring the object of philosophy before the eye of the mind."[2] Insofar as all knowledge of essence is founded in knowledge of value, *no* act of phenomenological reflection can be value-indifferent; each involves the participation of the investigator as an emotional, value-open being. Phenomenological investigations into the value essences themselves require an even higher degree of moral commitment. But what is the nature of this "moral commitment"?

Insofar as the essences intended in phenomenological reflection are grounded in an ideal sphere of being — the *Wesensreich* — which both transcends and is independent of the act of knowing, the phenomenologist, in his reflective acts, participates in this ideal sphere. Hence Scheler's frequent metaphor: knowledge is the "having" or "taking part in" the object of knowledge by the knower. The highest mode of this participation in the ideal sphere of being, Scheler assers, is *love*. This emotional confrontation of essence is the means by which the phenomenologist can best bring himself to grasp essences in themselves; essence gives itself most adequately to him who loves it. An adequate phenomenological description even of value-indifferent essences would seem thus to be dependent upon the moral capacity of the investigator to love. This, according to Scheler, is Plato's *second* rule for philosophers. He asserts: "This act [of the person that brings the object of philosophy before the mind] is founded in an act essentially characterized by *love*."[3] As we shall learn later in this study when we turn to Scheler's phenomenological exhibition of the essence of love, the capacity for loving is the most essential characteristic of man. We can now appreciate the importance for Scheler of the consideration we rejected above, that the act in which the value component was intended is the highest act logically presupposed by the act of perception, for it would follow from this that only because man is able to love does the *Wesensreich* open itself to him; only then are men able to perceive objects as carrying reference to these ideal entities. All knowledge, all language is hence founded in the capacity of men to love the world around them. Animals cannot love, they can experience only urge, *Drang,* and thus they apprehend their environment as devoid of meaning.

How do these Platonic speculations on the relation of love and knowledge bear upon the phenomenological method? Because the world of everyday experience, in which the *Wesensreich* is so vaguely intended, is so "everyday," the phenomenologist must try to reexperience the essences in which that world is founded by re-performing (*Nachvollziehen*) the primordial act of love more perfectly and systematically in order to open himself more perfectly to the realm of essence. The phenomenologist has to imitate methodologically that act in which men are first opened to the world *as meaning* something or other. Hence, in addition to the bracketing of the moment of reality and the attempt to abstract from all sensible elements involved in the perception or cognition that is the object of the investigation, the act of phenomenological reduction requires the performance of the "unified act of the whole person which is founded in love."

Again in *Vom Ewigen im Menschen*, Scheler discusses three necessary moral conditions for performing this "unified act of love," conditions that dispose the philosopher to the phenomenological *Wesenschau*. We might look upon these three moral conditions as the preliminary stages of the Schelerian reduction:

1. The love of the entire spiritual person to absolute value and being;
2. The making humble of the natural ego and self;
3. Self-mastery, and, by means of this and only by means of this, the attainment of a possible *objectifying* of the natural drives of life, which always and necessarily condition sensible perception, and which are given as "corporeal" [*leiblich*] and experienced as corporeally founded.[4]

The last of these conditions is, of the three, perhaps the most important for the theory of phenomenological method, and is most intimately involved in Scheler's notion of essence. It is the subject of the revision and expansion of his notion of method in philosophy that he undertook in *Die Stellung des Menschen im Kosmos*. In this late work, he discusses the necessity of repressing the vital drives, which condition our apprehension of the world, by means of *sublimation*, that is, by using the biological drives to produce an intensification of our spiritual capacities. He notes in another late essay that an "exact theory and technique" for putting out of action all practical attitudes and impulses for the purpose of the *Wesenschau* was planned for the first volume of his never-written metaphysics.[5]

Now the question might be raised: does Scheler's inclusion of "moral conditions" in the phenomenological reduction make phenomenological descriptions logically dependent upon the content of those conditions? Has he made an "objective," that is, value-neutral, methodology impossible?[6] Although Scheler makes knowledge of essence causally dependent upon the performance of emotional acts (such as, love, humility, self-mastery), he does not thereby subjectivize or irrationalize his method or the knowledge founded upon it. He does not "irrationalize" knowledge because the sphere of the emotions is by no means to be interpreted as a source of irrationality in our more "rational" thinking. As he establishes in *Der Formalismus,* the emotions intend values according to *a priori* laws. These laws of the order of foundation of emotional acts are no less rigid than the order of foundation of nonvalue essences, and these values are given in emotional acts as clearly and distinctly as are nonvalue essences to phenomenological intuition. And thus it follows that Scheler does not "subjectivize" knowledge, because his *Gesamtakt* is an intuitive act; it can be performed in any case only by an individual subject, and has no external or psychological "signs." Objectivity, in the interpersonal "scientific" sense, is possible only on the basis of the "subjective" evaluation of evidence. Finally, it should be clear from our discussion that the soundness of any phenomenological description is not logically dependent upon the moral commitment of the investigator. The "moral conditions of knowledge" given above are quite general and do not require commitment to specific ethical norms or world views; in fact Scheler claims that the only way of attaining the insight into values required for the establishment of ethical norms is an attitude that is loving, humble, contemplative.

Nevertheless, it is not yet possible to rest satisfied with this description of the phenomenological approach to knowledge. Clearly, if Scheler is going to claim that it is possible for a man to detach himself so completely from the values and norms to which we are consciously or unconsciously committed in our everyday existence so as to be able to contemplate values and essences themselves, apart from their appearances on objects, goals, and desires, he must present us with an account of our "everyday" ethical consciousness. Moreover, since phenomenological knowlege lays claim to apodicticity, to the *a priori* and necessary knowledge of essences, the phenomenologist must be capable of a vision that transcends the historical limitations of his own time and place. (We will report upon his attempt to justify these claims in our section on his sociology of knowledge.) Further, it is not sufficient to describe the attitudes of the investigator to the object of his investigation in order

to assure ourselves of the objectivity of his researches. The question
of evidence must also be raised. In the preceding paragraph we
noted Scheler's opinion that all phenomenological evidence is ultimately founded in "subjective" awareness. But how then is it
possible to judge upon the truth of the phenomenologist's claims?
Is a criterion for the truth or falsity of phenomenological knowledge claims possible?

II   Phenomenological Evidence

Because Scheler insisted upon the exclusion of observation and
perception as modes of phenomenological evidence, he will be
called upon to provide an analysis of the phenomenological way of
experiencing objects, which he calls reflective intuition, or, meta-
phorically, "seeing with the eye of the mind." It is clear from the
preceding discussion that we can discuss the nature of this mode of
experience and its expression in language as a phenomenological
description or "exhibition" (*Aufweisen*) apart from the means to
its attainment, namely, the fulfillment of its "moral conditions." If
we thus bracket questions of Scheler's reduction, the general structure of the phenomenological method becomes apparent. Scheler's
essays on the phenomenological attitude parallel Husserl's analysis
of the same theme:[7] one turns one's vision away from the world of
changing things, the world of the "natural standpoint"; one directs
one's mind upon what is given to consciousness, refraining from
judgments about the existence of the given; one attempts to bring
what is given to perfect adequation, to self-givenness: *self*-given,
we recall, because given in one intentional act, thus without any
further elements of meaning, symbol, or sense in terms of which
the given could be thought. But what are the characteristics of the
phenomenological mode of experience? Scheler himself speaks on
this issue in a rather long passage, which is the best summary statement of his position:

> Phenomenological experience... can be sharply distinguished from all
> other kinds of experience, e.g., experience from the natural standpoint
> and from the scientific point of view, by *two* characteristics: It alone gives
> us the facts "themselves" and therefore immediately, that is, not mediated
> by symbols, signs, or directives [*Anweisungen*] of any kind. So, for exam-
> ple, a given color red is capable of determination in the most various ways:
> as *the* color that is denoted by the word "red"; as the color of *this* thing or

this surface here ... as the color that I see now, etc. The experience appears here as the X of a formula or as the X resolving a sequence of conditions. Phenomenological experience, on the other hand, is that in which the particular totality of these signs, instructions, modes of determination, finds *final* resolution. It alone gives us red "itself." It makes out of the X a factual content of intuition. ... Thus we can say: all non-phenomenological experience is in principle experience through or by means of one or another kind of symbol, and hence is mediate experience, which never gives us the things themselves. Only phenomenological experience is in principle asymbolic and for that very reason capable of resolving *all* possible symbols.

At the same time, [phenomenological experience] is pure immanent experience, that is, only that belongs to it which is intuitable [*anschaulich*] *in* the particular *act* of experiencing, never anything that, through the content given in the act, is thought of [*vermeint*] as outside of and separate from the act. All non-phenomenological experience is in principle transcendent of its intuitive content, e.g., the natural perception of a real thing. In [this perception] something is "thought of" [*vermeint*] that is not "given" in it. Phenomenological experience is that in which nothing is intended [*gemeint*] that is not given, and nothing given is outside of the intended. In this congruence of "intended" and "given" the *content* of phenomenological experience is made known to us. *In* this congruence, at the point where the intended and the given come together and satisfy each other, the "phenomenon" appears. Where the given surpasses the intended, or the intended is not "itself" and thus not perfectly given, there is as yet no pure phenomenological experience.[8]

It is clear from this definition that the question of how we can be sure that an intentional object is self-given or not is inappropriate. Truth, Scheler quotes Spinoza, is the criterion of itself and of the false. To demand a criterion of truth — such as we have in the sciences — is to demand a pattern against which objects or propositions might be measured; a criterion, by its very nature, involves a weighing of things, a comparison with a standard. Scheler's point is, simply, that in order to cut the pattern or set the standard, one must already have some insight into the nature of those things that are being compared with the pattern or standard. But it is exactly that insight into the nature of things that the phenomenologist wishes to develop more deeply; and he wishes to reexperience things as they were experienced *before* all standardization, before the resolution of our experience of the world into concepts and symbols. "Even the idea of a criterion of self-givenness is nonsense," according to Scheler, "for all questions concerning criteria make sense only where the thing is not itself given, but only a 'symbol' for it."⁹

It is important to keep in mind that the experience of the congruence of the given with the intended cannot function as a criterion of the "truth" of phenomenological evidence because we have not yet to do with the truth of propositional knowledge. What is "apodictic" in pure phenomenological experience is not the *judgments* founded upon that experience but the *intuitive knowledge* of the things themselves that are given in that experience. Yet it is just that fact that many critics of the phenomenological notion of evidence fail to apprehend in their criticisms, namely, that the phenomenologist is not at first seeking to ground apodictically a set of judgments concerning the nature of the given by means of phenomenological intuition, such as, for example, Descartes in his grounding of the sentence *cogito, ergo sum*. Rather, he is looking for insight into our most fundamental experiences of a world that make *any* judgment possible. Still, the question remains: can there be no self-deception as to the congruence of the given with the intended? Can one not "see what one wants to see"? Furthermore, does it make sense to speak, as Scheler often does, of the "levels of adequacy" of a preverbal mode of experience? The notion of a "level" implies standards and measurement by them. Such objections are clearly dangerous to Scheler's claim to apodicticity for pure phenomenological experience. Yet his answers to them are not entirely satisfactory. The difficulty perhaps lies in his failure to think through the concepts of "truth" and "falsity" themselves to a point where it makes sense to speak of the "truth" of the given itself, and not simply as the truth or falsity of sentences. Heidegger's later studies of "unhiddenness" as the most fundamental insight into the essence of truth, is perhaps at the root of Scheler's understanding of truth and falsity in phenomenology, but this concept was never developed by him. Rather, he seems unable to escape the interpretation of truth as the correspondence between judgment and "reality" that was common in the "scientific" philosophy of positivism he was attacking.

Consequently, Scheler appears to have become more willing to speak of phenomenological claims as true and of judgments about a thing that is experienced as self-given as not liable to error as he grew older. He wrote, for example, in 1924: "There is no false knowledge [*Wissen*]. Knowledge is *evident* or *not evident,* or again *adequate* or *inadequate* in relation to the essential fullness of the object. True or false, on the other hand, are *sentences* alone, i.e., the *ideal meaning-correlates* immanent in our judgments. These sentences are true when they 'correspond' to the evident and most adequately intuited essence of an object of knowledge; false, when they conflict with it."[10] The growing confidence in the apodicticity of judgments based upon phenomenological evidence is a phenomenon perhaps parallel with his growing belief in the possibility of a speculative metaphysics. Still, this view is in contradiction both with his definition of phenomenological experience as preverbal intuition of the things themselves and with his conception of metaphysics. We will have occasion to return to these problems later. Now we must describe how Scheler proposes to apply the phenomenological method of reflective intuition to concrete philosophical problems.

Since Scheler has excluded the possibility of employing criteria in phenomenological investigations, it follows that he can offer his readers neither demonstrations (*Nachweise*) nor proofs (*Beweise*) of phenomenological "doctrines." Rather, in his books, lectures, conversations with other phenomenologists and with laymen, the phenomenologist attempts to help his readers attain the same intuitions of essence as he does. By means of the descriptive use of language, he seeks to "exhibit" or "present" (*Aufweisen*) to others the object he has before his intuitive eye. Generally, the author or speaker will begin by inviting his readers or hearers to adopt the phenomenological point of view, which involves before all else the willingness to think of all things (in the broadest possible sense, as in the German *alles Seiende*) as instances of essences. After having adopted this phenomenological point of view — the *Einstellung* — the phenomenologist will go on to describe the object he has in view, his sentences directing his audience toward that which is to be intuited, that which is asymbolic. Naturally there may be divergences in opinion between the phenomenologist and the audience concerning the descriptive terms used in the *Aufweisen;* then there is discussion, until clarity is reached. That such clarity is possible is the premise of phenomenology. That there can be criteria for judging that clarity has been reached is impossible, for the reasons just adduced. Admitting then that proofs and demonstrations are not part of the phenomenologist's tools, may we yet not point to recurrent patterns in the *Aufweisen?* It seems to this reader that we can distinguish at least three such patterns, or what we might call forms of Scheler's argumentation.

First of all, there is a parallel between the phenomenological method and the Kantian transcendental method in that Scheler is continually looking for what a cognitive act presupposes by way of other cognitive acts as the grounds of its possibility. Thus we noted earlier that the act of grasping something as a tree presupposes the previous apprehension of spatial relations. Thus again Scheler notes in *Der Formalismus* that the understanding of the concept of duty presupposes the understanding of what it is to give or receive an *order*.[11] In pointing such things out, he is not only giving us insight into the order in which we apprehend the things of this world but is also getting at the *essence* of these things and at their essential interrelationships with each other and with the mind that apprehends them; this search, of course, is one of the purposes of phenomenological analysis.

Second, Scheler attacks the phenomenon under investigation by looking into the usages of the words that denote it. Thus he notes in the course of his efforts to distinguish the essence of "person" from that of the "ego" (*Ich*) that " a person 'acts,' e.g., it 'takes a walk,' etc., but an ego cannot do that.... Of course language allows me to say 'I act, I take a walk,' etc., but [here there is a difference, etc.]."[12] Such applications of linguistic analysis are not uncommon in Scheler's phenomenological descriptions. Of course it follows from the nature of the method that at such times he is not trying to establish the logic of linguistic usage but is rather investigating usage in order to establish something about the fact described, or at least point us in the direction of the facts. Scheler's epistemological presupposition is, of course, that language reflects the way the world is experienced, and one may therefore attempt to go through language back to the original experience of the world in which linguistic usage is founded. Phenomenology is a science of the prelinguistic, as we have often noted; it is a study of that primordial intercourse with a "world" that is then expressed in language and logic.

A third "method of argument" deserving attention involves the calling upon of examples of the phenomenon under examination. These examples may be taken from everyday experience and are intended to illustrate the essences or essential relationships in question, which then must be intuited apart from their concrete instances: the mind must "leap" from the observation of real cases to the intuitive apprehension of that which is instanced. In *Der Formalismus* and the *Vom Ewigen im Menschen,* Scheler often takes his examples from historical sources; in the later works, they are often drawn from the sciences. One must be astonished at the enormous range of learning that Scheler possessed; his ability to call upon facts to help support a point he is making is staggering, even when we must question the value of the support rendered by the citation. The passage reproduced in footnote 13 occurs during his *Aufweisen* of the essence of the psychical phenomenon of "identification," and is an example of his occasional lack of discrimination in his choice of examples. It serves its purposes insofar as it is a *possible* event, however, and directs our reflection in a very specific way upon the phenomenon Scheler has before the "eye" of his mind."[13]

III   *Conclusions*

How does our discussion of the *Aufweisen* cast light on the frequent objection that phenomenological reflection is "subjective" and arbitrary in comparison with the methods developed by the natural sciences? Clearly, the phenomenologist can make no claims for publicity. Nevertheless, he believes his program is capable of being carried out with rigor and clarity. If, as Scheler asserts against Husserl, phenomenology is not a "science," the reason is not that there is publicity of inquiry in the natural-scientific sense of the term; this opinion rests rather on Scheler's analysis of the nature of the positive sciences as opposed to that of phenomenology. "Publicity" is a term appropriate to the natural sciences because of the peculiar nature of the sciences and their mode of investigation, and we should not feel that phenomenological intuition has less cognitive value than scientific observation because of the lack of appropriateness of this term to it. On the contrary, Scheler holds that phenomenology has a *higher* cognitive value than the sciences, because it reveals the ground of the possibility of the scientific mode of cognition.

However, there is a second possible objection that perhaps carries more weight. This objection concerns the apparent lack of substantive doctrines based on phenomenological inquiries, a lack that can be traced to the absence of criteria for the truth or falsity of propositions based upon phenomenological intuition. The problem seems to be that Scheler wishes to renounce the use of criteria as both impossible and superfluous, and yet wishes to claim that phenomenology can provide us with apodictic evidence for the truth or falsity of judgments. Scheler's position seems to justify only the apodicticity of the *intuitive* knowledge of the intended object, where that object is not a judgment but a pure fact. How is it possible to "translate" that perfect, intuitive apprehension of a pure fact into language, in which judgment is made concerning its nature? Our discussion of the process of *Aufweisen* and description strengthens us in our view that Scheler can claim apodicticity only for the intuition of essence (what Husserl called the *Erlebnis*), and thus only for the judgment *that* an object has been self-given in intuition, and *not* for any judgments concerning the nature of the self-given. The purpose of the *Aufweisen* is not the establishment of propositional knowledge, but merely the leading of other men to the intuitive apprehension of the given.

If Scheler nevertheless insists upon the claim made in an earlier quotation that "sentences are true when they correspond to the evident and most adequately intuited essences of an object of knowledge," then he is introducing a criterion, and thus passing beyond the limits imposed by the phenomenological method. In this case, it is the right of the critic to demand a justification of the claim of correspondence by evidence that can be made public. If, however, Scheler is content to restrict phenomenology to the attainment of knowledge that is nonpropositional, then the objection of the critic is nugatory, but the possibility of positive doctrines built upon phenomenological evidence and carrying the claim of apodicticity is eliminated. This is a paradox of Scheler's phenomenology.

Perhaps we could suggest a compromise settlement of the paradox. It is certain that *if* we can properly speak of "propositional" phenomenological knowledge, this knowledge will not be *exact*. Exactness, like publicity, is attainable only in the natural sciences, where abstraction is made from the fullness of the given. Furthermore, such knowledge would not be *apodictic:* we must insist that Scheler refrain from using this term when he is not speaking of what is given in an intentional act. The incorrigibility of judgments based upon reflective intuition directed toward objects cannot be maintained. Nevertheless, it would be unjust to insist upon the limitation of the term "knowledge" either to that attained by reflective intuition or to that attained by the observation of the behavior of concrete objects. The problem here is perhaps merely semantic and based upon epistemological prejudice. It should not inhibit us from earnest consideration of the doctrines Scheler claims — incorrectly, if we are right — are apodictic because founded upon the perfect givenness of the object concerning which the claim has been raised. If Scheler's doctrines do not increase our positive knowledge of the world, they still illuminate the broad chasm between the knower and the known in which experience and language interpenetrate, about which it is certainly possible to "talk sense" if not to found "truths" as defined by the correspondence theory. Yet this paradox plagues Scheler's efforts to present a consistent epistemological basis for his attempts to present a convincing case for the value of phenomenology for philosophical analysis and reflects the division in his own spirit as a philosopher on the one hand and as a political ideologist and moral teacher on the other.

Before we move to a description of the substance of Scheler's phenomenological philosophy, we wish to make a final excursus on the epistemological basis of his method. We will attempt an analysis of Scheler's program for phenomenology and its relationship to philosophy. We will ask whether he considered phenomenology to be the whole of philosophy, or whether there can be a philosophical undertaking that is both legitimate and outside the range of pure phenomenological inquiry; and further, whether the method itself is tied to any epistemological considerations that are not themselves justifiable by phenomenological evidence. These investigations should deepen our understanding of the problems of evidence we have encountered in this chapter, and, even more, should clarify Scheler's intellectual and political commitments as a man of his times.

CHAPTER 4

Phenomenology and the Problem of Knowledge

L ET us speculate for a moment from Scheler's point of view on the following problem. We are walking down the street with our dog. How does our "perception" of the houses and trees we pass by differ from that of our dog? We know from one of Scheler's last essays, *Die Stellung des Menschen im Kosmos,* that he viewed the higher animals as dominated by the biological principle of instinct and limited in their intellectual functions to the faculty of associative memory. Their reactions to the external world and the focus of their interest in the world are determined by elementary physical need and instinctual or learned response. Thus our dog "sees" — or perhaps better "smells" — his environment simply as a place in which satisfactions and dangers appear; he sees the houses and trees as "familiar" or "unfamiliar." But however else his "perceptions" of his environment may be structured — or, in a more phenomenological language, however his "world" is "constituted" — it is certain that he does not see the houses and trees *as* houses and trees, nor does he perceive the larger dog approaching *as* "dangerous," although he may respond by pulling his tail under. Perceiving things *as* something or other is only possible for those creatures who possess an understanding of essence.

Up to this point, we have described phenomenology as the method developed by Husserl, Scheler, and others, to explore systematically the content and logical order of the essences to which we make inexplicit reference when we refer in our everyday lives to things *as* being this or that. In this chapter, we are going to step back a bit and examine the horizon of meaning in which Scheler understands his method to operate. Thus we will be studying metaphenomenology: the picture of the world and man that emerges from this understanding of the nature of knowing. Scheler himself

74

would urge this task upon us, for just as he attempted to go back to the foundation of the world view in which his pragmatist and positivist opponents operate, so did he see the necessity that every attempt to think be self-critical, and go back to the original intuitions of essence and to the human goals that give, respectively, substance and direction to thought. Substantive doctrines about the world only "make sense" within a horizon of metaphysical commitment and human need. Similarly, his own moral and metaphysical commitments give sense to his methods, and although the method could operate without reference to them, a critical study of them will give us further insight into the essence of this methodology and the subjects he chose for phenomenological investigation.

I *Realism-Idealism*

The first of Scheler's genuinely speculative-metaphysical doctrines that we will consider involves his belief that essences are in some way real, that is, exist *extra mentem,* and that therefore knowledge — the intentional relation between a knower and a known, between "spirit" and "world" — is an ontological relationship, that is, an underived, primordial relationship between two things, not a construction of consciousness.[1] Yet his presentation of this doctrine is again unclear and paradoxical.

Scheler's theory of knowledge is an attempt to find a middle road between forms of idealism current in his day — including, perhaps, Husserl's later thought, to which Scheler makes veiled reference in the late essay "Idealismus-Realismus" — and epistemological realism in its classic form, which Scheler held to be untenable, given the facts of experience. By "classic realism" we are not referring to the theories that hold that a perception "represents," "copies," or "resembles" the object perceived. Scheler would reject all such theories as resting on the "sensualist" presupposition that *the* problem of knowledge is that of perception. Rather, a "classic" realist school in Scheler's sense would be represented by the claim that the mind passively receives its knowledge of the world; possession of knowledge does not involve the activity of the mind. On this interpretation, Plato is a realist, and Kant an idealist.

In "Idealismus-Realismus," Scheler localized the problem that he believed had usually led to the division between the "realist" and the "idealist." Both are struck by the fact that there seems to exist a rigid dichotomy between the thing as phenomenon and the thing *an sich.* This division, Scheler holds, is by no means a necessary one. We can distinguish between the *So-sein,* or "whatness," of a thing, the essence, and its *Dasein,* or existence. An existing thing exists as an instance of an essence or essences. When we perceive the essence carried by the thing, we "know" it, so to speak. "Knowing" and "naming" come at times very close together in Scheler's usage, at least when we are speaking about knowledge from the natural standpoint. But because the essence of knowing seems to be constituted by the perception of something *as* an instance of some essence — and Scheler will insist that all knowledge is ultimately of essences and not of things — we need not conclude that the essence is constituted by the act of knowing it or by Husserl's transcendental consciousness. Men may create symbols for the meanings they apprehend; they may place the meanings they apprehend in the context of a given body of knowledge or tradition; but neither they nor a function of their intelligence or their consciousness *create* meanings. According to Scheler, "The only thing to which a law [*Vorschrift*] in the strict sense of the term can be given, is not, as Kant says, 'Nature,' nor all of the objects and facts in Nature, but only the signs we use for them. Everything else must be looked upon as 'given.' 'Understanding,' contrary to Kant, does nothing, makes nothing, forms nothing."[2]

Now the fact that essences are objects of knowledge, that is, phenomena, does not exclude the possibility of their existence *extra mentem;* and it appears from our last quotation that Scheler posits this possibility as fact: for if essences are given to consciousness and yet are not constituted by consciousness, they must exist independently of the mind. Hence the concept of a *Wesensreich,* a realm of essence. But then the paradox arises: Scheler specifically denies that essences can be *given* as existing independently of the mind and that an *a priori* metaphysics of the really real is possible.[3] The only sensible question one might ask in the light of this is *in what sense* can we predicate existence of anything?

We recall from our discussion in the last chapter that Scheler holds that we are made aware of the existence of objects by their resistance to our will, or what he later called our *zentraler Lebensdrang.* Thus concrete, individual objects exist independently of their being known, and this empirical existence is best characterized by reference to their capacity to act. This mode of "givenness," that of empirical objects in the phenomenon of resistance, must be kept apart from the mode of givenness of essence, at least insofar as the former is not a cognitive act; rather, it is the ground of the possibility of our grasping cognitively anything *as* existing and *as* bearing reference to the *Wesensreich*. But most important for our discussion is Scheler's contention that this vital or noncognitive grasping of some indeterminate thing as existing is the *only* way that a thing can be given as real, and that this experience is the only justification for positing a thing as real. Reflective intuition alone will not reveal the existence of things to us; actual physical interaction of a subject with a world is required. "Even perception, memory, thinking, and all possible perceptive acts," declares Scheler, "are not able to give us this impression" [of reality]. What they give us is always only the fortuitous way things are [*So-sein*], never their existence [*Dasein*]."⁴ Despite the antimetaphysical flavor of this passage, Scheler uses this doctrine to make a metaphysical point in another work — he holds it to be evidence for the independence of the world from mental activity: "In every resistance that we experience, we apprehend the efficacy and strength of something else that does not originate in us, and cannot originate in us."⁵

It is most striking that Scheler does not apply this criterion for the existence of a thing to the *Wesensreich* itself. If essences exist *extra mentem,* and we can *know* that they exist *extra mentem,* should not we encounter them as resistant to our will? But of course essences by their very nature cannot resist anything, they are neither physical objects nor disembodied forces; and therefore they cannot possess empirical existence. The phenomenon of resistance may, indeed, bear witness that the world is something other than me, that it does not belong to my ego; but it is not the essences that are resistant to my will, but rather *physical objects*. I am forced in this matter simply to note the opinion of Maurice Dupuy, the leading French authority on Scheler, who observes that "essences[for Scheler] *are* without in any way existing as such. . . . He grants them a being that is not exhausted in being-an-object [*dans l'etre-object*]."⁶ That this is an extremely unsatisfactory solution, even leaving aside the paradoxical notion of a thing that *is* without existing, goes without saying. Thus we must conclude that Scheler's metaphysical realism is in fundamental conflict with his theory of knowledge.

If Scheler is confused concerning the metaphysical status of knowledge and the ultimate nature of the objects of phenomenological reflection, he is less so concerning the phenomenal character of knowledge. And this is of course what matters most for phenomenological philosophy. Thus when we turn to his account of types of knowledge, their conditions, and the modes of relativity of knowledge to a given subject, we find him again operating as a phenomenologist, trying to get at the essence of knowledge as it is experienced in our everyday lives — described in language, stated as a claim — rather than at its ultimate nature. His interest in this problem is motivated by what we referred to in the prologue as his central historical and ideological concern: the ethical and philosophical relativism of his times. This concern led him quite naturally to a phenomenological analysis of "relative knowledge" itself: what is knowledge said to be relative *to,* and does it make sense to speak of a knowledge that is relative to nothing? In our chapter on his sociology of knowledge we will again be concerned with Scheler's doctrine of world views, or *Weltanschauungslehre,* for there we will be studying the social and historical dimensions of world views, metaphysical systems, and "wisdom." But since this theme is relevant to an understanding of his analysis of the nature and kinds of knowledge, we would do well to introduce the reader to it at this point. It will provide us with a basis for a description and criticism of his efforts to counter "relativism" and to establish the conditions of metaphysical knowledge.

II   Weltanschauungslehre *and Relativism*

In 1922, Scheler wrote a brief article attacking a lecture by Max Weber concerning the positing of world views, or *Weltanschauungen.*[7] Weber's claim, Scheler explains, is that the positing of *Weltanschauungen* to, for instance, assert something about the nature of absolute reality, describe the highest human good, or posit the existence or nonexistence of God, is not possible on the basis either of science or of philosophy correctly understood (i.e., a philosophy concerned solely with logic and with the criteria of scientific argument and verification). Rather, the positing of *Weltanschauungen* is the affair of "charismatic prophets" who base their pronouncements upon the traditions of a people or a culture. Thus, Scheler proceeds, there is for Weber no "rational" way of positing *Weltanschauungen,* although such matters are, Weber admits, of even greater concern to men than the contributions of the physical sciences. The sciences, however, have the advantage of being strictly independent of all tradition and *Weltanschauungen,* and possess intersubjective validity (*Allgemeingültigkeit*).

Scheler comes out against this philosophical relativism by making some interesting distinctions. Relativism, he tells us, need not imply a single, absolute limit of knowledge. A *Weltanschauung,* or the view one has of one's own self or of God (*Welt-, Selbst-, oder Gottesanschauung*) may, however, be relative to some person, or some group of persons, or, in general, to some "carrier" of knowledge (e.g., to the person conceived as a corporeal living being, etc., as discussed earlier). The question to ask, in any case, is *what* the knowledge claim asserted to be relative is relative *to.* In the article attacking Weber, Scheler asserts that there are three levels of relativity of *Weltanschauungen.* First there is the *absolute natural Weltanschauung,* which he describes in this essay as a "historically and sociologically unchanging constant which philosophy must undertake to describe; a task which, however, can be accomplished only by means of a difficult peeling away of the 'real' and 'living' *tradition* that is always woven into every concrete social *Weltanschauung.*"[8] Scheler insists, however — in line with his opposition to Kant's belief that the understanding possesses a static categorical structure — that there is no single set of concepts or conceptual structure — (hence no single set of beliefs) — common to all men. On the contrary, Scheler asserts in the "Probleme einer Soziologie des Wissens" that "the hand-me-down concept of an *absolutely constant* natural *Weltanschauung* must be *rejected* by the sociology of knowledge. . . . [From the fact that what one group holds as obvious and not in need of any justification can be completely different from what another group holds] we learn that there is no *one* constant natural *Weltanschauung* 'of" men; rather, that the difference in world-views of men extends into the categorical *structures* of the *given* itself."[9]

However, insofar as the normal human biological organization remains constant, there will be preverbal, nonintellectual awareness of the world prior to and conditioning all conceptualization; hence "absolute" because dependent only upon the fact that men have this physical and biological organization and none other. Surely if men had bodies like ants, the direction of our conceptualizations would be quite different from what it in fact is! On the other hand, the ant is a corporeal living being, like a man, and if he could conceptualize at all, he would be capable of understanding the basic laws of mechanistic physics; in this sense, then, mechanistic physics is "relative" to a carrier of knowledge thus conceived. Similarly relative to the normal human organization are "all contents of the natural *Weltanschauung* of men, the moon and sun as visible objects there in the sky, or all normal artificial illusions."[10]

Now Scheler claims that one of the tasks of a phenomenological sociology of knowledge is to discover and analyze the levels of relativity of knowledge (i.e., belief in the reality of objects or in the value of actions or in the meaning of concepts) to the kinds of knowledge carriers. Just as we conceive of absolute knowledge as being relative to God, so knowledge may be relative to given races or to one sex or the other, or even, as in the case of the object of a hallucination, relative to one person. It is interesting to recall in this connection a discussion in *Der Formalismus,* where Scheler represents the doctrine that the "world" is relative to the individual "person": "To every individual person corresponds an individual world.... Each world, however, is in its essential structure tied *a priori* to the essential relation and relations of structure that exist between the essences of the things [in the world].... In addition, however, [the world] contains a final peculiar element, which cannot be grasped by the essential concepts that refer to general essentialities, an original trace of essence [*Wesenszug*] that belongs to the "world" of this person and to no other."[11] The interpersonal world in which men live together and can identify the same objects is a construction out of this personal world. This "world" of the "person" is irreducible; that is to say, it cannot be explained in terms of any other principle; perhaps better said, it cannot be founded in any other phenomenon. It is a "pure fact." As when we think of the concept of consciousness we must include reference to the intentional object that each act of consciousness is directed toward, so when we think of "person," we must include reference to the "world" to which *this* person is open. There is no act of consciousness without an object, no person without a world; these are *essential* relationships, as is *evident* in reflective intuition.

Basing himself upon these "essential facts," Scheler then adds to the above passage: "'The' truth, i.e., the metaphysical truth about the nature and existence of ultimate reality, can only be personal."[12] By this statement he means not that there are as many absolute truths as there are persons but rather that only those essences that can be given in phenomenological purity to the person as person (and not to the person as human being, living creature, German, etc.) can be considered to be "absolute" — not relative to a general *kind* of knowledge carrier, but only to a specific, concrete individual. For that reason Scheler holds that if there be a God, He must be a person. The truths relative to a person considered as, for example, a corporeal living being — that is, the truths of mechanistic physics — are derived from this primordial knowledge relation: a specific world is given to a specific individual.

That this should be Scheler's view will not surprise us if we consider his interpretation of the phenomenological method. We have noted that to him phenomenological research is by nature an undertaking in which evidence can be presented only to the individual researcher and that his public studies consist in an attempt to cause his hearers or readers to have the same intuitions of essence as he does. There is thus always a necessity of going back from the natural, intersubjective world of the everyday into a "private" phenomenological standpoint to dig out from the mass of data given to consciousness upon the natural standpoint those facts about what things mean, which are only implicitly given upon the natural standpoint, and to bring these facts to perfect givenness in reflective intuition. After that, it is a question of discovering how these essential facts serve as the building blocks for the meanings we employ in the everyday world in which we find ourselves in mutual understanding with other men; in other words, how the intersubjective "world" is constituted from the essence materials given to the individual.[13]

Nevertheless, what is individual in the primordial "world" given to the individual person is not reducible to anything else, and is hence indescribable, and can be grasped only in reflective intuition. The "person" can never be an "object" of knowledge. Nevertheless, the primordial relation of "person" to "world" is for Scheler the most fundamental ontological conception of what knowledge is: a person has a world. The philosopher who takes a position opposed to this view — who asserts that what is individual in the knowledge relation is a "subjective" element that stands in the way of "objective," universally valid knowledge — "will always think that one must brush *aside* the person, raise oneself over it, some-

how get *rid* of it, in order to come to Being itself," says Scheler.[14]
But this effort presupposes that "the" truth is something that *must
in principle* be given to or be apprehensible by all men — a presupposition that Scheler would deny, as we shall observe in our next
section.

Let us now return to the discussion of *Weltanschauungen* in the
essay on Max Weber. To recapitulate, Scheler was in the process of
distinguishing ways in which a *Weltanschauung* — a general view,
or a set of assumptions explicit or implicit in the intellectual world
of a person, concerning the nature of the world and man's place in
it — may be "relative." He first mentioned the absolute natural
Weltanschauung, which he understood, not as a single set of beliefs
about the world, but rather as the preintellectual *foundation* of
articulated *Weltanschauungen,* and relative to the person conceived
merely as possessing a human biological organization. The concrete
beliefs and presuppositions that are relative to the individual person, thought of this time as belonging to a specific human culture,
may vary from place to place, from tribe to tribe, depending upon
physical circumstances. The *relative* natural *Weltanschauung* is
then characterized as that set of (usually traditional) beliefs that do
not stand in need of any justification in the eyes of the people who
hold to them. These *Weltanschauungen* are of course not constant
in their specific content, but vary with the age and the group in
which they appear. Finally, there is the cultural *Weltanschauung,*
which "through conscious spiritual activity is created and, according to sociological laws, through the efforts of a 'few' personal
leaders and exemplary men and 'many' followers and imitators, are
spread and gain power."[15]

A system of metaphysics is a cultural *Weltanschauung.* The
knowledge it gives us is personal, but not absolute, for it springs
from a personal, finite vision that is conditioned by its time and
place; the "wise man" grasps certain essential characteristics of
reality and posits these characteristics as the existential ground of
all Being. Only knowledge of essence itself, of the whatness of the
given, can be said to be "absolute," because it limits itself to what
can be directly and immediately given to intuition. For that reason
it might seem that Scheler would wish to deny the possibility of
establishing the truth of a metaphysical system. And he does. A
description of his views on metaphysics will be the culmination of
our analysis of the horizons of the phenomenological method and

its relation to philosophy.

III   *Phenomenology and Philosophy*

The general conclusion that Scheler draws from his analysis of *Weltanschauungen* is that since knowledge may be relative to a given individual in various ways — depending upon how concretely the individual knowing subject is conceived — therefore there is no single *limit* to knowledge. If there are limits to knowledge, these limits must be sought in the givens themselves, and not in a formal definition of "knowledge" or "experience" or "validity." "There is ... no so-called ultimate limit to knowledge," Scheler states, "but solely limits that are relative to a given mode and capacity for knowing of any given carrier of the act."[16] These "limits" can be overcome with varying degrees of success if we devote ourselves to the unprejudiced examination of the givens in each case. Thus we noted earlier that it is possible for me to reexperience the world of the ancient Greek by studying the tracings left by the Greek people during their history and, most important, Scheler would add, by practicing the phenomenological reduction: the world of the Greeks will open itself to me in proportion to my love for it.

The problem of the possibility of speculative metaphysics is not simply a question of whether knowledge has limits, but whether we can state with certainty that we understand by the term "ultimate reality" can even in principle become an object of knowledge at all. And here the distinction between philosophy, understood as the attempt to speculate upon ultimate things, and phenomenology, understood as the attempt to obtain insight into the essences of things and their modes of givenness to knowing subjects, again becomes clear.

Scheler begins his discussion of speculative metaphysics in *Von Ewigen im Menschen* by noting a limitation of philosophy:

Philosophy is knowing, and the philosopher is a knower.... Were there a mode of participation by the essence [*Kern*] of a finite person in the most essential reality that was anything but knowledge ... it would not follow that the philosopher was not a knower, but that philosophy was *not* the *most immediate* mode of participation in the most essential reality that is granted to me.... The basic form of participation in primordial being [*Urwesen*] conforms by nature to the *content* of primordial being. The Orphic, to whom the "given" was, in the state of spiritual ecstasy, a

chaotic, unstructured, creative urging, would have to deny, of course, that
this participation could be possible for philosophy as an Apollonian art.
For him not knowledge, but the Dionysic frenzy was the method for the
highest and final participation in primordial being.... But just as
nonsensical as to deny the *formal* intellectualism of philosophy would be
the reverse, i.e., to want to attain or to infer something about the material
content of the most essential reality, in which the philosopher at first seeks
to participate (e.g., as to make inferences [about the nature of reality]
from such experiences as that of the Orphic mystic). For surely as the
philosopher is tied to participating in the highest reality through knowledge (or insofar as this is possible through knowledge), so surely is primordial being not obligated *a priori* to grant this highest and final participation to the knower *as* knower....

Those [proud philosophers] presuppose quite arbitrarily that primordial
being has such a content that it can be brought to complete participation
by means of its possible being-as-object [of knowledge]....

[But] being *can* reach *much further* than being-as-object. Only if the
being of the most essential reality and, especially, primordial being, is in
its content *capable* of being an object, will knowledge be the adequate
form of participation in it.[17]

The question with which we now have to concern ourselves is: How
did Scheler answer the question posed by this last sentence? Is
human knowledge and hence philosophy capable of participating in
(i.e., "cognizing") absolute reality?

His answer becomes plain if we recall his contention in
"Idealismus-Realismus" that the *existence* of an instance of an
essence is never given to phenomenological intuition, for intuition
is a purely spiritual apprehension of its intentional object. The
intentional object of an intuition is of course always an essence of
some kind. Existence can be "given" only to the senses, and never
to intuition, in the experience of resistance. For that very reason,
any sphere of being that is given to consciousness, be it given in the
experience of spiritual ecstasy of the Orphic mystic, or in the apprehension of intimations of divinity of the religious man, or in the
love of essence of the philosopher, is not, and cannot be, given as a
sphere containing empirically existing objects. As true knowledge,
for Plato, is knowledge of the Forms, so for Scheler knowledge is
always of essence and never of the existence of instances of
essences. This does not mean, of course, that the mystic or the believer or the philosopher may not in fact *posit* as existing the content of the spheres of being revealed to them, as Scheler apparently

does with his *Wesensreich* (although he never makes the claim that the *Wesensreich* is the "most primordial being"); nor that the essences implied in the content of what is given in such revelations may not be studied phenomenologically (i.e., the attempt may always be made to describe what is given to, e.g., the Orphic mystic in his ecstasy). Does this, however, mean that a metaphysics that attempts to know primordial being both as to its essence and as to its existence is impossible? Yes, Scheler concludes:

An *a priori* metaphysics is out of the question ... because the knowledge of *essence never* can lead to the *positing* of an essence as real, and yet every metaphysical claim contains a positing of reality....

The possibility of "applying" the entire sphere of the *a priori* to the reality of the sphere of the absolute is excluded, because it is in the nature of all possible essentialities themselves, ... that nothing can be "concluded" as to the possible *reality* or unreality of the instances of the given essence.[18]

Thus it is incorrect to think of metaphysics as possessing the same evidence for the truth or falsity of its claims as does phenomenology on the one hand or empirical science on the other. The three activities are vastly different from one another with respect to the experiential basis in which they are founded (e.g., "intuition," "observation," "ecstasy," "religious experience"), and their modes of evidence are hence qualitatively different. It is further incorrect to say, as does Dupuy, that there is in Scheler a "quasi-identification of philosophy with phenomenological ontology."[19] Metaphysics, as an *a priori* study of the really real, is a striving for knowledge, but is not knowledge itself, which only science and phenomenology can attain. Metaphysics cannot know whether its "way" into ultimate reality is that "true" way, or whether those spheres of reality revealed to men that have been posited as the highest reality at various times and places are in fact real. This does not mean, however, either that metaphysics as this striving for knowledge of the really real has no role to play in human affairs or that phenomenology has no relevance to the ultimate concerns of men. Scheler assigns two roles to metaphysics.

The first task in metaphysics is the pure phenomenological investigation of that sphere of being which is the subject of metaphysical discourse. As is usual in phenomenology, the study has two sides: there is first the description of the essences revealed in the metaphysical sphere, and there is also the description of the order of foundation of the acts of grasping what is given in metaphysical experience. The attempt is made to repeat the emotional and intellectual acts in which the absolute existential Ground of Being is given to those men we generally classify as "mystics," "prophets," "seers," "metaphysicians," and the like, and to submit these acts and their contents to phenomenological scrutiny in reflective intuition. Here there is no question of positing as real the objects of the essence described. We learn *about* the beliefs of the metaphysicians, mystics, and so on, with respect to their essential structures. On the side of the object, this study is roughly parallel to an investigation of the "language of metaphysics" (also ideally carried out without prejudice as to the possible existence of the objects denoted by the terms of the language), which has been the subject of much debate in recent years in the Anglo-American schools of thought, however different the theoretical basis of such studies may be from that provided by Scheler's epistemology.

This phenomenological study is not, however, the only metaphysical activity. We learn in Scheler's "Erkenntnis und Arbeit," a late essay, that philosophy asks itself how the essential structure of the world, as described by the phenomenology of metaphysics, *is possible*. This is not a phenomenological question. We might recall here our earlier reference to a criticism Scheler directed at Kant in *Der Formalismus*. He accused Kant of concentrating on the question of *how* a certain type of experience is possible, rather than asking first *what* it is that is given in that experience. Kant's question is a *metaphysical* one; it asks about the reality that made another reality possible, and the answer to such a question depends always upon an inference (presumed valid) from a given reality to one that is not given. Thus it oversteps the limits of phenomenology in two instances. It posits, by means of an inference, the existence of something not given in the experiences of resistance. Insofar as metaphysics seeks to answer this question in its most general form, namely, how the essential structure of the universe is possible, it posits what Scheler has called a cultural *Weltanschauung*. In the essay on Max Weber discussed earlier, it was said that "philosophical metaphysics is a doctrine that posits *Weltanschauungen*." Its goal is to develop a concept of ultimate reality. In its efforts, the metaphysician may *draw* on phenomenology, which draws the map of the sphere of the Absolute without regard to the existence of the essential possibilities described there. Similarly, he may draw on the empirical sciences for knowledge of the factual content of the world. Any specific *Weltanschauung* posited by the metaphysician must be in conformity with the findings of these two disciplines, but they can never offer conclusive support for any *Weltanschauung,* because the claims they make go beyond the natural standpoint investigated by the sciences, and because they posit existence, which phenomenology cannot do. Hence such *Weltanschauungen* possess a "merely probable" truth value.

The fact that cultural *Weltanschauungen* do not possess adequate evidence for their truth should not lead us to the conclusions that (1) such systems of thought are "purely arbitrary," because their content must be in rigorous conformity with the findings of phenomenology and the empirical sciences before they are posited as "probably true"; or (2) that they are "merely subjective," because it is in the nature of things that "knowledge" of the absolute is alone possible as the intellectual response of the individual subject to the world. Absolute knowledge, as we have seen, is personal; intersubjective knowledge is always nonmediate and conditioned knowledge, and is possible only on the basis of an abstraction from the "world" given to a concrete human subject. It was undoubtedly Scheler's opinion that a system of metaphysics comes closer to representing the primordial world intended by the "person" than does the "abstract and bloodless" scientific picture of the universe.

Yet it is clear that the positing of a *Weltanschauung* will always involve a certain amount of arbitrariness, insofar as the positing cannot be adequately justified by its phenomenological and scientific evidence. Nevertheless, Frau Maria Scheler, the widow of the philosopher, tells us in her notes to the collected works that in later years the degree of adequacy Scheler was willing to grant to a possible metaphysics of the really real tended to increase, whereas in his early works Scheler limited himself simply to denying that a metaphysics could ever possess completely adequate evidence.[20]

Thus we must not allow ourselves to believe that knowledge of essence can give us insight into the way the world must be constructed. It tells us what existential possibilities the world possesses, but not what does in fact exist. In sum, what in fact exists is *either* a matter of speculation and not of knowledge, when it is a question of the Ground of Being, *or* is given to the senses in the experience of resistance. It then becomes clear that Scheler is not overstepping the limits of knowledge of existence set by his theory when, in a later essay, he approvingly quotes Hegel to the effect that knowledge of essence furnishes for metaphysics "windows onto the absolute."[21] Such knowledge functions only as windows — windows that one can see and describe with perfect adequacy without, however, being able to determine whether they give a clear and undistorted view of the universe onto which they look.

And thus we may conclude that for Scheler phenomenology is not the whole of philosophy, but it is the only area of philosophy in which true and adequate knowledge is available. Phenomenology may, however, furnish the materials toward the solution of speculative problems, but the results of such speculations are merely probable. The saint does not "know" things that the philosopher does not, but in his descriptions of his intercourse with the sphere of the holy, a knowledge of essence is implied that the wise man — the phenomenologist — may attempt to bring to perfect adequation without passing judgment upon the existence of possible instances of these essences. The experiences of the saint may be topics of inquiry for philosophy and the sciences (e.g., the science of psychology), but such studies presuppose, ideally, a phenomenological investigation of the meanings intended by the cognitive acts of the saint.

Yet there is one more issue we might raise that is not without interest. If the foregoing is a fair interpretation of Scheler's views on the possibility of a speculative metaphysics, then in the light of the fact that he held that a valid, intersubjective, adequately grounded metaphysics of the really real is impossible, why did he not only insist upon the right to live of metaphysics but himself wrote metaphysical treatises, even planned a work on metaphysics as his crowning achievement? He answers this question in another late essay, where he speaks of metaphysics as an *instrument for the realization of value.*[22] As the "human value" realized by scientific knowledge is the satisfaction of material needs, so is the human goal realized through metaphysical knowledge — and here we are speaking only of the value of "pure" metaphysics, that is, the phenomenological description of the givens of metaphysical experience, and not of metaphysics as a doctrine "positing" a cultural *Weltanschauung* — the perfection of the person. This concept of perfection is founded upon the epistemology discussed earlier in this chapter: knowledge is an ontological relation of knower and known, in which the knower "takes part in" the object known. In pure metaphysical knowledge, the knower "possesses" *in mente* some of the essential possibilities of the universe, even if only a small part of it, for to no finite mind can be given the entire *Wesensreich*. In phenomenological metaphysics, the knower makes the attempt to become a microcosmos, a reflection of the essential structure of the world; this is the ultimate goal of all moral endeavor.

Behind this general view of the role of phenomenology in the attainment of human ends stands a more particular intention. Metaphysics, this time understood as the positing of a *Weltanschauung,* is a means toward achieving *political* ends: it serves as a foundation of ideologies, and in many of his writings, Scheler functions as an ideologist. We will have frequent occasion to note his impassioned hope for the establishment of a general intellectual framework that might serve as a basis for a gradual reconciliation of the warring elements of his times — a reconciliation that would bring together East and West, *Bürger* and worker, the nations of Europe. This hope often finds philosophical justification in his writings. A critic of Marx, he believed that the solidarity of peoples and classes has as a necessary condition the prior reconciliation of ideologies. Servants of this end are metaphysics and, of course, phenomenology applied to the description of the essential content of the opposing nationalist and class ideologies and *Weltanschauungen.* The phenomenological analyses that we are now going to investigate were written, I believe, out of a love for all being and essence and a hope for the reconciliation of moral, intellectual, and, ultimately, political differences among men.

CHAPTER 5

Phenomenology and Value Theory

SCHELER's longest, most systematic, and perhaps greatest work is *Der Formalismus in der Ethik und die materiale Wertethik.* This book is not simply a phenomenological analysis of the "values themselves," as Scheler puts it, a task he refers to as the "most central concern" of value theory. In fact, such a "first order" ethical system is only sketched here. Rather, Scheler is concerned in *Der Formalismus* with an entire spectrum of problems in value theory and phenomenological method. We will be concerned in this section with establishing that value theory can be profitably carried out on the phenomenological basis that Scheler has established. And, despite some critical reservations concerning his efforts, we will illustrate the method in action with examples taken from *Der Formalismus.* Before we do that, however, we want to describe the nature of *Der Formalismus* itself — a book that, despite the number of topics it discusses, is a highly integrated work — and touch upon the theoretical and historical problems that determine the direction of Scheler's thoughts on value theory.

The central theoretical problem of *Der Formalismus* is provided by the philosophy of Kant. Kant's *most fundamental error,* according to Scheler, was to divide too sharply between the sensible element in cognition — which he imagined, following the English empiricists, to be constituted by atomic "impressions" given in sensation — from the rational element, which for him was constituted by the application of purely formal elements to the data given through the senses. This division resulted in an all-too-narrow concept of perception, in which no clear account of the meaning element given in perception is attempted. We have also seen that although the neo-Kantians of Scheler's youth expanded the concept of cognition to include further formal laws and categories of the understanding, this new attack was not radical enough to satisfy Scheler.

90

How do these epistemological considerations relate to ethics? As a consequence of Kant's belief that the *a priori* element in experience pertains to the element of understanding in a perceptual experience and never to that which is understood — that is, to the chaotic data given through the senses — Kant held that it is impossible to know *a priori* what is good and what is evil *in itself*, impossible to establish either a "highest good" or a "highest goal" of practical human activity, from which one could deduce ethical norms. For the "material" of ethical experience, according to Kant, consists of "unordered" feelings of pleasure and pain given with the phenomenon; the cognitive element is purely formal, namely, the "categorical imperative." Kant postulates freedom of the will to regard or disregard the flux of desires and impulses, pleasures and pains given in sensation, in choosing a course of action. Yet no *a priori* justification for a system of norms of moral behavior can be discovered either in the will or in the sensations. The moral subject who heeds the call of the noumenal sphere whence comes the categorical imperative receives merely a purely formal criterion for judging whether he has been "moral," that is, consistent in a dutiful application to his tasks, and thus he does not learn what his duty is, or what his tasks are, in a specific concrete situation.

Scheler agrees with Kant that all naturalistic and teleological ethics have questionable status; reason alone cannot justify the view that a given goal or object (happiness, pleasure, communion with God, etc.) possesses intrinsic merit. The difference between Kant and Scheler is that Kant denies that there is both a *stable* order of values and an ethical *a priori* that is other than purely formal — and thus ethics is incapable of giving us ethical advice, it does not tell us specifically what is valuable — whereas Scheler claims that there are *material* values *a priori*, and an *a priori* order of values according to their relative worth, such that we can indeed decide ethical conflicts by reference to these *a priori* values and their order. It is the ultimate task of *Der Formalismus* to exhibit the material content of the value essences themselves. And to do this, Scheler will have to show that Kant was wrong in his belief that a material ethics is not possible.

Scheler's insight is that a stable *a priori* order of *values* does not involve or imply a stable *a priori* order of value *carriers*, that is, of valuable things, or actions, or goals. We can reflect upon the essences of values themselves and discover a stable order of preference of certain value types over others. Of course, in making moral decisions we do not choose one value over another; rather, we choose one thing or course of action or goal over another, because we feel it to be more valuable than the alternatives. But Scheler's point is that such "everyday" ethical decision-making derives a material *a priori* from the understanding we already possess of the nature and order of values. This primordial knowledge of value "founds" our everyday perception of objects *as* "beautiful," *as* "holy," *as* "noble." Just as we are able to grasp a thing as being alive because we come to the experience of that thing with prior knowledge of the essence of "life," so can we recognize a thing to be beautiful because we come to the object with a concept of beauty. The content of that concept provides the *a priori* framework for our experience of the object; we can ask what is the material content of that concept and submit the concept to phenomenological analysis. In so doing, Scheler believes, we will be laying bare the essential content of value judgments.

In order to justify the possibility of such an attempt, Scheler must try to isolate the material in which are founded all judgments we make from the natural standpoint concerning the value of a given object. As the phenomenological analysis of nonvalue essences began with the material given in perception, so will a phenomenological analysis of value essences begin with the material given in what Scheler calls *feeling* —f we "feel" the value of a thing as we "see" its color. This assignment of cognitive value to the emotions was the decisive step in Scheler's thought; it affirmed that the emotional life of men is not a chaos of feeling states succeeding one another in time, but that feeling is actually a mode of knowing something, however imperfectly its object may at first be given. Furthermore, the fact that a thing is of higher or lower value than another thing is given in the experience of *preferring* or, the opposite, of *thinking less* of that thing than another, as the value itself is given in the act of feeling. The phenomenological analysis of these natural experiences, that is, their reperformance in phenomenological reflection, will disclose the pure value facts in which they are founded. Hence phenomenological ethics begins as descriptive ethics — in it we describe the phenomenologically reduced object of value experience, namely, value essences, the "intentional object" of everyday "feelings."

But now we encounter theoretical problems that must be handled before phenomenological-descriptive ethics can get off the ground. In order to support his view that it makes good sense to speak of *pure* values (e.g., "beauty itself") as opposed to concrete valuable things (e.g., "that beautiful painting"), Scheler must refute claims that the experience of value can be explained other than by assuming that the givenness of things as valuable is a primordial fact of experience and hence *a priori*. He presents us with ingenious and interesting arguments against the views of those "ethical empiricists" who hold that value is given in "contingent experiences," namely, of pleasures and pains, and that *either* human behavior is completely subject to psychological laws (avoidance of pain and pursuit of pleasure) and hence causally determined, *or* moral behavior is at bottom simply the product of striving toward arbitrarily selected goals. His own view will involve the phenomenological exhibition of moral behavior and ethical conviction as a *function* of primordial insight into the essence of values. What emerges from this analysis is a view of human moral behavior as *guided* but not *determined* by *a priori* laws of value. Founding all acts of feeling and preference is an *ordo amoris*, whose laws of loving and hating, while they may be ignored or perverted by the moral subject, are as rigid as those of logic, are discoverable in principle by reflection upon everyday acts of feeling, and are themselves not founded in any physical (e.g., in "biological drives") or psychical (e.g., in the "understanding") apparatus peculiar to men, but have the ontological status peculiar to the *Wesensreich* of which they are a part.

One final remark. It is one of the greatest contributions of Scheler's *Der Formalismus* to ethics that it does not begin with the question of the nature of the Good but rather with the question of the nature of the various value qualities. The moral good is not understood here as the highest ethical value, one that is indefinable and available only in intuition (Plato, Moore), but simply as the value that appears in the activity of realizing positive values. The positive values, on the contrary, are intuitable essences. Ethics begins, for Scheler, with the phenomenological analysis of these value essences as they appear "upon" the objects and actions that "instance" them. "Goodness," on the other hand, is not an intuitable value essence, and is thus not to be described phenomenologically. An act is good because we feel the values realized through it as higher than those that would have been realized had the act not been performed. Thus the *values* are then understood as indefinable, intuitable qualities, but the Good itself is not an independent phenomenon; "good" is simply a comparative term.

Now let us begin our study of Scheler's phenomenology of value qualities.

I *Modes of Value Givenness: Feeling and Preference*

If Scheler is to obtain value material for the study of a possible *a priori* lawfulness in ethical experience and behavior, he must attempt to disengage the value qualities from the essential and sensible elements that appear "on" some concrete object. Now it is clear, he begins, that a value can be given only in the act of feeling something. However, what is *felt* are the values that appear upon objects, and not simply feeling states.[1] Feelings are cognitive acts; that is, they possess intentionality: they are directed, according to laws peculiar to themselves, toward an object given in sense perception, and, in many cases but not in all, toward the external cause of the sense perception. Thus the *feeling* of a value is always given as different from the feeling state that may accompany it.[2] That the two may vary independently is evident from a simple example. One may take various attitudes toward one constant feeling state of pain: one may "put up with it," "find it unbearable," possibly even "enjoy it." What is varying here is not the state of pain itself, but rather what we *see in* the pain: we "feel" the "feeling state" in various ways.

Thus, feelings are what Scheler calls "functions," such as seeing and hearing; they are ways in which material given to the senses is taken up and given to consciousness. The cognitive act of feeling is thus the source of value consciousness; for what "appears" in the act of feeling is the value of things, or perhaps better said, things *appear to consciousness as valuable.* A feeling state, as opposed to a feeling, intends no object, although it is caused by some object, and although we may know what that object was that caused it. The "quiver of joy" that runs through me when I feel the beauty of a piece of music, for example, is not directed toward the beauty of the music, and, indeed, this feeling state is a mere accompaniment whose presence is not necessary; I may be as keenly aware of the beauty of the music the next time I hear it without experiencing a quiver of joy. Again remember that it is the *beauty* that is felt, not the music, which is merely "heard." Hearing is a function, like feeling, but it intends sound, not value.

Hence it follows that the emotional life of men is not constituted simply by the feeling of values in the physical feeling states of pleasures and pains and their modes. Scheler rejects the view that the emotional life — and hence all ethical behavior — is a simple function of human sensibility. This incorrect view, he notes, is common to various philosophers, including Kant, and it results in a terrible *poverty* in the description of the emotional life of men. The theory incorrectly identifies an emotion as a type of sensual feeling state, hence divisible into atomic parts. Rather, Scheler holds, an emotion is the subject and not the object of an act of consciousness. We do not "feel an emotion," as we "feel a pain"; rather, we experience the emotion of, for instance, sorrow, in which a negative value of, for instance, "loss" or "loneliness," is given.[3]

Scheler goes on to charge that the theory of emotional reductionism makes it impossible for us to feel several emotions at one time. He argues that there are many situations in which emotions neither succeed each other rapidly, as do feeling states, nor mix themselves together to produce one unified emotion. It is possible for a person to be both "cheerful" and "at peace" upon receiving news that he has just lost a fortune and is thus at the same time "unhappy"; one can be unhappy and at the same time enjoy the taste of a good cigar or a glass of wine.

These facts show that what we generally classify as "feelings" is not a homogeneous phenomenon, and that there exists a qualitative difference between types of feelings and emotions; indeed, that there are kinds of feelings and emotions that are by their very nature *essentially* incompatible with each other. The search for cases of such incompatibility constitutes a phenomenological study whose goal is to produce a *typology* of emotions and feeling states in which the essential characteristics of each type are described. Those feeling states and emotions that are not compatible with each other (i.e., which cannot be experienced simultaneously) are placed in one group. Scheler, beginning such a study, classifies feelings into four groups of incompatible emotion types. We have (1) sensual feelings, such as simple pleasures and pains — stinging, pinching, tickling, and so on (these are the physical feeling states we spoke of above); (2) vital feelings (*Lebensgefühle*), such as feelings of good health, weakness, refreshment, sleepiness; (3) pure ego feelings or emotions of the soul, such as sadness, cheerfulness, euphoria; (4) spiritual emotions, such as despair, beatitude, *serenitas animi.*

These four types are given in the order of their increasing "depth." The depth of a feeling type is determined by what could be described as the closeness of the emotion to the center of the human person. We might express this thought for Scheler by pointing out that the feeling of despair, for example, is "deeper" than that of sadness in that despair is a matter of more ultimate concern to us as persons; in the case of the former (where "despair" is thought of in the religious sense, as Scheler is here considering this phenomenon) our entire spiritual being is in crisis; in the case of sadness there is no such crisis, our entire being is not called into the affair, and the longing we feel in sadness seems far easier to cure than that experienced in true despair. It can be shown, in addition, that the feelings of greater depth intend values of higher worth than those of lower depth, hence, for example, the values typically intended by the feeling of good health (vitality, work as a value) are higher than those intended by the sensual value of tickling (pleasure, giddiness). The order of relative worth of values requires, of course, an independent phenomenological *Aufweisen.*

Let us turn briefly to the chief points appearing in the *Aufweisen* of the essential characteristics of each of the four types of emotion and feeling. In the case of the sensual feeling states (type one), it is clear that these are always given as extended over a definite area of the body. They are not affected by directing our attention toward them; they are more subject to the will than our other feeling states (i.e., one can take an aspirin, touch oneself, etc.);[4] they are tied to the *hic et nunc*: there is no true "remembering" of a past feeling state, although it may be possible to cause the "same" feeling in us again; and there is no true *sympathetic* experience of the sensual feeling of another person. What is "felt" when we sympathize with a man in pain is not the pain itself but rather the vital-emotional state of *suffering*. Still further, an essential characteristic of the entire scale is that a lower feeling cannot destroy or alter a higher feeling. Scheler holds that pain cannot put an end to the feeling of beatitude, for example. We might note with some skepticism that this will depend upon the degree of pain (or pleasure!).

This brief adumbration of a single example of Scheler's investigation of what he calls the "levels of the emotional life" is valuable in that it presents us with an example of a concrete phenomenological undertaking: it takes the notion of feeling as its theme, turns its attention to several concrete examples, and separates the meaning elements and their interrelationships from the individual synthesis of meaning, value, and sense data that made up the particular case. The analysis thus represents an attempt to describe what meanings and meaning relations are implied by the occurrence of a "feeling" or an "emotion" in a given subject, and how this feeling or emotion is related to other feelings and emotions with respect to a second type of meaning that is clearly involved in the meaning of the natural phenomenon designated by the terms "feeling" or "emotion," namely, the meaning of the concept of Person, that is, the concept of the subject experiencing the emotion. The investigation tries to grasp the essence of feeling through the medium of examples, rather than by comparing various cases of feeling and abstracting similarities; this would be the way of induction. Induction can render only laws descriptive of the behavior of objects, and it never describes the meaning or sense of those objects. Scheler's investigation is into the meaning of objects of knowledge. It is *a priori* in that it does not describe the actual occurrence of emotions and feelings in individuals and the causes of these emotions but describes rather the cognitive elements presupposed by our understanding of something *as* valuable. In the same way we must try throughout the coming discussions to think *abstractly* of the values themselves that appear in the feeling of an emotion or a feeling state, that is, apart from their realization in objects and apart from our behavior toward these concrete objects that appear to us as possessing positive or negative values.

Now we have access in feeling to a realm of values, but the relative worth of each value type with respect to the others is not given in the act of feeling itself; this phenomenon of "higher" and "lower" value is given only in the act of *preferring*. An act of preference must in no case be confused with an act of *choice;* one chooses between two or more possible *actions,* whereas one can prefer one *thing* to another, or, on a higher level, one value to another. The choice of one action over another is in fact founded upon a previous preferring of one value or thing that is to be realized or produced through the course of action chosen. Preferring, like feeling, possesses intentionality, and thus is a mode of value cognition; it is also directed upon the value material contained in the objects intended in its own peculiar way. In the act of preferring one thing to another, one value is given *as* higher than another. We do not prefer a value on the basis of its higher value; rather, the higher value first appears *as* higher in the act of preference. *If it is possible to study acts of preference phenomenologically,* that is, with reference to the acts of preference among values and not among objects, and *if we assume that acts of preferring occur according to stable laws of the emotional lives of all men, then out of this study will emerge a scale of values that is transcendent of all acts of preferring upon the natural standpoint,* and that contains no reference to the carriers of values. This analysis accomplished, Scheler then tries to make a case for the view that the actual acts of preference between things, courses of action, and so on, upon the natural standpoint are "functions" of this primordial preferring.

Thus it is Scheler's contention that values and an order of values are "known" by all knowing subjects who perform acts of feeling and preferring. That men do not all agree as to what concrete objects and actions are valuable is contingent upon some differences in their intellectual capacity and their material interests. That men can "pervert" *a priori* knowledge in their pursuit of happiness is granted by the theory of functionalization. Simply stated, Scheler's point on this issue is that some knowledge of the essence "treeness" is a condition of the possibility of misidentifying a thing as a tree as well as of correctly identifying it, and it makes sense to demand a description of the essence as well as an account of the conditions of the application of our knowledge of "treeness" to sensibly given data. Similarly in the case of value judgments, we are aware of a primordial order of preferring in which are founded our everyday judgments that one thing is more or less valuable than another. To show this relationship, Scheler must exhibit this stable order of preference among values on the level of pure facts concerning the affective life of men. This *Aufweisen* results in a typology known as the *ordo amoris,* the primordial order of loving and hating.

Scheler refers in his discussion of this expression to the saying of Pascal, "the heart has its reasons." How often, he observes, has this statement been taken, even by philosophers, to mean that "the heart should be allowed to speak after the understanding has spoken."[5] Such people wish to imply that the heart's "reasons" are not reasons at all but rather the impulse of sentimentality, which, nevertheless, it is often wiser to follow than the dictates of cold, inhuman reason. Against this interpretation, Scheler holds that Pascal's opinion is that the "heart," that is, the function of feeling, has in fact "reasons" in the strict sense of laws grounding preferences; and that these reasons are not "borrowed" from the understanding but belong to the heart alone: "Into it [the heart] are written laws which, as the ancients taught in their doctrine of the *nomos agraphos,* correspond to the plan according to which the world as a world of values is constructed."[6] The "reasons" of the "heart," that is, the *ordo amoris,* thus refer to the ultimate reasons for preferring one thing to another, reasons that correspond to an external and absolute order of the relative worth of values. However, we have yet to explain the role of love and hate in this analysis of our emotional modes of access to the *Wertreich,* although the acts of loving and hating constitute the *highest* level of human emotional life. These acts, unlike those of feeling and preferring, do not possess intentionality, and hence have no direct cognitive function; nevertheless, love and hate "found" the acts of value cognition, and, as Scheler puts it, "they represent a peculiar attitude toward value-objects."[7] His phenomenological analysis of the emotions of love and hate — in addition to and apart from the metaphysical role the act of love plays in his ontological theory of knowledge and in his reinterpretation of the phenomenological reduction — is quite interesting, if difficult, and deserves our careful attention.

First let us sum up the analyses of this section: value is given either in feeling (the value essences themselves) or in the act of preference (their relative worth). Phenomenology repeats these acts in reflective intuition, in the course of which it "brackets" all thought of specific objects on which values may appear. In this way, it wins for itself a vision of "pure" values. On the basis of this vision, it will attempt to describe these values and their relative worth. Phenomenology may also describe the emotional life of men, the levels of the emotions, and the interrelationships of these levels with the typical values given in each. The theory of functionalization reappears in the analysis of values in connection with the *ordo amoris:* the laws of loving and hating, through which all concrete acts of preferring and valuing upon the natural standpoint are founded in an independent, objective realm of values. The theory seems immensely promising for the study of values, and we await with interest Scheler's attempt at a phenomenological analysis of value essences.

II *The Phenomenology of Love and Hate*

An objection that is often raised against attempts to analyze the phenomena of love and hate is that such analyses usually assume that, for example, love of God and love of one's family and love of beauty are somehow fundamentally the "same," but that such an assumption is questionable; rather, it is added, there is simply a family relationship between them. But Scheler does not assume that these different kinds of love are accompanied by similar feeling states the way "rage," for instance, is pretty much the same experience each time. He is not asking what happens to me as a psychophysical entity when I perform an act of love. He *does* hold, however, that all these various experiences of love are instances of the same essence; that is, they involve the awareness of the same central core of meaning that founds my identification of a mental act *as* an act of love. He begins his analysis by asking, in effect, what I mean when I say that "John loves Mary," and what other meanings, what other essential possibilities are presupposed by the grasping of the meaning implicit in this judgment. Thus Scheler attempts to exhibit that central core of meaning by reflecting upon what meanings, if any (and he claims that there are none), I must have previously grasped in order to have grasped this thing as a case of love. Later, of course, he will place the fruits of his phenomenological analysis in a metaphysical context: he will ask, for example, what does the fact that I am able to grasp what love means — thus, potentially, to love — say about me as a human person and as a moral subject?

Now Scheler asserts in the *Wesen und Formen der Sympathie* that love and hate are *Urphänomene,* ultimate facts of interpersonal experience, in which experiences upon the natural standpoint can be shown to be most deeply founded.[8] We know from our earlier discussions that the phenomenon of knowledge itself contains love as one of its essential constituents. Love and hate themselves, however, are unfounded — they cannot be "explained" or "described" in terms of anything else. Thus he begins his *Aufweisen* of love and hate by making a case for excluding all other possible candidates as the "foundations" of these two phenomena. And our own analysis will begin there. For reasons of economy, we will refer only to love in our description of Scheler's *Aufweisen,* but the analysis also applies to the phenomenon of hate.

Love should not be confused, first of all, with the phenomenon of *sympathy:* love is not to be understood as the mere intensification of the feeling of good will. This confusion can be traced to various thinkers whom Scheler classifies as "reductionists," that is, those who attempt to explain all psychic phenomena on the basis of a few key concepts — usually taken from biology — and thereby obscure the fullness of concrete human experience. Scheler argues against this view of the nature of love by pointing out that love is not directed toward the "good" of the loved object: for example, we can love beauty or truth, but the thought of wishing good upon beauty or truth is nonsense. Sympathy, in any case, as Scheler will show in the *Wesen und Formen der Sympathie,* is a kind of attunement to other *persons,* and could not found the meaning elements constituting such forms of love as love of being and essence, love of beauty and truth.

Second, he attempts to exclude the element of *striving* as an essential element in the essence of love (and thus as its possible "foundation"). Love is not only not an intense good will, it is not a willing at all, he declares: "Love may leave various acts of striving, desiring, yearning in its wake, but it itself has nothing of these."[9] The correctness of this assertion is clear from the example of the act of loving the beauty of a piece of music, where quite obviously nothing is to be realized through this act. Similarly, all complexes of striving-acts and of feeling states of any kind must be rejected as the foundation of love. Striving has love as its source rather than the reverse. One strives only after that which possesses positive value for one, and thus striving presupposes a mode of value-relatedness to the object of striving.

In this same context, Scheler rejects Spinoza's definition of love,[10] which is "joy, accompanied by the idea of an external cause."[11] Not only is there implied in Spinoza's definition the "hedonistic" thought that the essence of value is to be sought in and is dependent upon our feeling states (which in Spinoza's thought function as either the objects of striving or as the Good in and for themselves, whereas Scheler insists that the act of love is independent of all alterations in feeling states), but it is also evident from Spinoza's definition that he makes the experience of love dependent upon the occurrence of the feeling state of joy, which is thought by Spinoza to be caused by an external object.

It is further incorrect to attempt to reduce love and hate to a form of "feeling" (of a value) or "preferring," that is, to a type of intentional act in which value or the relative worth of values is grasped. Rather, it is apparent that one can feel the value of an object *without* loving or hating it. One does not *know* value in love and hate at all, and therefore these cannot be counted among the cognitive acts, as we mentioned earlier. We have seen from our discussion of Scheler's analysis of knowledge that knowledge of value founds all other acts of knowledge; now we must describe how the acts of love and hate found the cognitive acts of value apprehension, namely, feeling and preferring. It is in this sense that love and hate become the root elements in his entire ontology; for love is thought of as the primordial form of "having an object," which is for Scheler the essence of knowledge.

We see from the fact that love and hate are not founded in feeling and preferring, but rather the reverse, that love and hate are the most *immediate* and *direct* modes of relatedness to the value content of an object, such that we can love a thing before we are aware of it as an object possessing a certain, specific value, and certain specific qualities, thus *a fortiori* before we can explain what it is about the beloved object that is of value to us. Scheler notes that it is because love and hate are such immediate modes of emotional involvement with the world that we are often so embarrassed by requests to explain *why* we love the beloved thing.[12] Thus the presence of certain value qualities alone does not cause the emotion of love in a person; rather the degree to which those qualities are valued will depend upon whether the thing is loved or hated, or merely liked or disliked. What is loved is not the thing because of its qualities but the *essence* of the thing itself; and the value qualities are valued to a greater or lesser degree for their being carried by that thing. Scheler writes that "love and hate are directed upon an individual center [*Kern*] of things, a center of value ... which does not allow itself to be reduced entirely to values that we can judge, not even to values that can be given individually in feeling."[13] In the case of human beings, this center of value is called the *Person,* a concept that thus becomes central to Scheler's phenomenological account of the essence of man.

In sum, then, Scheler's "negative" uncovering of the essence of love establishes the primordial quality of this phenomenon (and hence ultimately, for Scheler, its importance as a metaphysical principle); our sympathetic awareness of other selves, indeed our awareness of values, is founded upon our capacity to love. The positive description of the phenomenon of love characterizes Scheler's metaphysical dynamism: love and hate are essentially *movements,* specifically, movements in which the intentional act directed upon an object passes from a given value intended in that object, its carrier, to a higher (in love) or lower (in hate) value in that object. He writes: "Love is the movement in which every concrete individual object that carries values arrives at the values that are the highest possible for it according to its ideal nature; or in which [movement] it reaches the ideal value-essence peculiar to it."[14] Love "founds" preferring, Scheler continues: "Each act of preferring is 'founded' in love insofar as the higher value first appears in an act of loving, and which higher value may then be preferred."[15]

What concrete phenomena does Scheler have in mind in this rather complex and puzzling description of the essence of love? First we must recall that the act of love is always directed to the value center of the object loved and is not genetically dependent upon the values carried by that thing. We can feel the values of a person, for example, his beauty, piety, and so on, without loving that person; and these values can be diminished (a person loses his beauty, becomes arrogant and lazy; becomes, in a word, "unlovable"), and yet we continue to love him![16] What happens then, when on the natural standpoint an approximation of true love takes place, that is, a love that is a clear instance of that central core of meaning, the "having" of which is the ground of the possibility of our recognizing all the various phenomena we call love *as* instances of love?[17] Despite the abstractness of Scheler's description and the unavoidable obscurity of a discussion in which we try to think of love apart from all concrete cases of it, and where the object of the discussion, insofar as it is a primordial phenomenon, is in principle indefinable, we can nevertheless make a few positive statements in answer to this question on the basis of the text.

First of all, it is clear that Scheler intends to say that in being loved, the object attains a higher degree of individuality: that is, one comes closest to the value center of another person (or to oneself, in the phenomenon of self-love), to that "indescribable trace of essence" that is the foundation of the personality of a human being. The more we love a person, or thing, the more we discover in that person or thing those traces that make it the individual thing of value that it is, and the more we distinguish it or him from the mass of things or men. One can never love an abstraction. We can love a social class, or an idea (e.g., of a "nation"), or a race, but never a mere "class of things" artificially constructed by analysis; for here that "trace of essence," that *personality as a whole* that alone can be loved, is absent. On the other hand, when we hate a thing, it tends to withdraw into the "mass": we then think of, for example, a man, not as a person, but as "personifying" some negative value qualities.

Now the fact that such phenomena as these are essentially founded in the primordial act of love is established, Scheler believes; yet these phenomena alone do not take us to the core of the phenomenon of love itself. The above phenomena refer more to the being of the thing loved than to the element of movement that Scheler identifies with the act of love.

Let us consider the psychological fact that when we love another person, we tend to think of that person, not simply as the carrier of the values that we actually feel in him, but, in addition, as a carrier of values yet unrealized; we "put him on a pedestal," so to speak. This is not to say that the fact that we put the beloved on a pedestal means that we "create" the higher values and "project" them onto the beloved person. If this were the case, it would be impossible to have illusions in love. Rather, we open ourselves in love to the values *possibly* carried by the beloved. Scheler would dispute the old saying that "love is blind"; the case is, rather, that through the act of love we are able to see more, not less, objectively; we may become aware of values in the person to which people indifferent to that person are blind.

We may come closer to Scheler's meaning if we bracket from this everyday phenomenon of "putting the beloved on a pedestal" (1) the accompanying feeling states or other emotions that may or may not be present in a true act of love, such as "admiration," "despair"; (2) the *desire* to *realize* or to *discover* in the beloved person the values possibly attainable by him. Then we may understand love as the "movement" that takes the lover from the values actually felt (and which may or may not have stimulated his love) to the *appearance* of a higher value and to the *possibility* of its realization in the person loved. These values "appear" *as* possibilities; thus they are not actually felt by the lover; they are ideal, they "should be" and yet are not.

This last statement seems particularly perplexing. To whom is this "should" directed? Basing ourselves on the discussion of the "ought" in *Der Formalismus,* which we will take up shortly, it appears to be Scheler's contention that this "should" is directed toward no one; it is ideal. "Ought" in this ideal sense does not imply a *duty* belonging to someone. In love, one experiences this ideal "ought" at the end of the movement of love: we feel that the higher value revealed in love "ought to" belong to the beloved, but it is not experienced as incumbent upon us or upon anyone to realize this higher value; such "duty," such "striving" to accomplish one's duty, may be a *consequence* of love, but it is surely not of the essence of love. Indeed, Scheler points out that such striving may be incompatible with or even destructive of love: the search for or the attempt to produce in the loved one (i.e., through "education") higher values than one immediately feels leads to disillusionment. On the other hand, the *attainment* of higher values on the part of the beloved can obviously not be a *condition* of the continuance of love. No: the essence of love is the spiritual event that lies at the root of all its empirical occurrences in all its various forms; it contains neither an element of striving nor one of longing, yet it is an experience that is essentially incomplete; it is directed toward the *ideal perfection* of the thing loved, the possibility of which is revealed in love. Scheler notes that it is the possible being-higher of the value given on the thing toward which love "moves," and not toward a higher value itself, which we believe exists, but which we have not yet felt.[18]

Further, Scheler holds that the highest form of love — love in the ethical sense — is love of the value of a person *as* that person, and not as the possessor of such and such characteristics; rather, the characteristics of the person are loved *because* they belong to that person. This value of the person appears first in the act of love of an individual person, and, insofar as the person is unobjectifiable, his value cannot be felt (and hence from Scheler's standpoint, cannot be "cognized") but can only be grasped in an act of sympathetic imitation (*Mitvollzug*) of the cognitive acts of the loved person. Scheler clearly has in mind here as an example of such ethical love the "imitation of Christ" in which the ethical essence of Christ is revealed to his disciples.[19] Here he finds the most perfect realization of the pure essence of love in a concrete example; here there is no striving, but complete surrender; here most clearly the *possibil-*

ity of a higher value of the person of Christ than that which is actually felt by the disciple is given in the act of loving him.

One is led by this analysis to the remark that Scheler seems to have made the love of God impossible; for if, in the act of love, the possible being-higher of the values felt on the thing is revealed, and if God is all-perfect, then no movement from the actual to the possible is possible when we contemplate Him.[20] We will not go into Scheler's interpretation of the relation of men to God at this point, but we might well compare a remark by Scheler in which he noted that it was the analyses of *Der Formalismus* that brought about his metaphysical transformation, and that the transformation in metaphysics brought about no essential changes in his views on ethics, with the fact that he later *denied* the perfection of God.[21]

Scheler now pursues his *Aufweisen* of the essential moments of the phenomenon of love further by describing three essential forms of love, all of which share the primordial characteristic of "movement" described above, but which are differentiated according to the type of act they represent. They are thus phenomenally different movements of the spirit. His analysis is an application of the analysis of types of acts that we find in *Der Formalismus:* we have the vital act (thus vital love, opening us to higher values of the noble and the base); the psychic or ego act (thus love of the soul, opening us to higher values of knowledge and beauty); and finally, the spiritual act (thus love of the spirit, opening us to higher values of the Person, and ultimately of the Divine Person). There are further parallels with the analysis of act types in *Der Formalismus* in that these types of love acts are listed in increasing order of depth and value, and in that the types are incompatible — that is, that it is similarly possible to direct different types of love or hate acts toward the same object at the same time. Thus Scheler remarks that writers have often described the type of person who feels a strong passionate love for a person whose "soul" he at the same time hates. The consequence of this feeling is usually self-contempt. Notable is the absence here of the possibility of an act of love in the fourth and most shallow type of emotional act (or better, in this case, the "act of feeling a feeling state"), that of sensual feeling. Scheler's contention is that there can be no *purely* sensual love, for the purely "pleasant" values can only be felt and are not capable of an augmentation of value, such as is necessarily the case in a true act of love. The quantitative intensification of sensual pleasure is not something revealed through love, we might add, but rather is merely produced by an external cause. Upon the foundation of the above description of love and hate, Scheler further elaborates his doctrine of functionalization. We recall from our earlier description of his reinterpretation of the phenomenological reduction that its first and primary act is the "love of the entire spiritual person for absolute value and being"; for insofar as the ultimate act founding all other acts of knowledge is that of love, the phenomenologist must reperform this act in order to gain the clearest insight possible into these posterior acts in which essences are given. From our just-completed discussion of the phenomenology of love, we can see that the theoretical foundations of his method are logically consistent with, perhaps even derived from, this phenomenological doctrine that love is the principle that first makes the world as an object of feeling and knowing accessible to us. Love, we learned, is the movement by which we pass from the apprehension of a thing as possessing a certain value quality to the possibility of that thing's possessing a higher value. The capacity to love, among creatures peculiar to man alone, thus gives us the possibility of going beyond the apprehension of the things immediately given in sense perception as causing pleasure or pain to the apprehension of those things themselves as ideal possibilities. Out of this spiritual movement all our knowledge of meanings — not just of values — takes root. It is in this sense, I submit, that we must ultimately understand Scheler's statement that men become open to the world in love. Thus, again, it seems that the *amount* of essence that a given race or epoch or individual is able to grasp and to "functionalize" is dependent upon the depth of its love toward the world. Broadness of vision of a people or of an individual, as opposed to "intelligence," or the capacity to apply rules and to discover logical relations, is dependent upon the capacity of that people or person to love.

From a metaphysical point of view, acts of love and hate are thus the "spiritual events" in which the *Wesensreich* is expanded or contracted. When Scheler repeats the chief conclusion of his *Aufweisen* of love and hate in *Der Formalismus,* he asserts:

[The act of love] presents us with ... a *movement,* in whose course *new* and *higher* values, i.e., those still completely unknown to the given subject, light up and flash before his eyes. Thus this act does not *follow* the acts of feeling of value and of preferring, but goes before them as their pioneer and leader. Insofar as this is the case, we must ascribe to it a *creative* capacity, not of the values, which exist in and for themselves, but of the circle of values and their contents which can be felt and preferred by a subject at a given time.[22]

Thus the metaphysical conclusions of a difficult and suggestive, yet incomplete, phenomenological *Aufweisen.*

III   *The Phenomenology of "Ought"*

Scheler once contended that Kant's rigorous ethics of duty constitutes a "betrayal of joy," insofar as it depicts the morally good life as one of selfless pursuit of duty. This ethics is based, he holds, upon the doctrine that every "ought" is founded in a previous apprehension of a value as something that "ought-to-be." The *value* in which the "ought" is founded, according to him, is not first apprehended in the feeling of duty (Kant), nor in a previous striving to realize that value (ethical vitalism), but, on the contrary, the striving is a *result* of the awareness through love of a *higher possible* value; from this awareness we derive our concept of something-that-ought-to-be. The value essence thus *founds* the essence of "ought." First we must understand *that* something is valuable, yet does not exist, before we can understand what "ought" means. Thus, in all cases in which a possible value is revealed in the act of love as higher than the value already felt, the "ought" again appears. Here, however, the "ought" is not experienced as a negative principle, but as a positive principle: something ought to be. There is no notion of duty here, for there is no implicit reference in this "ideal ought" to the *will,* as Kant incorrectly assumed. This claim — that when we love something we immediately apprehend possible higher values in it without feeling any need to realize these values in the loved thing — is said to be self-evidently true. How is it, then, that we often do in fact strive to realize the higher possible values in the loved one (e.g., in a child we love)?

Scheler agrees that the possibility of an act of striving is founded on the prior possibility of grasping something *as* something that ought-to-be. But the fact that we know something *as* carrying an ought-to-be does not imply striving to attain it; the matter that ought-to-be may not be in our hands at all: for example, "there ought to be a hell for evildoers." This "ideal ought" carries no reference to a will. On the other hand, there is a specific sense of "ought" — a sense *founded* in that of the "ideal ought" — which he refers to as the "ought of duty": one "ought to conform oneself to a norm." Here we have for the first time in the order of knowledge an implicit reference to the will, and thus we have the beginning of morality. Only because we see, for instance, the child in the light of a *norm* — that is, as the possible carrier of a higher value — can we possibly feel that it is our duty to lead him there. This duty, however, is not a necessary consequence either of our love or of our apprehension of the "ideal ought." This appeal to the will is logically distinct from the "ideal ought" and the values upon which it is founded.

We can make this distinction between the "ideal ought" and the "ought of duty" clearer by again noting that the "ought of duty" is only possible on the basis of something being given to us as "possibly better." Scheler expresses the difference between the "ideal ought" and the "ought of duty" with the sentences "injustice ought not to be" and "thou shalt not commit injustice." Further examples from everyday usage will confirm the justice of this distinction, and it is apparent that the possibility of my apprehending something as my duty is contingent upon the possibility of my apprehending that thing as not-existing and yet as ought-to-exist, and this again upon my apprehension of that thing as valuable. We might further agree that it makes no sense to say that duty is drawn from "what conscience tells us," or "is the product of unconscious impulse," for whatever causal role these factors may play in determining our action in a concrete situation, both presuppose that some value is given as lacking. We can thus assent to the logic of the *Fundierungsordnung* however questionable we may find Scheler's apparent claim that there exists some *genetic* order of dependence among these acts.

The distinction between the "ideal ought" and the "ought of duty" is an important one for Scheler, for it draws a clear line between the apprehension of value itself, or of something as possibly possessing higher value, and the practical behavior directed at realizing values: the mere understanding of something as ought-to-be is not a sufficient condition for establishing what one's duty is; an act of will must intervene that is not determined by the "ideal ought" alone. Thus Scheler notes that the Kantian notion of a categorical imperative, that is, a type of duty that is not commanded by any authority, makes no sense. Duty is traceable to an *order* of some kind, to a willing by someone, whereas the "ideal ought" is not. Furthermore, various and even contrary imperatives (i.e., "duties") can be based on the same "ideal ought." This point is clear from the fact alone that the "ideal ought," *as* ideal, is directed toward the realization of the *pure* values without regard for the concrete carrier of values, or for the concrete situation of the moral agent to whom the ought is directed. Thus the value intended in the sentence "love thy neighbor as thyself" can be and has been expressed in imperatives dictating opposing types of behavior. This variability is due to variations in the historical and social situation and in the dispositions of individuals, and possesses no *a priori* lawfulness. Moreover, in any given people — or in individual persons, for that matter — one finds an abstract recognition of the *ideal* ought-to-be of a value, which nevertheless is not "functionalized" by that people or person (i.e., no specific imperative is formulated), and thus the "ought" remains ideal; it does not become a part of the living tradition of duties among them. This situation may occur where there is no temptation to do otherwise than to realize that value. On the contrary, we tend to look upon as our "duty" those actions and dispositions that counter what we hold to be evil but powerful tendencies peculiar to us. Scheler notes that Nietzsche was undoubtedly led to formulate such imperatives as "become hard" *because* he sensed a disposition in himself and those around him to do the opposite.

Now that he has discovered and clarified a basic distinction between two kinds of "ought," Scheler makes the attempt to establish the relation of the "can" to the "ideal ought" as the foundation of *virtue*. Virtue, he defines, is the ability (*das Können*) to desire and to realize something given and experienced as possessing the characteristic of "ought-to-be."[23] Scheler's point seems to be that virtue lies in an ability to desire to do what is perceived by the agent as something that (ideally) ought to be done. The "can" here must be understood not simply in terms of freedom of the will, that is, the abstract ability to choose to do something or not to do it, but rather as an immediate experience of my power to realize something of value. It is this irreducible experience — the joy of feeling it in one's power to realize something that ideally ought to be — that Scheler discovers to be the root of virtue. This is a remarkable insight. Its corollary is that "happiness is the root of virtue, not its reward."[24] Moreover, it follows from this analysis of "can" and "should" that one does not *choose* to be moral, that is, to live according to moral knowledge.[25] Knowledge of value obtained through positive moral insight "determines *immediately* my will without the necessity of going through an 'I should.'"[26] Virtue is not mechanical behavior according to norms; true virtue is a product of moral insight. Thus the problem of "why should I be moral?" *never arises* for Scheler; thus the question of the *binding power* of his scale of values — whose phenomenology we will take up in section V — never becomes a problem for him.

This thought that moral insight brings with it the determination of the will — which Scheler shares with a conception that Plato appears to maintain — is a central principle in his ethics. Yet it seems to lack *phenomenological* foundation. By his own principles, the determination of the will to perform a given action — which is an empirical fact — can only possess a "contingent" order; that is, it is a matter of study for empirical psychology which concrete acts of knowledge produce what sorts of behavior. Furthermore, it seems clear that a phenomenological scrutiny of "value apprehension" and the "determination of the will" will fail to establish a *meaning* relation between them in the same sense that such a relation exists between the meanings of the phenomena of "ought," "can," and "value." Scheler's opinion is perhaps based on his doctrine that love is the primordial act in which knowledge of value is founded, and that this act results at the same time in the positive determination of the will to realize that value; but it is clear from his own analysis that "desire," striving," "willing," and related phenomena are merely attendant circumstances of love, and are in no way necessary moments of the act such as must be present if we are to establish an essential relation between them.

IV   *The Phenomenology of Action*

Let us proceed to still another *Aufweisen,* one related to the problem just raised concerning the relation of *knowledge* of value to ethical *behavior.* Scheler's analysis of the essential moments in an act of will takes the form of a criticism of Kant's apparent presupposition that all material ethics must become an ethics of success, for example, a teleological ethics, which places the moral value of a human action in the consequences of that action. In this case, the moral agent is judged to be "good" or "bad" according to whether his actions have good or bad effects. The difficulty that arises out of this view is that a person can act with "good" intentions, but his actions may have "bad" consequences in the long run; yet we would not always want to judge him "evil" in that case.

Kant held — correctly, according to Scheler — that ethics must place moral value in the will of the moral agent and not in his actions: that is, in Scheler's language, the moral values "good" and "evil" *first* appear in the process of *realizing* values. However, Kant believed — incorrectly, according to Scheler — that such an ethics could only be purely formal. What Kant called the *Gesinnung* — what we might call an "attitude," but will keep in the original — is purely the empty form in which a concrete "intention" (*Absicht*) is posited; *Gesinnung* is understood in the Kantian philosophy as the condition under which the fact that there is some order and direction in our intentions first becomes possible. But because *Gesinnung* is thus a mere transcendental condition of this unity underlying our intentions, it cannot itself be good or bad. Scheler's mission here is to show that a material ethics such as his can locate the "place" of virtue in the person, especially in the *Gesinnung* of the person, and not merely in his specific intentions on specific occasions. He will demonstrate that the *Gesinnung* is an experienceable state of affairs and thus possesses its own "material." In order to do this he must "exhibit" the essential moments of a concrete act of will, show the *Gesinnung* to be a phenomenologically experienceable moment of it, and finally exhibit the relation of a "good" act of will to the *Gesinnung*. Thus we have a theme for phenomenological analysis.

The everyday experience offered as an example in which a *Gesinnung* is experienced is as follows. "If a man comes to us and tells us that he expects or does not expect us to do something for him, then the first thing that we experience is an act of *striving,* which has in view either "positive values" or "negative values" related to this man. This is entirely independent of whether we have formed any intentions of taking or not taking the step expected of us. We then say that this is a difference in the *Gesinnung* we have towards him."[27] Examples of *Gesinnung* are "goodwill," "love," "suspicion," "confidence," and so on. His point is that inherent in our directedness in *Gesinnung* toward positive or negative values in the person who approaches us is a type of "material" that will partially determine our inclination to perform or not perform the action expected of us. Our *Gesinnung* does not entirely determine intentions, but it does establish the *a priori* limits of possible intentions; the changing concrete situation also plays a determining role. Thus the intention to strike a child is compatible with a protective *Gesinnung* toward him, but the intention of letting him play with matches (*ceteris paribus*) is not. Scheler adds that a given *Gesinnung* toward a person, group, or thing is experienced as enduring and as independent of most circumstances of life, such that we tend to have the same tendencies of sympathy or antipathy toward a thing each time it is brought before us.

We must keep in mind that despite Scheler's examples, he seems to use the term *Gesinnung* not simply for the particular attitude one has toward a person at a given time, but for the very general characteristic of personality that we might call "temperament," a term that, however, does not come up in his discussion. Nevertheless, Scheler speaks of *Gesinnung* as something that cannot be affected by the results of our actions (obviously, insofar as the action is founded in *Gesinnung*), or by education. Still, when the *Gesinnung* spontaneously undergoes a change, it gives new direction to one's entire life. His thought here is undoubtedly that such a change in the *Gesinnung* is only possible by means of the experience of moral and/or religious conversion, in which the person — the center of moral value in which the *Gesinnung* is founded — gives new direction to itself. Does this state of affairs mean that all attempts at moral self-betterment are in vain? It appears to imply this; and Scheler, the Catholic, appears to hold at times that Grace and not works is the only means to "salvation."

Nevertheless, it is clear that he holds that the content of the *Gesinnung* of ourselves or of another person is immediately intuitable by an observer, such that the observer can *judge* that person morally. Scheler points out that in Kant's view, a person could be a criminal and yet be of good *Gesinnung* without anyone knowing it — hence the criminal would be a good person, insofar as the *Gesinnung* is the primordial carrier of moral values in the person, in both Kant's and Scheler's view. The Kantian view, he notes further, is parallel with Calvin's doctrine that there is to our eyes no difference in the behavior of the chosen and the damned.

We see from our discussion, in addition, that the *Gesinnung* is not only the carrier of moral values in the *individual* person but can also be common to a group of people: to construct our own example, a political party is a group of *Gleichgesinnte,* that is, people who are "of one mind" with regard to the political situation in general. Agreement as to their specific aims (*Vorsätze*), which are to be realized by means of concrete actions it is their intention (*Absicht*) to perform, is founded upon their "like-mindedness."[28] But now since *Gesinnung* is the foundation of specific intentions and aims, we can sum up Scheler's description of the act of *Gesinnung* by calling it the *primordial* moment of an act of will and hence the primordial carrier of "good" and "evil" in the moral sense. *Gesinnung* is the "carrier that *must* possess moral values, if intentions, aims, decisions and the action itself are to have them."[29]

Scheler gives us a concrete example of the fact that it is not only *Gesinnung* that is the carrier of the values of good and evil, but rather that a specific action in which the *Gesinnung* of an agent appears also contains elements that carry value. A man has fallen into a lake. A lame man, observing, is "of a mind [*gesinnt*] to rescue him," but of course cannot. It is evident, Scheler holds, that the lame man cannot even *want* (*Wollen*) to rescue him (although he may want him to be rescued), insofar as he is aware of the impossibility for him actually to perform the rescue. The point is that the moral worth of the lame man in this case is not the same as would be that of a man with the same *Gesinnung* who actually attempted to carry out the rescue; the moral worth of the second man is *higher.* If this were not the case, it would follow that the moral worth of a third party, who was not at the scene, but who "would have been" of a like mind as the other two men, will be the same as that of the first two; obviously this is not the case. Nevertheless, it is true that the moral worth of the man who attempts the rescue will be the same should he fail in his attempt or not; the point is that there is a "will to do" in the second case that does not and cannot appear in the former — unless the lame man *first discovers* his lameness in an attempt at a rescue. It is the element of striving given with an act of will (or "wanting"), it seems, that places the act *necessarily* in a concrete situation with a specific value content toward which it is directed, and that distinguishes this act from the phenomenon of *Gesinnung* and gives it its *own* moral value.

We will not follow Scheler further in his analyses of other candidates for becoming carriers of value within what he calls the "experiential unity of an action" (e.g., "performance," "disposition," etc.), or into the analysis of related notions such as that of the general nature of *objects* of wanting, that is, the "practical objects" and their "milieu," or again into the general nature of the "feelings" associated with the performance of an action — all of which make up the thematics of a phenomenological study of the fundamental meanings revealed in the ethical point of view. We should keep in mind, however, the nature of the problem with which Scheler is concerned here, and his general point of view concerning such problems.

Again, Scheler's analyses can be viewed from three aspects, the historical-critical, the broadly political or ideological, and the phenomenological; we have just been studying this latter aspect. The critical problem he directs at Kant does not simply question Kant's belief that moral worth must be sought in the will of an agent and that such ethics can only be merely formal. Rather, it is the corollary to Kant's view that bothers him: namely, that the *material* of an act of will, that is, the concrete elements determining the act of will as distinct from the purely formal element of *Gesinnung,* is constituted by the states of pleasure or pain that the representation of the proposed action inspires in us — a view in violent conflict with Scheler's belief that the material of the ethical standpoint is not reducible to the vital-physical and that the wellspring of human ethical behavior is a kind of love that is at first a spiritual phenomenon.

In order to refute the Kantian view, Scheler presents us with this phenomenological analysis of purposeful human action as executed within the framework of the value *a priori,* which it will be the business of our next section to describe. The central philosophical claim in this analysis is that the objects that prompt one to action — the "practical objects" — are not primarily objects given in mere sense perception, which excite one's senses and arouse one's desire to do something, but rather in an immediate feeling (*Fühlen*) in which an "ideal ought" appears. These claims, if justified, enable Scheler to deny that the striving inherent in any act of willing-to-do-something is founded in the prior representation to oneself of the sensual values of pleasure and pain that the moral agent intends to result from his action (such representation does not usually occur, in fact), and to affirm instead that this striving is founded in *any* of the value modalities that one immediately feels in the given object-to-be-realized. Insofar as the value modalities are not reducible in any sense to one another, moral action cannot be said to be founded upon striving for the realization of sensual values alone, as Kant's theory ultimately implies, in Scheler's interpretation. His point is obviously directed not only against Kant, however, but against modern schools of ethical vitalism, evolutionism, and pragmatism: striving, yes, even "impulse," does not obtain its "material" simply from the values given in sensual feeling.

V *The Phenomenology of Value*

On Scheler's scale, values are listed in four classes. We recall that values appear in each of the four levels of the emotional life (the four irreducible modes of *Fühlen*): the sensual, the vital, the ego-feeling, and the spiritual levels. Each class of values includes those that appear on each of these four levels. Each of the classes has subclasses; these are generally classified according to the types of carriers on which they necessarily appear. There are three fundamental types of value carriers: *persons* and their *acts, things,* and *functions.* Thus, for example, the value of the "holy" may be carried by a thing such as a crucifix, whose function as a symbol is to "point toward" the sphere of the holy. The crucifix carries a symbol value in addition to the values it carries as a material object — its dollar value — and as a human artifact — its beauty. Similarly, the value of the holy appears on functions, such as the *emotions* of beatitude and despair; these are psychophysical reactions to the feeling of the holy in such acts as "reverence," "prayer," "disbelief." Again, they may appear on the *type of person* that we call the "saint" or the "holy man," or upon the "typical" actions of such persons. One can feel the value of the holy *on* any of these persons, things, functions, or actions, and by reflecting on any of these examples, we may attain insight into the value of the holy itself.

By following this procedure, the phenomenological study of values results in a *typology* of values, whose most important feature is the claim that each type possesses a *relative worth.* Scheler's discussion is remarkably compact: that which "before all else must be demanded of an ethics" is sketched on five pages out of the 580 that make up *Der Formalismus.*[30]

The order of values is as follows: First and lowest are the values of the *pleasant* and the *unpleasant,* given in acts of sensual feeling; the former is higher than the latter, for pleasure *must* be preferred to pain. We will examine the nature of this "must" in a moment. Second, there are the values of the *noble* and the *base,* given in vital feeling; the noble is preferred to the base. Third, we have spiritual values of spiritual feeling, especially the *beautiful* and the *ugly,* the right and the wrong (or the just and the unjust), and the value of *pure knowledge of truth* (i.e., knowledge of essence as opposed to knowledge of "empirical laws," which latter serves vital and not spiritual interests). The evidence that these values are higher than and independent of those of the noble and the base consists partially in the fact that given with the higher values is the insight that the lower values "ought" to be sacrificed for them, and partially in the phenomenologically clear and distinct insight that we in fact do prefer the one to the other. Finally, the highest values are those of the *holy* and the *unholy* (or the profane), which are first revealed as objects of feeling in the primordial acts of love and hate.

Let us now direct some questions at this unique and, one might say, daring attempt at an ethical system.

First we must again make clear that the values in question here are being considered *as essences,* apart from their possible instantiation on carriers, and their positions on a scale of relative worth are for that very reason given *a priori,* prior to actual cases of value judging. Scheler is correct in his assertion that we would reject *a priori* any description of a race of beings about which it was said that they preferred the unpleasant to the pleasant; for *either* what such beings prefer is not the unpleasant but some higher value that commands them to renounce the pleasant (asceticism), *or* they prefer things as pleasant that "we" normally consider unpleasant, for the preference of the pleasant over the unpleasant "rests in the essence of these values and in the essence of sensual feeling."[11] Scheler views this meaning relation of the pleasant and the preferred as pointing to a *basic fact* about value and human biology.

Even when we are clear as to this point, however, other problems remain. First of all, it is not entirely clear to this reader to what extent the scale of relative worth of values constitutes a *Fundierungsordnung.* The *Fundierungsordnung,* we recall, is a relationship between the meanings that are implied by the act of grasping something *as* that something, such that the statement of a case in which a meaning A "founds" meaning B may often be expressed as a tautology. "All bodies are extended" is a tautology; "extension" *founds* "body." We now ask, are the statements "the pleasant is a higher value than the unpleasant," "the holy is a higher value than the beautiful" similarly tautologies in Scheler's sense? Or is the relative worth of a value independent of the order of foundation of values?

If we study Scheler's discussion of the essence of "higher" and "lower" values toward the end of this discussion of the values themselves, we may obtain some clarity in this matter. It is apparent that he does in fact understand the scale of values to be a *Fundierungsordnung,* although he does not say so explicitly; hence the above statements are tautologies. Indeed, it follows that the understanding of such a statement as "John likes vanilla ice cream" has insight into the nature of the holy as its necessary condition, for the possibility of grasping something as pleasant, that is, liking something, is founded upon the prior grasping of the value of the holy. Reinforcing this interpretation of the scale of values is the consideration that the cognition of the sphere of the holy as a value is said by Scheler, in *Vom Ewigen im Menschen,* to be one of the three most *fundamental* acts of cognition; these three acts, which we shall study in a later chapter, are said to "found" all other acts of cognitive awareness, perception, and feeling.

Now Scheler perhaps has a point here. He might indicate in justification of this claim, that the act of liking vanilla ice cream is not simply an act of sensual feeling, but involves an act of understanding, of cognition. Dogs do not "like" some foods more than others, it might be said, although they respond with greater enthusiasm to some foods than to others. But only "spiritual" beings *understand* a feeling *as* pleasant, and it is this understanding that is implied by the statement that John likes something. Again, we would not imply that a dog cannot discriminate between the pleasant and the more pleasant, the useful and the dangerous, but that he cannot *cognize* values the way men do. The difficulty we find here is simply that Scheler's *Aufweisen* of this *Fundierungsordnung* of the acts of cognizing value is a bit too brief to be completely convincing, but we leave that to each reader to mull over. Is the possibility of the act of feeling the value of, for instance, the noble founded upon the prior feeling of the value of the sphere of the holy? Of the beautiful? Would we not feel the beauty of a summer's day *as* beautiful, were we not open to the value of holiness? Did

Kierkegaard have a similar insight before the eye of his mind when he wrote, in *Either/Or,* "without courage I see absolutely nothing eternal, *and, accordingly, nothing beautiful*"?[32]

Another problem with Scheler's ethics concerns the incompleteness of the scale of values. Scheler believed that the scale could be worked out further, but in what direction?[33] Did he intend, for example, to subdivide the four modalities into further types of values falling under each heading, and rank these submodalities according to their relative worth? Now it is apparent that the practical difficulty of obtaining clear insight into the relative worth of value modalities becomes greater as the number of them increases, although the possibility of obtaining self-evident insight here is theoretically always present. Nevertheless, there seem to be cases in which it is not entirely clear even in which of the four categories a value falls. Scheler holds that the value of the virtue of courage (the courageous) is a vital value, because conditioned by vital impulse (*triebhaft*). Now one might ask whether the value of the virtue of temperance (the temperate) is similarly a vital value, or whether it belongs to the modality of spiritual values. Here the problem of adjudication becomes particularly intense; the question of whether the moment of impulse or similar vital factor belongs to the essence of temperance (a virtue Scheler does not discuss), and if so, whether its value as a human virtue is preferable to that of courage, gives us an example of how complex and slippery are the problems that Scheler has set for himself. The difficulty alone of performing the phenomenological reduction and disengaging the value of the virtue of temperance from its concrete manifestations is enormous, to say nothing of the problem of obtaining insight into its relative worth. We must admit this, however much we assent to as self-evident the order of relative worth that he assigns to the four value modalities. Yet it is hard to avoid the conclusion that it is the description of the submodalities that he has in mind as the central problem of ethics.

VI *Phenomenological Ethics as Normative Ethics*

In the circle of problems in ethics we have discussed up to now, the phenomenological method has been everywhere assumed. Scheler holds that the descriptions of the phenomena of "feeling," "love," "can," and "ought" are grounded upon the same reflective insight into self-evident data as are the typology of feeling and the descriptions of the values and their order themselves. In this self-evidence we have a check against *anarchy* in ethics, he believes. He reaffirms his ethical absolutism against those who proclaim the "right to freedom of conscience" — sophists all — by undertaking an analysis of "conscience." His problem is to establish the limits of conscience as a mode of moral insight and compare the value of conscience as moral *evidence* to the self-evidence in ethical matters afforded by phenomenological reflection. Here, however, he runs inevitably into what is perhaps his deepest trouble.

Conscience is first shown to have only relative value as moral evidence by means of a demonstration that conscience can *deceive*. Thus we can speak legitimately of a "good" and a "bad" conscience, but not of a "good" or "bad" self-evident insight. Insofar as this is the case, conscience is itself a carrier of values ("good" and "bad," "correct" and "deceptive") and thus cannot be the *final source* of ethical insight. Some other mode of evidence must enable us to judge the value of conscience. Phenomenological reflection, on the other hand, cannot be deceptive, as we have clearly seen in our study of the method; only a judgment that we have a case of self-evident insight before us can deceive. Now in addition, conscience functions essentially negatively: it tells us what we ought not to do, criticizes us, makes us hesitate, and so on. Thus it cannot give us insight into a positive good; indeed, an act of conscience is *founded upon* acts of value apprehension, rather than being the *source* of such apprehension. What is then the role of conscience as a source of ethical insight, and how should we understand the notion of "freedom of conscience"?

Scheler's answer is quite difficult, but his point seems to be as follows. Even granting self-evident insight into what is valuable, in a given situation I may not be able to decide on the basis of generally valid norms what is the "good" action *for me,* for it is possible that in the same situation the "good" action for each person will be different. Scheler says that

conscience, therefore, says something different for each person in the same situation the more purely it speaks, and it would surely err, if it said the same to each! For "conscience" in *this* sense, that *principle of freedom of conscience* is unconditionally valid which says that it is open to everyone to listen to his conscience in the case of questions whose solution is not regulated by the objective, generally valid kind [of ethical insight] and the norms based on it.[34]

We may assume that what Scheler has in mind in this passage is that each person may, in certain situations, feel that "his is a special case" and cannot be handled by general norms; in this case, he will do well to listen to his conscience. In doing so, however, he will not be questioning the validity of the generally valid norms. Undoubtedly Scheler saw in the phenomenon of conscience, as it is generally applied as a source of moral insight, a rather fickle, impulse-ridden whispering formed by one's personal experiences and psychological development, whereas the performance of the phenomenological reflection is an act demanding rigorous training and moral discipline.

Here now is the problem: conscience appears to speak from the natural standpoint, whereas phenomenological reflection does not; the latter considers essences apart from "carriers," apart from a concrete situation. Phenomenological knowledge of essence is hence not applicable to problems involving the objects given from within the natural standpoint. In Scheler's view, apodictic knowledge is available in phenomenological reflection upon essences alone, and not in what he calls "perceptual" knowledge, that is, our everyday understanding of the things we encounter in the world about us. For that reason, it appears that the notion of a phenomenological reflection that renders us self-evident insight into what we should do — as to what is "good" and "bad" — *in a concrete situation,* that is, where values appear "on" objects, acts, and so on, involves a contradiction; for it is of the nature of phenomenological reflection to intend, to direct itself toward, the *essential,* namely, the *meaning element* in any experience from within the natural standpoint. Reflection upon the givens in an act of feeling and preference may reveal the values intended, their order of foundation, and their relative worth, but such reflection can never enable us to judge *apodictically* in a concrete situation just what values are present, and what steps should be taken, what decisions made, to realize higher values. More generally, perfect evidence may be available concerning the content of an essence or a pure fact, but no such perfect evidence is available for the assertion that an *instance* of the pure fact is present in the natural object before us.

This final and, I think, most damaging criticism to be directed at Scheler's plans for a normative ethical system concerns the possibility of applying the phenomenological *description* of values to an ethics that imagines itself capable of employment in the solution of concrete ethical problems. This is in essence the same problem we raised in our discussion of Scheler's program for philosophy: does he expect phenomenology to establish a body of knowledge, that is, a series of propositions expressing some set of facts concerning essences? But phenomenology is said to obtain insight into phenomena that are given apart from and prior to all symbolic notation. How can the insight thus attained be expressed through language? All knowledge claims made on the basis of phenomenology, moreover, are in principle unverifiable in terms of any criterion of truth and falsity, such as are applicable from within the natural or scientific standpoints. Scheler has, in sum, created a gap between the phenomenological fact and the facts of perception, and he has failed to provide a bridge between these two kinds of fact.

Does the scale of values have *any relevance at all* for helping me to decide, for instance, whether I should contribute a sum of money to the university or to the hospital? The answer is yes, apodictic evidence for deciding correctly is available, *if* I can decide upon the values carried by the university and the hospital; a "good" action would then be to contribute to that institution which carries (or acts to realize) the higher value. But no apodictic evidence is available for deciding the latter problem; therefore the scale has no application here. It does not seem even to make sense to speak of feeling the values carried by a university, although it may make sense to speak about feeling the values carried by a piece of music, as Scheler does. An *a priori* ethics may describe the values themselves and their order of preferability, but it can have no answer to the question we have just raised, for apodictic insight into preferability is confined to the sphere of pure values. Again, simply, we may see that the holy life is better than the life of sensuality, but can we know *with the same degree of evidence* in just what activities the truly holy life consists? The fact that we cannot indicates that the latter problem is *not* a phenomenological problem.

Thus the effect of all Scheler's efforts in normative ethics is to perpetuate the myth of philosophy begun by Socrates: the philosopher is a seeker of norms of human action that shine in like beacons from outside history and from beyond the complex, changing situations of life. These beacons are used to fix the course of the philosopher and are the source of true moral behavior, culture, and the attunement and, consequently, the happiness of the philosopher's soul. Indeed, the secret of Scheler's philosophy is its Platonism, in which the phenomenological method has been substituted for the method of dialectics. What is Socrates searching for, if not "essences," in Scheler's sense? The wedding of these two is perhaps surprising but not entirely fruitless. If we "bracket" Scheler's epistemological realism and put aside possible claims to have discovered the basis of a normative ethics, Scheler's ethics teaches us to reflect upon the cognitive content of value terms. If this reflection can be made without illusions as to achieving finality or completeness, and if poets or thinkers as inspired as Scheler outstrip other men in depth of insight and capacity to describe values, still this attempt to understand what we know of beauty itself when we refer to a thing as "beautiful" or as "grotesque" should not be despised as nonphilosophy.

A further service resulting from Scheler's analysis of the relative worth of values is the discovery of the *irreducibility* of values. Through his *Aufweisen* of the various and independent functions of feeling and emotion, he can claim to have provided us with sufficient ground for turning away from attempts to "explain" the phenomenon of value on the basis of human vitality or biological organization, or in terms of such trite theses as that sytems of morality and aesthetic norms are functions of the human attempt to cope with our environment, and so forth. The relation of men to the values they discover about them is too complex to reduce to such simple formulae. Naturally, the argument is metaphysical; to the claim that, for example, the act of valuation is the product of biological impulse, Scheler opposes his metaphysical thesis of ethical absolutism. But there are uses of metaphysics; while the vitalist's thesis leads him to the investigation of human psychology and ethical behavior, Scheler's thesis leads to the description of meanings in ethics. Here, as everywhere in his work, what is to be investigated is not the causes of ethical behavior but rather what understanding of value is presupposed by actual ethical behavior, whatever its cause.

Scheler's thesis has a further consequence: if ethical absolutism is correct, if men value and prefer according to an *ordo amoris,* then the fact that there are enormous historical variations in systems of valuation must be explained in terms of pathology; where values are not apprehended, there is blindness; where a positive value is taken as a negative value, there is a *perversion* of the *ordo*. Again, this blindness, this perversion is not a simple function of human needs, but involves a *spiritual failure* as well; and thus Scheler sets himself to a study and description of the sociological and spiritual disease he calls *ressentiment*. These problems take us beyond *Der Formalismus* and presuppose a familiarity with Scheler's concept of man and society. A study of these categories will proceed a reintroduction of the concept of the perversion of knowledge of value through *ressentiment* in our chapter on the sociology of knowledge.

CHAPTER 6

Sympathy and Community

I *Sympathy*

S CHELER's studies of the phenomenon of sympathy have been interpreted as an attempt on the part of a philosopher and phenomenologist to contribute to empirical psychology by providing a conceptual framework for experimental studies. While this interpretation has a firm basis in Scheler's own intentions, it is clear that *Wesen und Formen der Sympathie* is, essentially, propaedeutic to ethics and metaphysics. He is investigating the mode in which human beings are *immediately aware of other persons.* Thus its phenomenological studies — which were completed before *Der Formalismus* — supply the foundation for later investigations of the nature of society and knowledge as a social phenomenon. Indeed, insofar as man's relationship to God also involves a form of sympathetic awareness of His presence, the studies in *Sympathie* offer a key to much of Scheler's later work, and represent as well the turning point in Scheler's thought from neo-Kantianism to phenomenology.

The title of this study of the phenomenon of sympathy is "Essences and Forms of Sympathy," indicating that we have to do both with a phenomenological investigation of sympathy and with its typology. As a phenomenologist, Scheler is trying to *intuit* and *describe* the essence of his theme. He compares his study of the essence of phenomena to the empirical-psychological comparison of actual instances of a given phenomenon with the purpose of discovering similarities and dissimilarities in the modes of its genesis, the classification of "pathological" types, species-genus relationships, and so on. Whether Scheler is correct in his assertion that science *qua* science cannot discover of itself the distinctions within the phenomenon of sympathy that Scheler presents under the title

125

of phenomenology is still a question. He is in strange territory when he claims that the phenomenology founded on his method may "of itself" result in knowledge useful for the guidance of science; generally he does not hold up his method as an aid to science or as providing scientifically useful knowledge. It is clear, however, that his analysis of sympathy, with its strange mixture of empirical, metaphysical, and phenomenological elements, is highly interesting not only for the insight it gives us into this phenomenon but also for its "usefulness" for psychology and sociology — as at least one worker in these fields has borne witness.[1]

Thus it comes about that Scheler's first "opponents" as well as his sources in the matter of the nature of sympathy are not the scientists but rather the "metaphysicians" who have concerned themselves with the problem. For example, Scheler spends many pages discussing and refuting the monism of Schopenhauer, who saw in the phenomenon of sympathy evidence for the fundamental *unity of egos* behind their apparent plurality. Scheler's refutation is based upon his *Aufweisen* of what in fact appears in the act of sympathizing with someone: in the true act of sympathizing, of "feeling with" another person what he feels the "otherness" of the person sympathized with is not negated[2] — as would have to be the case if the phenomenon of sympathy were to serve as "evidence" for a metaphysical monism — indeed, this "otherness" is a necessary element in the experience of sympathy. What is "given" in sympathy is not the other person, but rather his emotion and the *value given in it*. This metaphysical skirmishing is, of course, of interest to those who wish to understand Scheler's own metaphysical speculations. It may seem, indeed, that for Scheler, phenomenology and metaphysics are inextricably interrelated. As we shall see from many examples in the pages to come, Scheler viewed the history of metaphysical speculation as a repository of insights into essence. Phenomenological analysis may therefore profit from these ideas without itself becoming speculative.

A more modern view of sympathy than that of Schopenhauer with which Scheler enters into dialogue is contained in the various genetic theories of sympathy that attempt to explain the origin of this phenomenon on the basis of an inference from or a projection of one's own feelings into the foreign self with which one sympathizes. Scheler claims that the "foreign" emotion is *directly and immediately given* in the outward expression of emotion and that intuitive reflection upon what is given in an act of sympathy will reveal no "projection" or "inference" involved either in fact or as a logical precondition of the act of sympathy. Moreover, the thought that we "go" from our own ego "to" the foreign ego in the act of sympathy contradicts the phenomenological facts: we first come upon the ego in our understanding intercourse with other egos; we discover "ourselves" in discovering "others": the "we" *founds* the "I."

Whether or not one prefers the metaphysics of naturalism — in which the so-called argument from analogy first makes sense — to Scheler's idealistic metaphysics, it is clear that his description of what is given in an act of sympathy and what is logically implied by that act is more accurate than that implied by the analogical or projectivist "explanation" of how an act of sympathy is possible. An intuitive examination of the phenomenon of, for example, pity fails to reveal either an act of projection or an act of logical inference, except in unusual circumstances, in which we often no longer have a true case of pity. We can make Scheler's general point here clear with an example to which Scheler refers in passing: we observe a child "screaming himself blue in the face." It is one thing to look upon this child's head simply as a physical object, another to understand that head *as* an expression of an emotion. In the second case we need not, of course, *sympathize with* or pity the child, but when we do, our sympathy is based upon our understanding of the head *as* an expression of emotion of a "foreign" ego, and not on the basis of our mere perception of the head *as* a set of physical characteristics.

Phenomenological reflection reveals the following *essential characteristics* of the true act of sympathy:

(1) Pain must be given to me *as* the pain of another person before I can perform an act of sympathy. I do not discover the "otherness" of the pain in sympathizing, nor do I "pity myself in pitying him," but rather sympathy is one possible reaction to the discovery of pain in another person.[3] According to Scheler, "The feeling of foreign feeling-states precedes feeling-with." Sympathy is, of course, not the only possible result of grasping a foreign feeling; we can just as well examine it scientifically, attempt to "relive it" in order to understand it more deeply, all without sympathizing with the person who feels it. As Scheler correctly points out, the good historian is often a man who has a highly developed capacity for re-

living the emotions of historical personages in order to better understand their actions and decisions, but he need not thereby "sympathize" with their failures.

(2) Second, the otherness of the person is *maintained* in the act of true sympathy. The fact that there are such sympathetic phenomena as that of complete identification with the feelings and emotions of another person merely shows that sympathy is not a single, simple phenomenon, but has subforms and perversions.

(3) Thus, although the emotional acts of the person with whom one sympathizes are not given in themselves in the act of sympathy, still they are understood and possibly "relived" or "reperformed" by the sympathizing person. The sympathizer "puts himself in the place of" the person sympathized with, and "tries to feel what he feels." These are, of course, highly spiritual and voluntary acts.

(4) Finally, the act of sympathizing with the emotions of another person is a *cognitive* act, whose material is given in the emotion of sympathy in which, as we see from paragraph (1) above, what is intended is not one's own feeling states but the feeling states of another person. What is cognized is the value that appears on the foreign feeling state. Thus we see that it is essential to the act of sympathy that a value pertaining to another person is given in it.

Up to now we have been examining a "true" act of sympathy for its essential content. Scheler, as we noted, divides the phenomenon into independent but interrelated *types,* all of which share at least some of the general characteristics of true sympathy. This was for him the most important undertaking from the point of view of empirical psychology, for in it we discriminate between those types of observable human psychological phenomena that we generally classify under the heading of "sympathy." Scheler undertakes a phenomenological investigation of the essential moments of three such types, in addition to the "true" sympathy we have been discussing.

(1) The first category of sympathy — which Scheler appears to hold to be the *highest* form of sympathy insofar as it is possible only on the basis of the "highest form of love" and insofar as we come in this case as close to the spiritual center of the other person as is possible in an act of sympathy — Scheler calls the "immediate feeling-with" of the same single emotion with another person. Scheler gives us the example of parents standing over the lifeless body of their beloved child:

They feel *with each other* the *same* suffering, the "same" pain; i.e., not that the one feels this suffering and the other feels it also, and in addition they both know that they are feeling it, but rather this is a *feeling-with-each-other.* The suffering of the one is not given to the other in any way as an "object," as is the case with the friend who comes up to the parents and sympathizes "with them" or has pity "on their pain."[4]

The case Scheler has in mind is clear, but one may wonder whether it is distinct from other forms of sympathy with respect to its *depth.* It is indeed clear that a truly deep emotion is described in Scheler's example; the parents "feel themselves together" in their sorrow over the loss of their child. However, from a purely structural point of view, the situation is parallel to the case in which I miss the bull's eye at the fair and thus fail to win the kewpie doll for my girl friend. In this case, we both share the same emotion — simple disappointment — and this emotion is, as in Scheler's example, different from that of our friend who wished us well, but who had no stake in the doll. In his case, there is no sharing of a *single* emotion; the friend is, so to speak, "alone in his pity." It is possible that Scheler has been guided too strongly in his *valuation* of this phenomenon of "feeling-with" by the single example he discusses. We can allow him in any case his point that we have here an emotional phenomenon with a unique structure.

(2) The second category of sympathy phenomena that Scheler describes is that of genuine sympathy, which we have already dealt with in our general discussion. What is peculiar about the structure of this type of sympathy is that the pain or the joy for which one sympathizes with another person is not one's own — as in the case of the parents' both suffering the same loss — but rather one "takes part in it" as something belonging to the other person.

(3) The third category presents us with a radically different structure. Here it is no longer the case that pain is not itself given to the sympathizer (in the sense that he himself feels pain), but rather *actual* pain is transferred to the sympathizer from the foreign ego. This form of sympathy is called "contagion" (*Gefühlsansteckung*), and occurs, for example, when we enter a room filled with happy, laughing people; we tend to get "taken up" by the prevailing mood, we become gay almost against our will — in fact, when we are in a bad mood, we may even seek out a gayer company in order to "snap us out of it." The difference between this type of sym-

pathy and that on the second level is obvious: there is *no previous knowledge* presupposed by contagion of the *cause of* or the *reasons for* the joy felt by the happy group, whereas we cannot rejoice with another person unless we know what he is rejoicing about. What is given in contagion thus takes place on the level of feeling states and the sensual or vital values revealed in them, and not on the level of the higher emotions, whereas true sympathy can occur on both levels. Scheler adds that one's moods can be affected in this way not only by the moods of other persons but also by the "moods" we find expressed in the things about us. Thus one can be affected by the brightness of an early morning in spring so that one becomes also "bright."

It is not to the point to object to this analysis that the lines between contagion and true sympathy cannot be so clearly drawn in actual experience. It is clear that the most careful self-analysis will not reveal, for example, what part of our total aesthetic reaction to *Hamlet* is a case of true sympathy with the hero and what part is due simply to the contagious effect of the surroundings, the behavior of the actors, their weeping, and so forth. However, what Scheler is after is the essential characteristics distinguishing the possible sympathetic emotions felt in that *total* experience. That he has succeeded in describing these characteristics is clear, even if the techniques for identifying instances of these phenomena are unclear.

Again, however, it is hard to avoid the conclusion that whatever the "usefulness" of this analysis for scientific studies of the human psyche, Scheler's *primary* interest in this analysis is the problem of *value*. For example, he concludes his analysis of contagion by criticizing Nietzsche for his well-known thesis that pity is one of the sources of decadence. Nietzsche failed to see that in the phenomenon of pity are elements of the spiritual phenomena of love and knowledge (i.e., of the cause of the suffering and the value intended by the person pitied) to be found; but neither love nor knowledge is an element in contagion. Thus Nietzsche's erroneous valuation of pity is a product of his *confusion* concerning the nature of pity. A correct valuation of the phenomenon of sympathy would point out that contagion and the fourth category of sympathy, ego identification, *deaden* the spirit, whereas "feeling-with-another" and "true sympathy" *enhance* spiritual receptivity and are hence not causes of decadence.

(4) The form of sympathy farthest removed from true, spiritual feeling-with-another is at the same time a limiting case of emotional contagion and is called by Scheler *Einsfühlung,* the emotional identification of one ego with another. Its characteristic structure has two forms: one can feel as if one has become the person identified with, as in the case of the child who had lost his cat and transformed himself into the cat, walked on all fours, refused to eat at the table, and so on.[5] On the other hand, one can feel that another person has taken the place of one's own ego, as is occasionally the case in schizophrenia. Scheler identifies ten case types of ego identification taken from the widest sources: totem worship, childhood play, sexual intercourse, hysteria, animal behavior. A case of the latter type has been quoted from Scheler earlier in this work.[6]

In conclusion: although the applications of this analysis to empirical studies in psychology are not clear, on the epistemological level its results are more promising. Scheler has in effect turned us away from viewing the "problem of other minds" as a purely logical problem of finding evidence for an inference in which the existence of egos and thought processes foreign to our own are posited, by pointing out — correctly, we must agree — that this problem of other minds can only arise once we already have the object of our "search," namely, the foreign ego. The real significance of Scheler's study of sympathy is that it brings us back to the things themselves, and attempts to describe the concrete phenomenon in which such abstract conceptual problems such as that of other minds first take their point of departure. The analysis exhibits Scheler's fundamental presupposition that feeling is as much a mode of cognition as is conceptual thought. The acts of understanding foreign thought processes are treated not as involving an inference or any other covert "movement of the spirit," such as the projection of my feeling states onto others, but as a single act of perception in which elements of thought, emotion, and feeling are present.

In another direction, the study of sympathy has consequences for sociology. Scheler has been describing other-relatedness, or the peculiar kind of openness of men to other men, in its most general form. The sphere of *Mitwelt* is founded upon this phenomenon; it is only because men have a capacity for grasping foreign egos at all that the phenomenon of human sociation becomes possible. This phenomenon has its own peculiar essential structure, and, as we will see in the following section, is divisible into a set of irreducible types.

II   *The Phenomenological Foundations of Sociology*

P. A. Schlipp once pointed out that in Scheler's philosophy of sociology, as it is developed in *Die Wissensformen und die Gesellschaft,* the philosopher appears more systematic, more painstaking in his approach than in the earlier works, but that it is nevertheless difficult to pass judgment upon what we find here; for, as Scheler constantly reminds us, the "strict scientific grounding" of the doctrines outlined here were to be presented in a later work, which he never lived to complete.[7] Whether or not one agrees with the first part of Professor Schlipp's judgment, it is clear that in the essays we have under the above title, Scheler is occupied with the propaedeutics of a type of sociological study he was recommending not only to himself for later study but to sociologists — that is, to empirical investigation — as well. Thus Scheler engages in an empirical study that is based in phenomenological methodology and is not, as in the case of the *Aufweisen* of sympathy, a purely phenomenological enterprise.

However, prior to this study of the "material principles" of the sociology of knowledge, Scheler engages in what is clearly a study in "pure" phenomenology: this is where he presents, in *Die Wissensformen und die Gesellschaft,* the three "highest principles" or "axioms" of the sociology of knowledge. These axioms are based upon intuitive reflection upon the nature of knowledge *as a social phenomenon.* Moreover, all three axioms are variations and adaptations of earlier phenomenological studies that Scheler presented in various works, but chiefly in *Der Formalismus.* Apparently, Scheler was in the process of rethinking these studies and giving them a more final, systematic form when he outlined these three *a priori* axioms. We will draw on all the available sources in our description of them and try to present a balanced if unfinished picture of what Scheler considered to be the fundamental elements constituting the *essential* relationship, knowledge-society. Then, at the beginning of the next chapter, we will begin with a study of the empirical-phenomenological science of the sociology of knowledge, which takes these axioms as its point of departure.

(1) The first axiom rests on the view that the knowledge that I am a part of a social entity is *a priori*: it states that before "I" can come to givenness, the *sphere* of *Mitwelt* — being with others — must already have been given. The view that we come to the discovery of our own selves only after having discovered selfhood in others — indeed, even in physical objects — has been represented by psychologists, notably by Piaget. Scheler's view, however, does not simply assert the priority of knowledge of other selves over knowledge of our own self, but is conjoined with the assertion that we have primordial knowledge that these other selves — and our selves — constitute a "society." How is the apriority of this knowledge established by Scheler?

In his article — which until very recently was one of the few attempts at a critical discussion of Scheler in English — Schlipp refers to the central example that Scheler calls upon to ground this doctrine as "unconvincing." Scheler refers us to an "epistemological" Robinson Crusoe, who has lived on his island since birth without any human contact, and who asserts that "I know that there is a community (*Gemeinschaft*) and that I belong to one (or to several), but I do not know the individuals who constitute them, nor the empirical groups of them that make up this existing community."[8] Robinson would be aware, Scheler asserts, of an *emptiness* that would be present when he performed certain elementary conscious emotional acts, and in this experience of emptiness the *sphere of the other* would appear. It does not seem to be clear in just what acts of consciousness Robinson would experience this "emptiness," this "lack of fulfillment" (in the sense that an act of consciousness is "fulfilled" in the content given in it). It is clear that Scheler does not have in mind an "unfulfilled longing" — for someone to talk to, for example — on the part of Robinson; but rather that Robinson would always experience a lack of unity of *meaning* in these acts of consciousness. He writes that "Robinson would always experience according to essential laws a state of 'unfulfilled consciousness' when he performed intellectual and emotional acts that can only come to an objective unity of meaning together with possible social *counter*-acts."[9] This statement appears to mean that Robinson would feel something like the emotion of sympathy, without, however, being able to understand its directedness. Perhaps we can take this rather obscure assertion to refer to the thought that many of the meanings that we intend in our daily life involve an implicit reference to social existence. Such meanings as those denoted by the terms "obedience," "promising," and "trust" would not be understood by an imaginary being who was not aware of the self as a social entity. He could not "unify" the diverse meaning elements that constitute the meanings of these terms.

But what is it, then, that leads Scheler to the belief that Robinson would perform such an intentional act in which the social element or simply the element of the foreign self was implied yet not given? There is never a question of Robinson's intending something, parts of which he had forgotten — Scheler expressly excludes the interpretation that the knowledge of foreign selves is innate — and the notion of the order of foundation excludes the possibility of Robinson's intending a meaning content founded in a phenomenon that by hypothesis has not been given. In fact, Scheler's "example" of Robinson is not an unconvincing exhibition of an essential relationship between the "I" and the "we"; it is a faulty metaphysical argument, one founded upon the assumption that the human mind develops according to laws that bear no reference to the physical environment.

Were it nevertheless possible to show an *essential* interrelationship between the phenomenon of the "I" (or the act of my grasping "myself") and the "we" (or the act of my grasping another self as foreign), there would not necessarily be any mention of the *social* dimension of these "selves." Clearly, Scheler's intention is to assert nonetheless that, directly and without inference, the social dimension of the "we" is grasped by Robinson in the *same* act in which he becomes aware of the fact that he is not alone: "I know that there is community, and that I belong to one." The grounds for this assumption, we must assume, are a phenomenological intuition of the essence of the "I," but no attempt is made by Scheler either to exhibit or to ground this assertion. Certainly the apriority of our knowledge of community is not evident from the argument built around the example of Robinson as we have interpreted it.

(2) The second axiom states that there are various *essential* ways in which an individual person takes part in the life of his community — or communities, for it is normally the case that a person is a part of various social entities at once, from the family to the nation. These modes of participation can be classified with the help of the categories descriptive of the modes of other-relatedness in general, which were outlined in *Wesen und Formen der Sympathie*,

although we are dealing here not with the abstract form of other-relatedness but with the social institutions, traditions, customs, and so on, in which such forms typically appear. Thus Scheler states that the possible ideal-typical modes of social intercourse extend from the ego identification characterizing certain primitive institutions to the most abstract and impersonal relationships between individuals, such as are regulated by contracts. In between are the various other typical modes and their forms of social expression. An exact description of these is the task of several analyses in *Der Formalismus*.

Here the import of Scheler's studies of the phenomenon of sympathy becomes apparent: a *social* entity is constituted in some form of other-relatedness, that is, in sympathetic apprehension of foreign egos. This is to say that in order for there to be social groupings, the individual must understand himself as being a part of the group, as existing in a certain sort of relation to another person. Knowledge of itself and of common goals and traditions belongs to the *essence* of "society." This fact distinguishes a community from a mere statistical agglomerate of persons. This profound insight into an essential-phenomenological characteristic of community in general was used by Scheler to ground what he held to be the highest political goal, namely, a society characterized by a specific mode of other-relatedness, which he calls the "solidarity" of each member with each other and with the whole.

This type of society is distinguished in *Der Formalismus* from three other modes of sociation,[10] each of which is founded in a type of sympathetic understanding that the members of this group have of each other and that makes this group a social entity and not a mere "collection" of individuals. Since this phenomenological *Aufweisen* is not developed further in *Die Wissensformen und die Gesellschaft*, we will not discuss it here. But a concept appears in the analyses of *Der Formalismus* that became important for the later work. The "highest essential type of community" represents Scheler's own social utopia — a term we may fairly use, insofar as these categories represent essential and not practical possibilities, possible and not actual communal forms — and is referred to as "the unity of independent, spiritual, individual persons 'in' an independent, spiritual, individual collective person [*Gesamtperson*]."[11] What of this *Gesamtperson,* however; what sort of entity does this term describe?

At the time of *Der Formalismus,* Scheler conceived of the *Gesamtperson* as a parallel concept to that of the individual person, which we mentioned in Chapter 4; the *Gesamtperson* is the irreducible, unobjectifiable and hence indescribable essence of an individual social entity, which is constituted in those intentional acts of the individual person that are properly *social* acts, that is, acts only possible on the basis of the *interaction* of individual persons with each other, and to which corresponds an equally individual and irreducible social world. But now if we look back for a moment at the discussion of the second axiom in *Die Wissensformen und die Gesellschaft,* written some eleven years after the typology of social forms in *Der Formalismus,* we find that this notion of the collective person has disappeared. In its place are the twin concepts of the "group soul" and the "group mind," concepts that Scheler calls "indispensable for the sociology of knowledge."[12] Here the collective person is thought of as the *subject of the knowledge* that is *produced in* the interaction of the individual persons who make up the given community. They are distinguished from each other with respect to their spontaneity: thus verbally reported myths and fairy tales, folk songs and costumes, dialects, customs, and the like, which are the products of "semi-automatic psychophysical activity,"[13] are the objects of knowledge of the group soul. The bodies of knowledge falling under the headings of law, philosophy, science, and so on, are the products of spontaneous, fully conscious acts performed by the members of a community, especially by its spiritual elite, and this knowledge is said to be that of the group mind.

What could be the reason for Scheler's development of these two categories and the subsequent neglect of the notion of the collective person? The answer seems to be as simple as the fact that Scheler's intentions and thus his needs in the way of theory in *Die Wissensformen und die Gesellschaft* are different from those in *Der Formalismus.* The fact that the group soul and group mind are conceived impersonally as subjects of knowledge, and not ethically, as spiritual Persons intending a world, signals the fact that Scheler is not preparing a political ideology here but is occupied with the sociological problem of the transmission of knowledge. The additional fact that the knowledge intended by the group mind and the group soul generally belongs to different social levels in the community provides Scheler with a framework for the most general problem of the sociology of knowledge, namely, that of the *transformation* of knowledge — more specifically, of relative natural and cultural *Weltanschauungen* — in history. And he understands this transformation as consisting partially in the interaction of the lower levels with the cultural elite in a given community.

(3) Let us return to *Die Wissensformen und die Gesellschaft* and complete our study of the sociological *a priori*. In the case of the third axiom we can again find sources in an earlier phenomenological analysis. A brief preliminary discussion of this earlier analysis will assist us in obtaining insight into the various standpoints, each grounded in different goals and purposes, from which Scheler seeks a solution to similar problems.

In *Vom Ewigen im Menschen,*[14] Scheler presents us with a description of what he considers to be the three most fundamental *insights,* that is, those three insights possessing the greatest evidence, and which may therefore serve as the point of departure for philosophy. The problem that Scheler has tackled in preparing this description is that of establishing the "order of givenness" of insight into reality. Unfortunately, the evidence for the correctness of the list of insights in the order of their evidence is not clear; Scheler has again put off the phenomenological grounding of this thesis for a later, unwritten work. Nevertheless, we can assert that the claim that an insight is the *first* insight carries with it, for Scheler, the claim that (1) it is the first in the order of foundation of knowledge, that is, that piece of knowledge that is implied in *all* other knowledge; it is thus the knowledge without which all other knowledge would be impossible, or what we can call "presuppositionless knowledge"; and (2) that the truth of the insight is the "least questionable" of all other knowledge claims; evidence for it is the most perfect. This is not to say, of course, that we are "more convinced" of its truth than of anything else, but that the thing itself is most completely self-given in intuition. The phenomenological grounding of such a list would be a most difficult task; indeed, Scheler notes that the very process of attaining these insights is a task that requires the highest moral perfection, despite the fact that their being known is presupposed by all other knowing and despite the degree of givenness to which their objects can in principle be brought.

The three most fundamental insights — which we will merely list, in view of the fact that Scheler's denial to us of a more complete

phenomenological *Aufweisen* leaves us with little material for critical analysis — are as follows. The *first* insight into a "state of
affairs" in the order of evidence and givenness is that *there is something at all,* or, expressed more sharply, that there *is not nothing at
all.*[15] The priority of this insight is indicated by the fact that the insight is available in reflection upon anything, existing or non-
existing. The *second* insight states "that there is an absolute
being," or a "being through which all other non-absolute being receives that [type of] being to which it is due." One would like to object to the thought that the insight that all "non-absolute" beings
owe their existence to an absolute being possesses the *same degree
of evidence* as does the insight that there is an absolute being; but
since neither *Aufweisen* nor argument for this claim is presented
here, and since Scheler apparently abandoned this doctrine of the
immediate relationship between the two insights, objection is
beside the point. Finally, he asserts that the *third* insight is into the
fact that every possible thing necessarily possesses an *essence* and
an *existence.* This insight is again attainable in principle in reflection upon any example we may choose to reflect upon.

If we now ask ourselves why Scheler wished to ascribe such
priority with respect to the evidence and order of givenness of this
insight, we may ourselves attain some insight into the *historical*
dimension of what Scheler is doing here, and what the purpose of
discovering an order of evidence is. We should note that the problem that underlies Scheler's investigation is not unprecedented in
the history of Western philosophy. Scheler points out that in fact an
answer to his question of the "first" insight in the order of evidence — however consciously or unconsciously the answer is given,
however variously the problem and answers to it may have been
stated — determines the point of departure of philosophy.
Descartes' positing of the *cogito ergo sum* as the fundamental self-
evident insight marked the transition from the classical and medieval philosophy of being to the modern philosophy of knowledge.
Scheler's doctrine of evidence can thus be interpreted as an effort
to reverse this direction and to establish philosophy as philosophy
of being; philosophy of the Ground of Being; philosophy of
essence, or strictly phenomenological philosophy. Each of these
three disciplines corresponds to one of the three fundamental self-
evident insights.

It is thus not surprising that we find an attempt to establish the order in which the world is given at various places in Scheler's works, and at various times during his career: he quite clearly considers this to be *the* most fundamental philosophical problem. We came across a similar concern in our second chapter, where we observed Scheler in the attempt to establish the priority of the givenness of value in the order of the genesis of knowledge to that of non-value essences. We noted the relevance of this doctrine to his analysis of the problem of the nature of philosophy as opposed to the nature of scientific knowledge. We are about to see him perform a similar analysis of the order of givenness of "spheres of being," and we will note the relevance of this doctrine to his analysis of a fundamental sociological problem.

Returning to *Die Wissensformen und die Gesellschaft,* Scheler holds that it is an axiom in the sociology of knowledge, as it is a theorem in the theory of knowledge, that "there is a rigid law establishing priority in the order of the origin of our knowledge and in the order in which their correlate spheres of objects are filled [i.e., with specific items of knowledge belonging to the spheres]."[16] This is clearly a different kind of order from that of *Vom Ewigen im Menschen;* we are apparently not concerned here with the *evidence* with which a thing presents itself to us, nor do we deal here with specific theses or "insights" but rather with "spheres" of objects and our knowledge of the spheres. The important difference is that the order is not an order of knowledge of the specific empirical items that fall under these spheres. The knowledge that he has in mind is parallel to the "knowledge" of Robinson *that* there are other men before he knows any specific cases of societies and men. The point is clear: knowledge of an essence — in this case, of the "sphere of others," of what Scheler calls the *Mitwelt* — precedes and makes possible specific empirical knowledge of objects belonging to the sphere. What makes the list of the spheres of knowledge and of being an order of precedence — makes it, in fact, *the Fundierungsordnung* under which all others must be classified — is that before one can have knowledge of a lower sphere, one must have knowledge of all the higher spheres. *In addition,* one can *doubt the reality* of the objects in a lower sphere when one can no longer doubt the reality of the objects in a higher sphere. This conclusion is clearly parallel with Scheler's claim made at the time of the analysis of the order of insights that one insight "follows" the other in the sense that "it is still logically possible [*sinnmöglich*] to 'doubt' one when we can no longer doubt the one that went before."[17]

He begins his list of the spheres of being with the sphere of the Absolute. No longer do we have to do with the thesis "that there is an absolute being"; rather, what appears to be in question is the phenomenon of intending the Absolute itself and not of what object with what essential characteristics is given in that intention. Here phenomenological reflection directs itself upon the *sphere* of the Absolute *in which* the existence of "things" holy and profane may be posited or denied. Similarly for all the other spheres: the sphere of *Mitwelt*; the sphere of the internal world and the external world, along with that of the body and its environment;[18] the sphere of living things; the sphere of "dead" things — that is, physical bodies in general. As examples providing evidence for this scale — especially for the position of high priority given to the sphere of *Mitwelt* — Scheler again draws upon the history of Western thought: there have been many thinkers — he takes Plato, Berkeley, and Kant, among others — who have argued against the thesis that there is a real extended dead world — although such is, of course, "given" to the natural standpoint — but few who have

questioned the real existence of an animal, even of a plant. Even Berkeley, the radical, "idealist" doubts even in the case of plants whether he may perform his "*esse-percipi*" with respect to them. Even more, never and nowhere has there been a "solipsist." This shows clearly, in addition to the great number of proofs for our law that are brought in from all areas of the psychology of development, how much deeper the belief in the *reality of society* is rooted in us than in the reality of any other object in all the other spheres of being and knowledge.[19]

What then, is the relevance of this list to the sociology of knowledge? Scheler argues that the "sociological character of all knowledge" is apparent from his list; not only are specific bodies of systematically acquired knowledge in the three general areas of knowledge — science, philosophy and religion — conditioned by the nature of the societies in which they appear, but all knowledge that makes up what Scheler refers to as the "relative natural *Weltanschauung*" is also *socially conditioned*.[20] This social conditioning of knowledge does not proceed according to any simple or single rule, although it can be said that the content of knowledge will depend to some extent upon the dominant interests of the society possessing that knowledge. The discovery of the laws — structural, *a priori*, and empirical — by which knowledge is socially conditioned and the description of the laws according to which bodies of knowledge are transformed in the course of its *social* transformation are the general task of the sociology of knowledge.[21]

But is Scheler's effort to discover an order of givenness of "spheres of being and knowledge" a *phenomenological* undertaking? Of course it is as hard to judge in the case of *Die Wissensformen und die Gesellschaft* as in *Vom Ewigen im Menschen*, because here too, the "systematic grounding" of the order was left for an unwritten work. Apparently, however, Scheler considered that he was dealing in both cases with a metaphysical problem with the help of phenomenology, and not with a phenomenological study *per se.* It is nevertheless a point in favor of the view that we have represented throughout this work — that however unclearly or with however little rigor Scheler may have practiced the phenomenological method, he was nonetheless constantly aware of the chasm that separates phenomenology from metaphysical speculation and from political ideology — that he does not make the *claim* that his order of spheres of being is founded in phenomenological intuition alone, and even leaves its "argument" for a work on metaphysics.

CHAPTER 7

The Sociology of Knowledge

HAVING thus established the social nature of knowledge, Scheler concerns himself in four ways, at various points in his writings, with the problem of the dynamics of the transformations of knowledge. First, he studies the most fundamental modes in which knowledge can be said to be "relative" to a particular society, social group, or individual person. Second, he considers the role of human biological needs and drives in the transformation of knowledge. His well-known essay on the phenomenon of *ressentiment* is an example of this attack. Third, he is concerned with the dynamics of interaction of types of knowledge. These questions he groups under the heading of the "material problems" of the sociology of knowledge. Finally, Scheler is concerned with criticizing established societies in the light of ethical norms; thus his discussion presupposes a concept of social critique. Each of these topics provides us either with examples of applications of the phenomenological method or with further descriptions of the epistemological framework within which phenomenology, and Scheler's thought as a whole, operates.

I *The Phenomenology of "Relativity"*

Scheler often points to the fact that his ethics, as opposed to that of Kant, is able to account for variations in the ethical beliefs of the various individual persons, peoples, and societies of world history, and is able to do this without abandoning the fundamental thesis of ethical absolutism. His point, however, seems at first sight to be radically relativistic: he asserts that what has varied throughout history are not only the *objects* that people have valued but also knowledge of the values themselves and the rules of preference according to which specific values and goods are rated higher or lower than others.

This thesis seems to imply a more radical ethical relativism than that of the various schools of "vitalists" and "pragmatists" that Scheler opposed. Such theories assert that the rules of preference between values can be reduced to one basic rule, usually that the more pleasurable object will be chosen over the less, or the more useful over the less. Such a thesis necessarily leads to absolute relativism, insofar as each age and people have found different things to be the more useful, the more pleasurable, or the more productive of social welfare, and there is no rule for deciding who is "right," or even which ethical theory is "correct."

The paradox in these theories, Scheler claims, is that their promulgators are *unconsciously* ethical absolutists; their theories posit, in effect, the given "rule of preference" as that which in fact determines ethical choice in all cases, albeit behind the scenes, so to speak, of developed systems of practical morality, aesthetics, and so on.

Now Scheler's point is that this projection of what he calls the prejudices in the ethical thinking of the nineteenth-century liberal bourgeoisie over the moral conduct and the value receptivity of all peoples and ages not only gives an incorrect picture of the rules guiding value preference (which he identified, of course, with his *a priori* scale of values) but also serves to prejudice inquiry into the history of man's consciousness of value. Variations in ethical beliefs should be thought of as ultimately founded in insight into the eternal scale of values and their order of relative worth, albeit with variations in the application of that insight — its "functionalization" — to practical moral problems. Each society has its peculiar capacities — its sharpness of insight and blindness — for apprehending value essences, for feeling the values in the persons and things around it, and for applying knowledge of value in judgments.

It is by no means clear what produces this sharpness of vision in one area and blindness in another — why the Greeks, for example, never produced a technological culture — but it is obvious that if we are to obtain any insight into the ways in which the values of a people undergo change, we must first become clear as to the various modes and levels in which insight into value functions in human thinking. Thus Scheler presents us with the following typology of what we will call the levels of functionalization of value insight, in order to guide inquiry into the history of human valuing.

In addition, this phenomenological inquiry will give us insight into the "dimensions of ethical relativity,"[1] that is, it is an analysis of the ways in which a moral judgment may be "merely" relative.

The five primary levels in which variations in the moral consciousness of a race, people, individual, or other social unity can occur are as follows.

The highest level is that of the *ethos,* or moral *Weltanschauung.* Here it is a question of the individual variations in the number and kind of pure values one feels and the *a priori* laws of loving and hating; that is, of the *extent* of the individual unit's *ordo amoris.* This level must be distinguished from the second level, that of *moral judgment,* which is founded upon the pantheon of values contained in the ethical *Weltanschauung* of a people, but here we find that primordial ethical insight functionalized as a set of rules, norms, and duties, which Scheler calls the "ethics" of that social unit. This is the set of rules implicit in the actual judgments made in the practical dealings of the people whose moral consciousness is being considered. In these "rules" for judging the ethical content of the concrete situation are now founded the concepts of the various types of ethical actions, goods, and institutions that appear on the natural standpoint in the explicit moral consciousness of a people, such as "theft," "celibacy," "betrayal," and so on. This is the level of what Scheler calls the "morality" of a people. Awareness of the meanings of such types of ethical relationship between men "founds" the specific definitions of what constitutes theft, celibacy, and betrayal, but is not to be identified with these definitions; these definitions belong to the fourth level of "practical morality." The unity of any possible definitions depends upon the essence of the thing being defined. On the third level on which the concepts appear, we are concerned with the moral awareness that appears in the way men understand the nature of that peculiar relationship between value objects, which they call, for instance, "murder."[2] As much as there can be variations in the fundamental understanding of the nature of murder, so can there be variation in the specific, concrete definitions of what constitutes murder, for example, that a certain type of killing of men (in certain situations in war) does or does not constitute murder, that killing at a certain time by certain persons, does or does not constitute murder, and so forth.

Such variations, dictated by custom, religion, the given historical and natural circumstances, and so on, will take place within the framework furnished by the prior intuition of the value intended in the abstract understanding of the concept of murder by this social unit. This concept, as we have seen, is again relative to the ethics of that social unit. Scheler maintains that the lower levels are not *reducible* to the highest, that is, we cannot "deduce" definitions of moral concepts, such as murder, from the *ethos* or even from the practical morality of a given social group. The higher factor furnishes only an *a priori* framework, a set of possibilities, which come to realization in the historical process. Still, he holds, the practical morality of a people must be understood and judged within the framework provided by the deeper levels of their moral consciousness, especially their ethos; "external" critique is as unfair as it is scientifically fruitless.

To conclude the discussion of the levels of ethical relativity, Scheler speaks of a level of "customs and manners" as the fifth level. These are relevant to a discussion of ethics insofar as the choice of customs and manners is to some extent dependent upon the ethical insights of a social unity and the rules of value preference founded upon them.

Scheler seems to realize that despite the sharpness of his definitions of the five levels, any analysis of the ethics of a social unit into these five categories on the basis of whatever material for an intuitive investigation we have at our disposal would be extremely difficult. In fact, it would seem that it would be impossible in principle to carry out this analysis with any finality; for quite often it will not be possible to judge which of the historical data we have at hand concerning any given people is *representative* of the moral consciousness of the people or culture in which it appears. There is the difficulty of deciding upon what constitutes a cultural unity (although, as we will see, Scheler occupies himself with related questions in his sociological studies). The sociology of knowledge of value (as an intuitive science) is thus faced with many problems at the outset that will alienate those who desire an *exact* sociological science. Nevertheless, if we accept Scheler's schema as a guideline for a historical investigation, it may indeed prove fruitful; and, in any case, Scheler has made the epistemological point that ethical relativity is not a homogeneous concept. An ethical belief can be relative in any of the given ways, and it is irresponsible to conclude from the fact that ethical beliefs have varied throughout history

that they vary according to some simple rule and are relative to men
(or to "life," etc.) in some one simple way.

II   Ressentiment

The essay on *ressentiment* represents Scheler's efforts, at a time
shortly before the writing of *Der Formalismus,* to reduce the phenomenon of value perversion, that is, distortion of insight into
values and their relative worth, to a single principle. The study involves a phenomenological exhibition and offers an interesting contrast with the procedures introduced later in *Die Wissensformen
und die Gesellschaft* to handle the phenomenon of the variation in
value systems among the peoples of the world.

We might begin our study of this essay by asking a natural question: did Scheler view *ressentiment* as the moral failure that leads to
the denial of "his" *a priori* scale of values and that thus all those
who are blind to the truth of his scale, who profess that the value of
sensual pleasure is higher than spiritual values, for example, are
guilty of *ressentiment?* It seems to this observer, despite passages in
which this becomes unclear, that Scheler was himself committed to
the view that on the level of the *ethos* — which is that of value insight itself and of insight into the "eternal" *ordo* — *no* deception is
possible as to their relative worth. What alone is variable on this
level is the *number* of values felt and the *clarity* with which they are
cognized, and not the order in which they are felt. If the people in a
certain time and place understand and are capable of feeling the
values of beauty and of the noble, they will in all cases prefer the
former to the latter (even if they generally prefer pleasurable *things*
to beautiful things), once, of course, they are brought to a point at
which they can consider these values apart from goods. The possibility that this people has no sense of beauty or nobility is the only
possibility of variation that Scheler is willing to allow on this level.
Ressentiment, as he understands this term, is a source of deception
for the grasping of that order of eternal values and its incorporation into life.[3] It seems then that if we are to make sense of the phenomenological theory surrounding the notion of an *a priori* order
of values, we must understand *ressentiment* as active in this process
of "incorporation," which we have described as the process in
which the primordial insight into values and the *ordo* is "functionalized," that is, expressed either correctly or "deceitfully" in

actual rules of moral judgment and choice on any of the lower four levels of moral consciousness. In brief, *ressentiment* causes a confusion of the *ordo amoris,* but not its reversal; what is confused is the application of *true* moral insight — the insight expressed by Scheler's value scale — to the concrete life situation.

What is the essence of *ressentiment?* Scheler begins his exhibition by noting that *ressentiment* is not the only cause of deception in matters of value and the resulting variations in the value judgments in various historical social units. The most general cause seems to be *striving:* we tend to assign the higher value to those things for which our desire is most intense and which our attempts to attain are fiercest. The usual result of this simple deception is imagining that things productive of sensual pleasure — toward which our biological impulses impel us — are in fact preferable to things carrying spiritual values. The deception here is "simple," insofar as the deception concerns only "goods," that is, things carrying values, and similar matters of practical concern, and not the rules of preference among values themselves. Nevertheless, striving is also an essential moment of *ressentiment* itself, and this latter phenomenon is productive of a confusion of the *ordo amoris* on a deeper level, the level upon which it is incorporated in our everyday value judgments and prejudices.

The process of *ressentiment* begins with the *frustration of striving* by other men whom one views as one's competitors for values striven after. This feeling of *impotence* produces a tension that can be released in any one of three central ways: (1) by means of a frontal attack on one's competitors in the face of one's feeling of impotence, with eventual success in the realization of the values desired (failure might result in a recurrence and even a deepening of *ressentiment*); (2) By means of an act of resignation to the fact that one will not be able to realize the values desired; (3) By means of developing a *secret desire* for revenge against those who possess the value objects one is incapable of attaining. In this third possibility we have the point of departure of *ressentiment.* The frustration of the impulse toward revenge may lead to the inhibition of one's desire for the goods possessed by the stronger; one denies their value and, quite often, but not inevitably, one affirms the contrary value. In this way, the stronger no longer is an object of envy, but rather of *pity.* The classic example of this process is that described by Nietzsche, who introduced the term *ressentiment* to the German language in the technical sense in which Scheler is considering it, in the *Geneology of Morals*. The envy and impotent hatred of the Jews against their oppressors gave birth to a new doctrine of love in the person of Jesus Christ, and led to the loss of value of the things previously desired by the Jews themselves: power, nobility, "happiness," and the affirmation *as higher* of the values of humility, poverty, and weakness. Early Christians, Nietzsche points out, pitied their Roman oppressors because they believed that the possession and use of unlimited power would lead to their damnation: a "love" nurtured by *ressentiment*.

From this example — which Scheler takes very seriously — of the essential dynamics of *ressentiment* in action, we observe that what was "overthrown" by the Jews was not Scheler's scale but the *specific* rules of preference among goods of a hatred rival culture, and that what the Jews had previously learned to admire and respect and to desire for themselves was transformed into a negative value by the power of frustrated hatred. Nevertheless, Scheler takes exception to Nietzsche's account of the birth of so-called Christian morality: he undertakes a phenomenological analysis of the Christian concept of love and attempts to show that *ressentiment* is *not* an essential moment in its constitution, while granting the correctness of Nietzsche's claims that *ressentiment* was a *causal factor* in the development of certain specific Christian doctrines and character types.

The difference in the procedure of the two thinkers, Nietzsche and Scheler, in their studies of Christian *ressentiment* is clear, although Scheler does not mention this difference in his critique of Nietzsche. Nietzsche's problem is to explain the human motives behind the development of the specific doctrines related to the Christian notion of love in the concrete historical setting of their development; that is, he is out to present a causal explanation of historical ideology, whereas Scheler, the phenomenologist, examines the essence of the Christian concept of love to see whether the act of *ressentiment* is a necessary moment in its essential structure. He makes, in effect, the distinction between the content of an idea and the energy with which men rally behind it. The latter question involves a study of the historical, psychological, and sociological reasons for that energetic rallying, whereas the first question is phenomenological. This distinction is not evident in Scheler's writings and we must give it special emphasis here, where it appears so clearly. The thought involves the claim that we can isolate certain essential, hence timeless, constants in intellectual history, which can be investigated apart from the historical situation in which they appear.

This doctrine of the interpretation of historical materials had been hotly debated in Germany since the time of Hegel and had been discussed under the heading of "hermeneutics" by Dilthey in Scheler's own day. Opponents of Scheler's view claimed that *any* historical doctrine can only be understood in the light of the culture that produced it: this doctrine has become known in English as "historical relativism." Scheler saw his problem as a phenomenologist in his critique of Nietzsche as one of discovering just what *new* value insight "founds" the Christian "law of love" as a rule of value preference, and of establishing whether the dynamics of *ressentiment* are a condition of this new insight. He finds that the preachments of Christ on love are completely independent of the political interests of the Jews, however quickly His words may have been perverted by the earliest Jewish and Gentile Christians in their pursuit of practical ends. Obviously, Scheler has tackled a different problem from that which we find at the center of Nietzsche's concern, although both investigations are based upon the same concept of *ressentiment*.

Whereas Scheler's diagnosis of the essence of Christian love and the morality founded upon it is that it is healthy, he finds that in the essence of the *bourgeois* morality of his own age appears a perversion of insight into value that is only possible on the basis of *ressentiment*. His argument, which, like his analysis of Christian love, we will not undertake to describe, is of interest to us for its identification of modern bourgeois morality with ethical relativism: Scheler's own opponents in the philosophical struggles of his day are driven by *ressentiment!* This, of course, invites the fallacy of *tu quoque:* and how often have we heard Nietzsche called a *ressentiment*-laden man; and Scheler has already been called this by one of his commentators.[4] This is perhaps merely a symptom of his lack of modesty concerning his own ideas, which led him to see in the phenomenon of *ressentiment* not simply a suggestion that might serve as a framework for investigations into the moral consciousness of individuals and peoples but ultimately an instrument of the external critique of the morality of a people, that is, a world-historical principle in terms of which one may pass approving or damning judgment upon the moral consciousness of an age.[5]

III   *The "Material Problems" of the
Sociology of Knowledge*

In the study that Scheler calls the "material problems" of the sociology of knowledge, there is a radical departure from his customs of analysis up to this point. In this later work, his studies of the relationship of knowledge to its social and biological determinatives exhibit less markedly the desire to provide a set of categories with clear moral implications. Perhaps more important, he is looking for a means of introducing empirical evidence into philosophical investigations. We are thus presented with a mode of inquiry that is less clearly phenomenological but that deserves our attention both as an example of what Scheler considered to be an application of phenomenology and for the insight it gives us into the later development of his thought. Rather than attempt to outline all of the problems he develops here, we will take only one of them for detailed discussion. First, however, we must try to establish what he means by a "material problem."

It is instructive to consider the way Scheler compares his procedure in the "material" sociology of knowledge with that of "empirical" studies of a single specific problem in this field, namely, the question of the mutual promoting and hindering influences of religion upon philosophy and science, the latter two taken as a unit:

Up to now the friends and enemies of religion and churches have simply described — usually in a one-sided manner — the inhibitory and promotive influences which occur between religions and churches and the development of the other forms of knowledge, by listing historical facts. The laws of typical relations between them, and the exact distinguishing of the forms of knowledge by means of the method of comparative sociology, have seldom been attempted. They [the laws] do not show themselves when one simply looks at such single historical facts such as the fact that in the West the Christian churches and their cloisters devotedly kept in safekeeping the treasures of ancient authors, [etc.].... Here we have a reckoning and counter-reckoning without end, and we will never come beyond our own *parti pris* by this method. Only by means of comparing larger, interrelated culture-unities do we come upon the unified style that exists between the religious systems [of a given culture] and the content of the other systems of knowledge. . . . The art of macroscopic and not of microscopic observation is needed here.[6]

What is so highly significant about this passage for an interpretation of Scheler's thought is that it allows, on a theoretical plane, a legitimate role to empirical investigation in a study that is itself not strictly empirical. Here it is no longer a question of simply using empirical facts as examples with which to lead reflective intuition toward the apprehension of the essence of the thing, but rather the facts of cultural history themselves serve us as partial evidence for a type of essential law abstracted from them. This notion of a "material" thesis that is descriptive neither of essence nor of an empirical law or object is peculiar to the direction Scheler's phenomenology took in the later period. He is searching here, it seems, for a synthetic *a priori.* We will now set ourselves about an investigation of the four examples of these "laws of typical relations" that Scheler discovers in the circle of problems in the sociology of knowledge that concern the reciprocal relations among the three highest categories of modes of knowing, namely, religion, science, and philosophy. This discussion will serve us as an example of Scheler's *conscious extension* of phenomenological methodology to empirical inquiries. For that reason, we will be most concerned in the course of our discussion to question the *nature of the evidence* that Scheler uses to "ground" his theses.

The first thesis:

In the sphere of *religion,* an anonymous . . . religious group consciousness, i.e., a native family or tribe or folk religion always precedes personal religions having a "founder" . . . Only the arrival of a *homo religiosus,* be he a prophet, be he a conqueror basing his authority upon religion, be he a "magician" or a conscious founder of religions, who appears as distinctive, "charismatic," i.e., as eminently "believable" . . . due to his personal extraordinary experience and contact with the divinity, is able to break religion from its original blood ties *in the political era.*[7]

The first part of this thesis — that a prophet can only appear within the framework of a specific religious consciousness — is at first sight a historical generalization; religious prophets, whether or not they later become the "founders" of a religion, have always spoken from within a certain tradition, have always drawn upon the thought about the holy of the people among whom they appear.

Nevertheless, there seems to be more than simply an appeal to all the cases of the historical past involved in Scheler's claim, but it is hard to say just what evidence he had in mind. Certainly there is not an element of apriority here; despite the reference to "priority," Scheler did not wish to affirm that the possibility of the appearance of the *homo religiosus* is "founded" in the prior presence of a religious tradition. On the other hand, there does seem to be a certain meaning relation contained in this assertion, insofar as the act of prophecy implies having a peculiar relationship with an aspect of the Transcendent that has already been "revealed" in some way. One can't be a *prophet* without a God who was "known" before the prophecy. Even in the case of Gautama, there had to be some notion of what "enlightenment" *is* before the future Buddha could begin to seek it.

If there is at least this much of an *a priori* element in the first part of Scheler's thesis — there seems to be something of a logical relation in it that goes beyond a mere historical generalization — this is hardly the case with the second half of the thesis, unless one takes it as asserting that the act of "breaking a religion from its blood ties" is in itself a political act (e.g., breaking the monopoly power of a native priestly class), and hence only possible in a so-called political era. It is possible that Scheler had such a thought in mind, but undoubtedly he did not wish to imply only this; his thought seems to be centered upon the idea that only an *individual* can bring about a universal religion, that is, one that is not tied to one people, language, and tradition, and that can therefore first win converts among members "foreign" to the tradition from within which the "founder" first spoke. This claim goes beyond not only the concept of an *essential* relationship but the sphere of historical generalization as well; we hardly have enough data to justify the claim that an individual prophet is a necessary condition of a universal religion. Moreover, what constitutes the "breaking of blood ties" and a "political era" requires a clarification that is not to be found in the text.

The second thesis:

The sources of the ideas contained in the [notion of the] Godly appear in each case in highly varying combinations. They lie (1) in the usually inflexible *traditions* of tribal communities (folk religion); ... (2) in the *living perceptions of God* of the charismatic *"homines religiosi"* and their manifold types, in their "holy words," deeds, doctrines and directives which can be either merely "traditional," or written in "holy scriptures" (book religion); (3) in the special new experiences that are had concerning the divinity and its attitudes toward men by means of cult practices and ritual; ... (4) in the ideas on salvation and divinity coming from a *metaphysical* source (e.g., Plato's and Aristotle's metaphysics for Christian theology), which occasionally add themselves to the above three and which, when they do not come only to serve and modify, but attain instead the upper hand, tend to replace the positive folk religion and the authority of the *"homines religiosi."*[8]

This second quotation adumbrates a typology that is rather different from those we have encountered thus far in our discussion. We do not have here descriptions of essences; instead we have a list of the *sources* of religious knowledge. Scheler adds to this list the thought that items one and three are more socially conditioned than the other two. He undoubtedly means that this knowledge is more a product of the group soul than the other, insofar as it is produced in the everyday "living together" of the individuals in the community, and is not a product of the spontaneous activity of the *homines religiosi* or of the independent metaphysical genius. Such knowledge that is an unconscious product of communal living will reflect the structure of the community in which it was developed more perfectly than the wisdom of the inspired genius, which tends to burst through the boundaries of the community. The thought here is sound and contains the valuable insight that not all the elements in any given system of religion and religious thinking are relative to its "social basis" in any homogeneous way; certain aspects are "more relative" than others. To show this relationship is a reasonable task of historical analysis; Scheler himself attempts a brief study along these lines elsewhere.

The third thesis:

What shakes the prevailing religion is never science, but the drying up and dying out of the content of its beliefs, of its living *ethos* itself: that means that "dead" belief, a "dead" *ethos* takes the place of the "living" belief and *ethos,* and primarily that a *new* inchoate form of religious consciousness, perhaps even a new metaphysics that wins the masses over to itself, *displaces* them. The taboos which the religions have placed upon the various areas of human knowledge by declaring them to be "holy" and "articles of faith" must always lose their character as taboo for reasons *peculiar to* metaphysics and religion themselves, if these areas are to become objects of scientific inquiry.[9]

We have here one of the two "laws of typical relations" between religion and the other modes of knowledge. Scheler may have had the belief of many people in mind, when he wrote his thesis, that the discoveries of Darwin had shaken, to a greater or lesser extent, the foundations of traditional Christian beliefs. That belief gave rise in certain quarters to efforts to suppress or refute these theories in the hope of saving Christianity. The point of the above thesis is not only to deny the possible effectiveness of such efforts but to assert that the investigations of nature by Darwin would never have come to pass had not the belief that true religion prohibits — or makes unnecessary! — the scientific investigation of the origin of life *already died* before Darwin took up his studies.

Other applications of this "law" are less clear, however, and there are counterexamples. It is certainly far from being clear that a religiously grounded belief in the evil of certain types of sexual behavior had died out before Freud and Krafft-Ebing made their investigations into such matters. What makes Scheler's thesis so terribly unclear and difficult to apply is that he nowhere attempts to show what constitutes the "dying out" of a belief. Otherwise, the thesis that religion possesses an autonomous evolution from that of science or metaphysics — such that the discoveries in the positive sciences cannot influence the further evolution of religion in the community — is predicated on the assumption that the two lines of development can be kept apart in any accurate description of the changes in belief in a given historical community; but surely the lines between the two are too fluid to permit the assembling of evidence establishing this thesis with any reasonable degree of certainty. Yet Scheler is surely correct in his assertion — made in this section — that the nature of religious belief in the West, with its emphasis on a single, transcendent creator-God, has had a tendency to open Nature to scientific investigation, and that similar coordinations among the three modes of knowledge and their practice can be discovered in the Eastern traditions of thought. His effort to use such insights to explain the rise of science in the West and the failure of science to grow in the East is nevertheless essentially a shift into a speculative mode of thinking. This belief is predicated in part upon the unfounded and somewhat dubious premise that human thought energy is limited, and that the development of science in Europe left little energy for the spontaneous religious-metaphysical thought that the East relied upon for the salvation that was promised "for so little effort" to Europeans. Scheler's difficulty in both cases lies in his efforts to formalize as "laws" some good, very general insights into specific historical events. We will say something about the *nature* of the *evidence* for this law in our discussion of the fourth thesis.

The fourth thesis:

... modes of possible mutual hindering and fostering influences between religion and the other modes of knowledge appear only when on the one hand, religion appears as a formulated "theological" *dogma* as the object and the first principle of a "science of belief," and on the other hand, when knowledge is either *genuine metaphysical* knowledge, or positive-scientific knowledge oversteps its limits and raises certain results of its own investigations to the *metaphysical* sphere.[10]

The first law of typical relations between religion and other modes of knowledge stated that religion has a development in history peculiar to itself. The law further implied that religious knowledge possesses a *content* independent of science. The fourth thesis gives us Scheler's answer to a question that has been frequently debated in English-speaking circles, partially, perhaps, as a result of Wittgenstein's well-known suggestion that talk about religious matters constitutes a "language game" with criteria of truth and falsity, sense and nonsense of its own, and that therefore we must not condemn religious assertions for not conforming to standards that may not be applicable to them. Scheler is of course not concerned here with linguistic distinctions or with criteria of truth and falsity, but his thought is parallel with Wittgenstein's in that he holds that science and religion have nothing to say to each other; one cannot be used to judge the other, nor can the two come in *conflict;* they deal with fundamentally different spheres of human concern. Scientific ideas can be incorporated into a metaphysical or religious body of knowledge only through misapplication. Thus, Scheler mentions the supposition that Galileo was condemned by the Inquisition only because he refused to accept the pragmatic interpretation of his theories — that is, that they represent merely an efficient description of the data at hand — and insisted that they represented the actual workings of nature. On the other hand, if

religion has tended to *foster* the development of the sciences, metaphysics, at one time a great contributor of religious ideas in the
West, has, from a sociological point of view, *lost all its battles* with
the religious *Weltanschauung* and with organized religion, so that
spontaneous metaphysical thinking has *atrophied* in the West.
What is especially interesting about the formulation of this
fourth thesis is the obvious *contrast* it makes with the third thesis.
Whereas both are expressions of laws of typical relations between
religious knowledge and the other modes, the doctrine expressed in
the third thesis is empirical in nature — whatever use Scheler may
have made of it, and however recondite the evidence for or against
it may be. This new thesis, in comparison, seems to possess certain
a priori characteristics. It depends, in the first place, on the ascer-
tainment of the limits of the various modes of knowledge. Scheler
declared the investigation of such problems to be one of the "formal problems" of the sociology of knowledge, the adequate completion of which is apparently presupposed by Scheler here. In the
second place, the correctness of this thesis depends upon his use of
language. One might ask whether or not this conception of
"dogma," along with the definitions of the limits of the modes of
knowledge, allows him to claim that this law is a true essential relationship. If so, this is then a case of an attempt to employ a formal
principle — a rule, so to speak — as the "highest principle" of the
historical-sociological investigation of the concrete relationships
between the churches and the scientific and secular communities in
Western civilization, which Scheler begins in this section and which
he expects others to carry further.

It is fair to say, I think, that each of the four theses we have been
discussing represents a struggle on the part of Scheler to discover
formal and semiformal principles in the sphere of the sociology of
knowledge and to relate them to analyses of historical facts.
Scheler, instead of simply using history to make ideological points,
and instead of carrying on sociology in the "scientific" manner of
collecting data and comparing them in the hope of discovering
regularities in them, is seeking a "middle road" between these two
methods. He desires insight of a philosophical nature and not simply "laws of behavior"; he wants knowledge that is not simply inductive and yet not simply formal and tautologous. This effort is
peculiar to the later period that began at the time of the writing of
Die Wissensformen und die Gesellschaft; its theory is related to the

declaration in the essay on Weber that metaphysics as a "possibly true" discipline must be built upon the results of both scientific and phenomenological studies. We will reencounter and discuss this thought in our concluding chapter on Scheler's theology and metaphysics, and we will attempt to show there that his efforts are misconceived.

IV *Scheler's Concept of Social Criticism*

Frequently during his lifetime, Scheler directed his attention toward concrete problems of the contemporary political scene. He saw as the most fundamental world-historical problem of his age the establishment of a spiritual reconciliation among the nations of the world; and, in politics as in metaphysics, he hoped for the eventual triumph of spirit over power, the loving soul over the vital drives of the body. A political conservative, he yet welcomed the wave of modern, progressive ideas that entered Germany after the war: the women's movement, the resistance of youth to parental authority and youth itself as a positive value, the interest in mystical and non-European philosophies and suspicion of "over-civilization," the liberalization of sexual mores. He welcomed these ideas because he believed that the expansion of the individual's experiences can only lead to better mutual understanding among all men and ultimately to a "balancing" of beliefs and ideologies upon which, he believed, the peace of the world depended. Indeed, since political accommodation is only possible by means of spiritual reconciliation, and not simply through a balance of power, practical politics in each nation must concern itself with the problem of the cultivation of a farseeing, spiritually cultivated ruling elite. Scheler concluded his lecture "Der Mensch im Zeitalter des Ausgleichs" (1927) with the following words:

Concerning the last and highest type of reconciliation in the coming age, i.e., the reconciliation of the content of metaphysical doctrines on God, the world, and man, I will be silent here. Yet I dare say that even in this highest objective sphere one may observe an increasing, almost strange *convergence* of the fundamental insights among the spiritual elite of thinkers of all peoples. And I dare say as well that here a reconciliation of great size and import is well under way — although unrecognized by many.[11]

The question we wish to raise here concerns the relationship of Scheler's politics to his phenomenological method. Was Scheler speaking as a philosopher in these political and moral lectures, or did he, as did for example Bertrand Russell, make a strict distinction between his philosophical and his "popular" writings? I think it is clear that Scheler believed that phenomenology was indeed relevant in the way of providing *evidence* to social philosophy. The problem is to discover how Scheler himself understood this relevance; that is, we must raise the question of his concept of *criticism in general* and of social critique in particular. Since he did not himself develop an explicit theory of criticism, we have had to go behind actual cases in which he performs a critical analysis to speculate on the theory standing behind it, and refer to the epistemology in which the theory is grounded.

Scheler's idea of critique is a very old one; it can, as can so many of the ideas in his work, be traced to Plato. *Theoros,* to the ancient Greeks, was originally a man sent by one of the Greek cities to observe the performance of religious rites at public festivals.[12] Later the term came to be understood by philosophers as *Theoria,* vision of the cosmos. In Plato's thought, the object of philosophical vision is not the physical cosmos but rather the *Wesensreich* he calls the realm of Forms. The knowledge of the forms is "theoretical" knowledge, as opposed to "technical" knowledge of the physical world; this latter is not knowledge at all, strictly speaking, but mere opinion, *doxa,* or what Scheler refers to as knowledge for the control of nature.

Philosophical knowledge is not without practical consequences, however. The commitment of the entire spiritual being of the philosopher to the object of philosophical vision, which Scheler takes from Plato as one of the moral preconditions of philosophy, involved for the ancient thinker the act of *Mimesis,* the attempt to "imitate" the forms, to re-create himself and his society according to the eternal and perfect models of man, society, and virtue, which are revealed to his "theoretical" vision. This doctrine of an intimate relationship between philosophy — or, in Scheler, the morally interpreted phenomenological *Wesensschau* — and ethics of social practice is, I submit, fundamental to Scheler's concept of criticism: the world is to be measured upon the essences described by phenomenology. Philosophy of essence is philosophy of possibility, that is, the possible realization of what things are essentially; hence the easy transition to *normative* philosophy. The results of this idea upon Scheler's practice of social critique are evident: existing social institutions are measured against the essential possibilities of human sociation as revealed in an essential-phenomenological analysis of possible social forms and of the human natures that constitute them and are constituted by them. Perhaps it was this capacity of phenomenology to discover the essential possibilities implied by the meaning carried by a phenomenon that most intrigued Scheler about its possible application to social problems. In Scheler the "essential possibilities" implied by the various social and other interpersonal phenomena often become the "essential ideals" society should set itself to realize, much as, for example, the essential possibility of a love toward another person that is never-dying — a capacity for which, Scheler asserted, is implied by the fact of the openness of men to the essence of love — becomes, for Scheler, an ideal that so often fails to be realized in the affairs of men. Becker quotes Scheler as referring to the essential possibilities of right and wrong preference revealed in the scale of eternal values as *evidence* for his assertion that "peace is the most noble goal to which a statesman can aspire" in a speech to a group of German military officers after the First World War.[13]

As opposed to this mode of social criticism, we can take Marxism. Scheler attacks Marx at various points in his work; his attacks are directed for the most part against the specter of Marxism as the negation of Western values and as the purveyor of a technological mass culture, and not against his social criticism as such. Nevertheless, the two make an interesting comparison. The Marxist develops analyses of the structures of prevailing systems of social production. These analyses are intended to reveal built-in mechanisms of class bias, oppression, and alienation in the social and political institutions of the society under analysis. Unlike Scheler's critique, the Marxist critique need not commit itself to any specific social ideal. Furthermore, insofar as the Marxist critique begins with an analysis of the actual political and economic forces present in the society in question, there is necessarily a historical moment — specifically, a question of the causal interaction of existing historical forces — injected into the criticism, which Scheler's social criticism can dispense with.

Thus we observed in our discussion of the doctrine of *ressentiment* that Scheler's critical investigation of the Christian notion of love abstracts entirely from the question of the actual motivation of the specific men whom Nietzsche accuses of bad faith, and inquires only into the constituent meaning elements of Christian love. Again, Scheler's insistence that philosophy should question its own nature and value — a question that, in our own day, seems to have been forgotten by most philosophers except the European Marxists, who wish to discover and criticize the function of philosophy in the *Lebenspraxis* of present-day capitalistic systems — is based upon his description of the essential possibilities of knowing, of the essential limitations of metaphysical knowledge, upon the doctrine of the relativity of knowledge, and similar considerations founded in phenomenological investigation. Finally, Scheler's typology of communal forms, which we mentioned in the last chapter, is an historical study of the essences of essentially possible ways that men can live together, arranged according to the nature of the interpersonal relationships practiced in each. Out of this typology emerges Scheler's ideal of a society of men who incorporate the highest possible social and personal values. Scheler undoubtedly had this society in mind when he pointed out inadequacies in his own society, and his suggestions for social change were intended to move society in the direction of this "theoretical" ideal.

Now this mode of social criticism need not be utopistic, that is, simply involve the comparison of an incomplete and evil reality with a speculative "ought-to-be." Many of the "utopian socialists" in Marx's day and the revolutionary socialists of our own time do just this, however: their "norm" of social organization is not tied politically to the historical possibilities and facts of power in the society under criticism. And it is well known that many revolutionary critiques are directed backward in hate toward the criticized society rather than forward in love to some ideal to be realized. Although Scheler's theory of criticism suffers from the danger of lacking concreteness, he avoids sterility by insisting upon a sharp cleavage between the norm and the reality, the knowledge and desire of the spirit and the needs of the body. For that reason he is indulgent in his moral and political criticism; he realizes the limitations of men. Yet his criticism is built upon a great and burning hope for the social betterment of man; indeed, how could it be otherwise in a man who believed in the power of the spirit to overcome the "vital interests" of concrete men?

Yet it must be said that some of the difficulties we experience with his sociology of knowledge arise, perhaps, from the fact that he is constantly obsessed with the practical problems of salvation and social order, problems that demand broad theoretical solutions, while phenomenology, even as Scheler himself interprets the method, can by nature only proceed in piecemeal fashion; it abhors systematization. But insofar as Scheler is not true to this basic claim to neutrality implied by his notion of method and raised so often by him, and enters the political arena with an Ideology of the Spirit, he does "little more than demonstrate the brilliance of his enormous intellect."[14] Then we are left with a series of insights whose value must be judged not in terms of their phenomenological evidence but in terms of their ability to realize the value of enlightenment by means of the inspiration of speculative metaphysics, or in terms of their capacity to create a consciousness of the unity of knowledge in all its manifold appearances among the nations and peoples of all the eras of world history, and a desire for solidarity with one's brothers on the part of all persons.

CHAPTER 8

From the Phenomenology of Religion to Speculative Metaphysics

IT is clear from our discussion of the applications of Scheler's methodology that practical concerns often carried him beyond the limits prescribed by his own theory of phenomenology into speculative metaphysics and political ideology. Occasionally we have observed him in the search for a theoretical foundation for philosophy beyond the limits of phenomenology. In this chapter, we will follow him further in these efforts and reconsider with him the nature of metaphysics and the relevance of phenomenology to a "possibly true" metaphysical system. Our concluding critical point will be that metaphysics, as Scheler conceived and practiced it in *Die Stellung des Menschen im Kosmos,* cannot be built upon the phenomenological method and is in fact incompatible with it; and that it is on this point that Scheler's philosophy ultimately miscarries.

Now the general direction of Scheler's thought beyond the limits imposed by the phenomenological method concerns the problem of God. It may help our understanding of this thought to consider that his struggle with this problem occurs within the framework of the more general problem of the relationship of the spiritual to the nonspiritual. This problem is often handled by him within the framework provided by phenomenology, of course. We recall our earlier discussion of his phenomenological analysis of the relation of "spirit" to "world" in *Der Formalismus.* He notes there that just as to every intentional act there corresponds an object, so to every concrete human person there corresponds a "world," and that world is an individual world, given only to the person who intends it: only John Doe knows just what it's like to be John Doe, and only he sees the world just as he sees it.

This point is central to Scheler's "theology," which we are now about to discuss. He holds that if one posits a single, existing, concrete world apart from the individual world that is accessible to one as a person, then it would be counter to the senses of the terms "world" and "consciousness of" — counter but not contradictory — not to posit along with this world the spirit who intends it, namely, God.[1] It is *evident,* he holds, that the thought of a concrete, objective, superpersonal world is essentially related to the thought of a concrete spirit intending that world, and if the first is posited, the second must be posited as well — a little hint from phenomenologists to any metaphysicians who might be listening!

Thus at the time of *Vom Ewigen im Menschen,* we do not as yet have an attempt at a metaphysical investigation of the nature and *existence* of God such as we find in *Die Stellung des Menschen im Kosmos.* In the earlier work, evidence of a purely phenomenological sort is presented, an *Aufweisen* of the essential meanings connoted by the term "God" is performed, and the positing of existence is avoided. Nevertheless, Scheler tries to combine a phenomenological description of the essence of God with a phenomenological description of what are essential acts of the *religious consciousness* so as to provide himself with a basis for distinguishing between "correct" and "incorrect" predicates of God, that is, for practicing natural theology. We will describe in a moment just how this phenomenologically based "natural theology" is supposed to work.

Our discussion in this chapter will have the form of a comparison of these two ways of talking about God, the phenomenological and the metaphysical. We will ask ourselves which of the two methods is the more clearly conceived and the better executed. We should nevertheless keep clearly in mind that the two attempts are not strictly parallel with respect to their material and their intent. We might characterize their differences by saying that the phenomenological studies of *Vom Ewigen im Menschen* have a more *religious* character; they have religion as their material and are written from a religious point of view.[2] This fact is not simply a consequence of Scheler's adherence to the Roman Catholic Church at the time he wrote this book, but its reasons lie in the nature of the analyses themselves:[3] while *Vom Ewigen im Menschen* is an attempt to describe our specifically religious (as opposed to our metaphysical and theological) understanding of God and the specifically religious intentional acts in which God is given to the religious person, the analyses of *Die Stellung des Menschen im Kosmos* do not take the notion of a specifically religious understanding of God as a point of departure for their investigations into the sphere of the holy. Such differences in the *material* analyzed by the two works will become more apparent as we progress.

I   *"The Essential Phenomenology of Religion"*

Let us now turn to the particulars of Scheler's analysis, and attempt to describe the direction and intent of his admittedly incomplete philosophy of religion. Scheler divides his theme into three types of material with which the phenomenologist is concerned: the phenomenology of the objects of knowledge, the phenomenology of the intentional act, and the phenomenology of the relationship itself between subject and object, between intentional act and thing given. In the case of the phenomenology of the *object* of intentional acts, Scheler is concerned with the description of the content of the phenomenon "God" itself; he recognizes the phenomenological value of, and builds upon, Rudolf Otto's *Idea of the Holy*. Scheler's specific task here is the description of what we may call three classes of attributes of that which is given as holy: the *formal* attributes, the *positive* attributes, and the *concrete* attributes. As always, his investigation begins by reflecting intuitively upon a given concrete, historical embodiment of the concept of God. He takes the religious beliefs and practices of Christianity as his point of departure, but he could have used any theistic religion for the same purpose.

The phenomenology of the subject-object relationship concerns itself in the phenomenology of religion with descriptions of the *forms of revelation*. Scheler has in mind here a typology of the typical "places" in which God reveals Himself to religious persons. For example, God may reveal Himself to men in Nature — as when Beethoven felt the trees in the forest calling "Holy! Holy! Holy!" to him; or as in the symmetry of a leaf to those who know how to look for such things — or, on the highest level, according to Scheler, God may reveal Himself in the Word of the *homines religiosi,* the prophets of the Lord. These men are not of a single kind; a typological analysis is needed here also, one that will reveal the essential characteristics not only of each type but also of the type of divine revelation peculiar to each. Thus Scheler names among others the visionary, the holy lawgiver, the savior, the king and hero; each type is essentially related to a peculiar type of message it brings about the sphere of the holy.

The third group of problems within the phenomenology of religion concerns the description of the *religious act itself,* that is, the essence of the process in which the material of revelation is taken up in belief by the religious person. Central to this problem is the question of the nature of the *evidence* with which the holy is given and the distinction between true and false belief. The possibility of a solution to such problems of "criteria" of religious belief is contingent upon a description of the essential constitution of the religious act itself and of the direction of its intentionality. Scheler holds that the specifically religious act distinguishes itself from all other intentional acts in that it (1) intends something that transcends the world; (2) is an intention that can be satisfied only by that which is holy; (3) is satisfied only passively, that is, by a Divinity who reveals Himself through the intentional act directed toward Him. God is never "discovered"; He "reveals Himself."

But the analysis can go further than these three criteria: we can consider the symbolic form in which God is worshiped within a given religious tradition — as "father," "protector," "conserver," and the like. By reperforming, in reflective intuition, the acts in which God is thus given to the believer, the phenomenologist may arrive at an intuition of the *a priori* order in which God is cognized. Scheler contrasts the religious act of knowledge in which revelation is received with the metaphysical knowledge act, in which the knowing subject is *active,* and moves toward God by means of logical operations.

Now although each of these three groups of problems calls for a separate phenomenological analysis, they are yet interrelated. Note that Scheler's analysis above of the essential characteristics of the religious act may serve as a basis for distinguishing "true" religious acts from "false" ones, for accepting and rejecting ascriptions of specific characteristics to God. Now the question of what is and what is not a legitimate ascription is, of course, the central question of theology. Yet if we reflect a moment on the nature of the phenomenological method, the possibility of *its* supplying an answer would appear to be excluded: phenomenological descriptions, after all, have the purpose of aiding the reader to intuit the thing intended by the author, and are not a list of the "attributes" a thing possesses, such as theology would like to develop with respect to God. Furthermore, natural theology is in essence an attempt to develop through rational argument grounds for or against the assertion that God possesses such and such attributes, whereas phenomenology does not proceed by argumentation at all but rather by intuition.

Scheler, however, introduces an interesting distinction. He points out that the phenomenological method is in many respects quite similar to that of so-called negative theology, which tries to "define" the indefinable *Ens a se* in terms of what it is *not*. This procedure is none other than the attempt to direct the vision of the reader or hearer in a certain direction, namely, away from that which is an element of everyday, "concrete" experience toward that which is in principle only intuitable, and not definable or even describable. "The method of 'negative theology,'" declares Scheler, "is derived from the profound insight that the divine and holy as such is a primordially given quality that can only be exhibited by means of the peeling-off of other qualities that it does not possess and by means of analogy."[4] Whatever positive assertions may be made by the phenomenological natural theologian concerning the nature of the holy, then, must be in agreement with — if not based upon — the self-givenness to intuition of the quality itself. As must always be the case, the self-givenness of the phenomenon is the final court of appeal for all assertions that the phenomenon possesses a certain constitution.

Now both pure phenomenology and natural theology will agree that the *Ens a se* is not simply another essence that can be unambiguously described in terms of its properties. Still, Scheler believes, we can take some steps toward establishing a "possibly true" description of God, that is, toward a *positive* natural theology. He notes, first of all, that the religious consciousness searches in the world for signs of its creator. But the "signs" that God leaves upon his creation are to be found, not in the concrete things of this world, but rather in its essential structure — and it is just this essential structure that is investigated by phenomenology.

Thus the religious consciousness has the results of phenomenological investigation to use as a basis for its imaginative venture toward God. But in addition, we have at our disposal a phenomenological investigation of the *a priori* structure of the religious consciousness itself to serve as a check against perversions or distortions of genuine or "authentic" insight into the nature of God. Thus "natural theology" operates upon the principle that it is irrational to ascribe to God characteristics that have no basis in the essential structure of the world or in the fundamental structures of the religious consciousness of mankind. Thus we have two checks against *anarchy* in religion. The results of such a dual operation will be a list of attributes of God that possess only analogical and not literal validity; for insofar as God is utterly transcendent, no adjectives referring to the things of this world could ever be properly applicable to God. Therefore, the descriptions lack even what could be called "metaphysical" validity — it was the error of medieval theologians to imagine this — for there is no question here of "arguing" from the essence of the world to the essence of God; no act of discursive reason is performed. Scheler insists upon a sharp distinction between the metaphysical and the theological imagination.

Thus the two disciplines involved in Scheler's procedure, the description of the way men come upon their symbolic pictures of God, and the search for God in the essential structure of the world, are actually complementary investigations, which together constitute his program for the philosophy of religion. True to his phenomenological procedure, a normative discipline — positive theology — is founded upon a descriptive. This theological method thus reflects the two modes of access we have to God: through the human reason, which is lighted by the infinite reason, and through the things of things of this world, out of which the divine light shines. The point of Schelerian theology is to redo what the religious consciousness itself does, and to do it *systematically and hence better*, so that theology can be used to criticize the concrete content of a religious belief. Something must be *given* before it can be *believed*, and Scheler is using the tools of his method to get at the essence of what is given in the act of belief. We will begin our discussion by distinguishing among the formal, the positive, and the concrete attributes of God.

The *formal* attributes of the holy are simply those that are *highest in the order of foundation* of all acts of intending the holy, and are hence its most essential characteristics. Scheler believes that there are three such formal characteristics of the divine. It is first given as *value*: something is Holy. It is given as *absolute*: there is something that is an *Ens a se*. It is given as *omnipotent*: there is something upon which the world is *dependent* for its existence and essence. These three attributes are not merely asserted as self-evident by Scheler;[5] he takes considerable pains to perform a phenomenological *Aufweisen* of the essences he is intuiting, and we shall use that of the third attribute — God as omnipotent — as our example of Scheler's procedure.

To help us along our way, we might consider that Scheler apparently holds that the primordial act of intending the Holy is in some sense an "unfulfilled" intention, insofar as what is given as holy, absolute, and all-powerful is merely an undetermined "something." The mind goes out to God in an undifferentiated act of love; much like the plant blindly impelled toward the light, the soul directs itself in love toward a God it yet knows nothing of. This primordial love, this direction of the spiritual eye toward the transcendent, is the decisive act in the determination of the *ethos* of a people. True to his doctrine of functionalization, Scheler holds that the way in which the three attributes are grasped in the primordial act of love is variable, but insofar as these attributes are few in number and very general in content, the range of their possible concretizations is small. Differences in the religious beliefs of the various peoples of the world are to be traced, not to this level, but rather to the level in which belief in God receives symbolic expression. The development of this new level first takes place *after* the development of a specific *Weltanschauung* and *ethos,* that is, after the establishment of a specific spiritual tradition within which God reveals Himself to the religious consciousness.

As we have seen from our description of Scheler's sociology of knowledge, the philosopher held, quite correctly, that all religious revelation presupposes a certain specifically structured religious tradition. The revelation takes place within the limits of this tradition. As all religious change is a religious renewal, a going back to the roots of the religious tradition, so does all religious revelation presuppose not only a divine entity Who reveals Himself but also a "world" in which He reveals Himself. The attributes of the Deity that are no longer merely formal, but that are founded in the consciousness of a specific people — in a consciousness that need not be merely the consciousness of a religious tradition, but is primarily on the level of their relative natural *Weltanschauung* and their *ethos* — are called by Scheler the *positive* attributes of God. Those attributes of God that are founded in the specifically religious traditions of a people — on the level of their conscious cultural *Weltan-schauung* — are called by Scheler the *concrete* attributes of God, that is, the attributes that constitute the living idea of God that is grasped upon the "everyday religious standpoint" by the individuals that make up a specific religious community. The study of these attributes would take us into the sociology of knowledge, and we would have to pursue an empirical study of specific religious communities to obtain material for description here. The theologian is concerned only with the formal and positive attributes of God; but these categories, again, describe the limits of possible authentic, "everyday" religious experience.

Now that the distinction among the three attribute types has been clarified, let us try working with some examples of a phenomenological "contribution" to positive natural theology: first, Scheler's *Aufweisen* of a "formal" attribute of God; second, his "reperformance" of the act in which the religious mind goes from the essence of the things of this world to the symbol representing the essence of God. This method will give us one example of the phenomenology of the intentional object and one of the phenomenology of the intentional act.

(1) This first example concerns the religious concept of the omnipotence, or of what Scheler calls the *Allwirksamkeit,* of God — the thought that God's power is not only almighty but also ubiquitous — and the corollary concept of the dependence of all things upon God's power. A problem concerning this occurs to us immediately; for while this category belongs to the class of the "formal" attributes of God, supposedly given before all else, the human subject seems nevertheless to depend upon certain other experiences of essence to attain this insight. It is difficult to make a case for the view that the experience of dependence is presuppositionless, in the way that the experience of Holiness springs from the primordial directedness in love of the soul to the Holy, the Absolute; and Scheler does not claim this, despite his belief that omnipotence is a formal attribute of God. Even more telling against the primordiality of omnipotence is the thought that dependency is a *relationship,* whereas holiness and absoluteness are not; therefore the term implies that something else besides God is given to the religious imagination before it can come upon this notion, namely, the world, which is then seen to be dependent for its essence and existence upon God. But, as we discovered in the last chapter, the

world is given only *after* the essences of the Holy and the self; thus almightiness and dependency cannot be formal attributes of God but must be either positive or concrete attributes.

Overlooking the problem, we may ask what is, then, the nature of the intentional act, that is, the nature of the experience of essence that leads the mind, in religious contemplation, to apprehend the world as dependent upon God for its essence and existence?

Scheler maintains that the *fundamental* essential experience here is that of *Wirken,* causal action-reaction. He takes great pains to distinguish this experiencé of the causal relation in a given specific case, in which one thing acts upon another, from the logical notion of causality, which is founded upon the merely symbolic notion of regular succession. His thought is that the causal relation of God-world is of course not itself experienced, but the *symbols* for this relation are founded upon the intuition of the meaning of causality upon a specific empirical case of it, much as the logical notion of causality as regular succession is ultimately founded upon such an intuition.

The symbols of the religious imagination are quite different from those of logic, however. It thinks of causality, not abstractly, as a relationship existing between types of events, but rather in terms of the relationship *artist-artifact.* As always, the religious imagination does not operate with the bloodless categories of metaphysics; it revels in symbols, analogies, suggestions, and always has the intuition of its living God before the eye of its mind as the reference within which it understands these "symbols," "analogies," and "suggestions." The experience of dependence of the world upon God and upon divine omnipotence, which occurs when the religious consciousness moves from the thought of any empirical action to that of the holy *Ens a se,* may thus be symbolized in the expression "God the artist, world the artifact." This very general symbolic description may, of course, receive very specific representation in a given religious tradition: the description of the six days' labor in Genesis, Michaelangelo's "Creation of Adam," the Enlightenment metaphysics of the mechanic-God, all are examples of how God's omnipotence and the world's dependence may be given concrete symbolic form within the formal pattern of artist-artifact. Scheler's point is simply that in all these cases, the lived experience of causal action-reaction is presupposed, and that this experience is thought of as occurring between God and world *analogically,* as artist to artifact; the world is thus experienced not only as dependent upon the creativity of its artist but also as the field of expression of its creator, as a painting carries the traces of its master. For that reason, the religious imagination is bound to look to the world as a source of knowledge about its maker. Following the act of religious imagination further, Scheler notes that the source of the typical religious experience of one's own finitude and contingency is to be sought in this primordial experience of God's omnipotence.

(2) Let us pass on without pause to a second example. The religious knowledge that God is spirit is the first and most central positive attribute of God in natural religion. By "natural" religion Scheler simply means that its beliefs are not a product of a religious tradition nor are they first given in the "revelations" of a *homo religiosus.* Nor does the belief that God is spirit follow analytically from the "formal" attributes of God. However, he tells us, the metaphysical thought behind this belief can be expressed in the form of a syllogism: the first premise states that the world possesses existence and essence independently of the occurrence or nonoccurrence of my spiritual acts or those of any other men; not only does the existence of the objects of this world transcend that of my mind, but also their essences are given only partially and, usually, inadequately to me.

The second premise states the interdependence of being and spirit, a doctrine we have had occasion to discuss earlier in this chapter. Scheler holds that it pertains to the essences of "cognitive act" and "cognized object," that to every possible act of knowing there corresponds a possible object known, and vice versa. This phenomenological doctrine is now taken as a starting point for the metaphysical speculation we mentioned earlier in this chapter: if we posit an existing, intersubjective world, we must posit a spirit to whom this world is given, and which cannot (by premise one) be the human spirit. This spirit, the metaphysician may conclude, is what we identify with God.

Now what is the relationship of this metaphysical argument to the process in which the religious consciousness attains the knowledge that God is spirit? Scheler writes:

It is not this conclusion [from the above argument] that is drawn by the person who performs the religious act in which he becomes certain of God as spirit. One can only say that the religious act itself operates analogously *according to* the premises just developed. It immediately carries over the *idea* of the prototype of the spirit, which it intuits in the human spirit, as it intuits the essential relation between spirit and world in the relation between the human mind and the world, to the holy *Ens a se,* of whose existence it is already certain.

Yet, he adds, an *Aufweisen* of this process in the religious imagination is extremely difficult: "It is like an unspeakably mysterious drama in the deepest depths of the soul in which the *religious* knowledge that the holy *Ens a se* must be of spiritual nature is procured."[6]

It is clear that the grasping in intuition of the truth of the first premise has as its "practical" condition that the human subject believe that the most intimate part of him — his Self, that which Scheler had called the "core" of the person — is "located" in his spirit and not in his stomach, as Scheler quotes the Apostle Paul. The man who imagines himself to be a succession of impulses and desires — not an unusual type of personality — will rarely come to the religious insight that God is spirit, although he may be an idealist on metaphysical grounds. The effort to attain the religious insight may be aided by the "moral precondition" of *humility,* especially insofar as the premise implies a recognition of the finitude of the human spirit, its complete incapacity to be in any way responsible for the existence and the essence of the things of the world. Yet despite this, one must have experienced, as does every truly religious person, something of the "dignity and nobility" of the spirit itself, in which experience it becomes *evident* that the spirit cannot be simply a part of this world, another "object," but must be that through which the essential natures that the objects instance first *become* objects.

The third and final act in this process of religious understanding is that of

attributing the essential attribute of "spirit" to the holy *Ens a se* of which we are already certain, and experiencing the illumination, the revelation, of the infinite reason within all the activities and actions of finite reason, or rather the illumination by the ideas and values themselves together with the order of those ideas and values, which stand before the acts of infinite reason as its correlates, of the objects of the world and their meaning content.[7]

Scheler's procedure is similar for what he considers to be further positive attributes of God, especially those that are intuitable in the fact that God is spirit: thus God is given as understanding, will, love, and most important, as an infinite Person.

Instead of merely following Scheler further in the *Aufweisen* of the essence of God, let us reflect critically upon this peculiar effort to provide a new beginning for the philosophy of religion. His analysis appears to be two-sided, as we indicated at the beginning. On the one hand, he is practicing "natural theology," insofar as he attempts to discover a criterion of the true and the false in religion, apart from all revelation, and insofar as he develops his thoughts in the form of a logical argument. On the other hand, his analysis is not founded upon criteria peculiar to logic; rather, these criteria are derived from the religious understanding itself. His point of departure is, as always, from natural experience, from the fact of something given from within the natural standpoint, and is directed toward discovering the "moments" of that experience: namely, what is given in and what is logically presupposed by the performance of that concrete act of knowing something upon the natural standpoint — in this case, by the performance of an act of knowing God. This much should be evident from the two examples we have chosen. Thus Scheler is not *defining* God — a process that antimetaphysical thinkers of Scheler's day correctly branded as the arbitrary speculations of unbridled reason — but is describing the essence of what *can be given* to a human subject who adequately prepares himself to experience the sphere of the holy of which he is primordially if imperfectly aware. Scheler is, in other words, not trying to work out what is logically implied by the idea of God alone (i.e., the phenomenological description of the object of religious consciousness), but is also trying to work his way back into the logical preconditions of a natural, "everyday" experience. He bases his analysis upon the personal performance in intuition of those acts we call religious, acts of "knowing God."

And yet, what is perhaps the weakest point of Scheler's analysis from a phenomenological point of view is this very fact of a double criterion of authentic religious belief, the fact that he is doing two things at once. Had he simply presented a description of the peculiar way in which the religious imagination apprehends God, how it passes from the contemplation of the essences given with the things of this world to the Deity who previously revealed itself to that imagination; if he had merely attempted to go from the concrete picture of God of living religious practice to the intuitions of essence and the movements of the spirit presupposed by them, the descriptions we have just been studying would have been less muddied by the heavy jargon that he brings in from other areas of this thought. Our last quotation from *Vom Ewigen im Menschen* is a good example of how Scheler's entire philosophical system provides the framework for his "essential phenomenology of religion," from which he was to build his criteria for a system of positive theology. Furthermore, what he fails to make evident is how the "positive" attributes of God are involved in concrete living ideas of God. This is, of course, a parallel problem to that which we encountered earlier, especially in our discussion of Scheler's normative ethics: this concerns the nature of the evidence with which it is asserted that a given thing instances a specific essence. As a phenomenological analysis of the religious consciousness, his descriptions in this section, and especially his interpretations of the historical experiences and doctrines he uses as springboards for his contemplation of essence, include profound and often persuasive insights into the essences intended in that "profound and unspeakable drama" in which the religious mind obtains that final and highest evidence that Scheler has attempted to bring us to see here, an evidence that, *as* the final and highest evidence, lies outside the arena of rationalist critique.

II *Phenomenology and Metaphysics: Scheler's Final Attempt at a Synthesis*

If *Vom Ewigen im Menschen* represents an effort to build theology upon phenomenology, *Die Stellung des Menschen im Kosmos* is an effort to draw upon both science and phenomenology in an effort to establish a "possibly true" speculative metaphysical doctrine of man, that is, one that does not contradict scientific and phenomenological knowledge. The Christian view of God and the Holy, so evident in *Vom Ewigen im Menschen,* has been partly abandoned, partly relegated to an inessential role in the discussions of the problem of God at the close of *Die Stellung des Menschen im Kosmos,* where a new line of speculation is taken up. Although the theme of the inquiry is the same, the concrete phenomena from which God is approached are quite different, and the argument is no longer religious or theological but rather metaphysical. The metaphysical tone is clearly set by a simple transformation: in *Die Stellung des Menschen im Kosmos,* Scheler is no longer trying to establish a *Fundierungsordnung,* that is, a description of those mental acts and the essences intended by them that are the logical presuppositions for the occurrence of other mental acts and the essences intended by them. Rather, he speaks here of the essences that are the ground of the possibility of the *existence* of other essences: the transition to metaphysics has been accomplished by considering the *Fundierungsordnung* from the point of view of epistemological realism. Thus, essences are not thought of simply as the ground of the possibility of a subject's cognizing an individual thing *as* an instance of essence, but as the ground of the possibility of the existence of empirical things themselves, and of "lower order" essences. In *Die Stellung des Menschen im Kosmos,* the metaphysical viewpoint has thus become an essential part of the analysis. Scheler is out to explain how the world comes about, and not simply to exhibit the order of insights according to which we grasp the things of the world from within our natural standpoint. One feels the enormous change in emphasis: in the period of *Vom Ewigen im Menschen, Der Formalismus,* and *Wesen und Formen der Sympathie,* the problems in phenomenology receive careful analysis, to the neglect of metaphysics; in the transition period of the "Probleme einer Soziologie des Wissens" and in the later period, phenomenology is neglected for the sake of metaphysics; and yet on a theoretical level, the epistemological basis of, and the knowledge acquired by, phenomenology remain untouched! Scheler is not forced to renounce his "essential phenomenology of religion" for his new metaphysics, nor did he in fact renounce it. As essential knowledge, it can be left intact. Clearly, Scheler's apostasy from the Roman Catholic Church left him without the instrument of religion that he had hoped would furnish the broad basis upon which the peoples of the world could assemble.

Thus in the later period, metaphysics, and not religion, is to play the chief role in the practical-political matter of providing a replacement of the "relativistic" philosophies of pragmatism and positivism on the level of theory. In the essay "Philosophische Weltanschauungen"[8] (1927), *Heilswissen,* or the knowledge of how to achieve salvation, is no longer referred to as religious knowledge; Scheler has stopped speaking of "revelation" as a passive

receiving of knowledge from God and is instead actively "thrusting
forward" to knowledge of the absolutely real. Metaphysics must
therefore become more than just a mode of theoretical knowledge;
it must become a *Heilslehre,* a means of attaining personal salvation. The following quotation typifies the later period:

[Metaphysics] shares with religion the attempt to take part in an "absolute
Being," but not, as does religion, by means of belief in and discipleship to
a person to whom one attributes a special ontic relationship with a deity
... but rather by means of spontaneous acts of knowledge of the thing
itself, whose evidence everyone can attain by reperforming those acts....
Thus metaphysics is also always a way of salvation, but a spontaneous
way.[9]

   Yet metaphysics is originally the property of an elite; and Scheler
realized that metaphysics, even in the form of mass ideology,
cannot bring the masses of men to their personal salvation. The
quality of metaphysics that makes possible salvation is just that it is
a personal mode of knowledge; salvation lies in the spontaneous act
of apprehending metaphysical truths. Its truth can be *apprehended*
by others in the reperformance of the metaphysical knowledge act;
but when its truths are simply "fed" to the masses, it will neither
bring about their salvation or produce a "community" among
them, in Scheler's highest sense of the term "community," such as
we described it in Chapter 6. Religion therefore remains in
Scheler's practical *Weltbild;* it maintains its priority in the scale of
spheres of knowledge and values, but Scheler's own politics and the
thrust of his researches have changed. The religious establishment
in Germany comes under attack, and Scheler places political leadership in the hands of those small elites who are metaphysically
productive: "Only the primarily *liberal* democracy of relatively
'small elites,' fighting themselves upward, is an ally of science and
philosophy: thus the facts now teach us. The presently dominant
democracy, which even extends itself to women and half-grown
children, is not a friend but rather an enemy of reason and
science."[10] The concept of God and the *Heilslehre* toward which
Die Stellung des Menschen im Kosmos now leads us is a confirma-
tion of the view that metaphysics is, as he puts it, a road to salvation open only to the few. It is "the *hazardous attempt of reason to
thrust forward into the absolutely real.*"[11] Indeed, *Die Stellung des*

Menschen im Kosmos presents us with the outlines of a very "hazardous" belief.

This late work is all we now have of Scheler's never-completed philosophical anthropology. It goes directly from speculations on the nature of man to speculations upon the essential nature of the really real. Man is conceived here as the microcosm in which both higher and lower forms of being come together in mutual self-creation. Scheler goes about this task coldly and methodologically, occasionally ascending to dizzying heights of metaphysical speculation, only to retreat and solemnly return to his analysis.

The essay, as I understand it, deals with three central problems, all related to the general theme of man's "place" (i.e., both his essential nature in comparison with other kinds of things in the universe, and his role in the development and change within the universe) in the cosmos. There is *first* the question of whether there is an essential difference between man and the other animals with respect to their relative capacity to perform certain tasks, or simply a difference in degree. *Second*, the "Cartesian" problem of the relation of mind (*Seele*) and body is analyzed. *Third*, Scheler attempts to establish the essence of the Spirit (*Geist*), and, from this, to draw metaphysical conclusions concerning its relationship to the life principle and its "place" in the universal scheme of things. It is not our purpose here to present a thoroughgoing description of his views on each of these matters; we are interested, however, in indicating his procedure in this work, for his analyses here contrast in many respects quite sharply with those we have encountered up to now.

Let us first turn our attention to the problem of whether there is an *essential difference* between man and the other animals. Scheler asks whether there is any faculty that man possesses that is not present in the other animals, even in the most inchoate form. He attempts to answer this question by describing levels of psychic or intellectual development of living creatures in terms of what is physically observable in them, that is, their behavior and the physical constitution of their bodies, especially of their nervous systems. On each level, a different essential principle can be discovered as the mode in which the creatures belonging to that level are "open" to their environment, that is, are able to perform certain actions directed toward the things about them for the purpose of satisfying their biological needs. Thus on the level of the plants, we have the blind *Gefühlsdrang* or the impulse toward the satisfaction of felt needs. The urge is "blind" insofar as there is no conscious awareness of the thing "needed," that is, the thing toward which the plant is impelled.

The second level of the psyche attained in nature, which Scheler calls "instinct," can be contrasted with the first level as an example of what he means by an "essential difference." In what sense does the fact that plants are related to their environment by means of the *Gefühlsdrang* while the lower animals have the additional faculty of instinct at their disposal constitute an *essential* distinction between plant and animal? Just in this sense, that the faculty of instinct is *irreducible* to that of *Gefühlsdrang;* the fact of instinctual behavior cannot be shown to have developed genetically out of the lower stage of *Gefühlsdrang,* or to be merely a highly developed *Gefühlsdrang.* On the contrary, it is a primordial phenomenon with a structure of its own that is not in any sense a function of a more primordial urge.

Scheler now attempts to ground this point in biological facts. *Gefühlsdrang* is "ecstatic": it is directed only outward toward things in its immediate environment; there is no reflex of the *Gefühlsdrang* upon some central nervous organ as we have in conscious sensation (for plants lack all trace of a nervous system) and as is presupposed by instinctual behavior — behavior, in order that it be instinctive, must be founded upon a consciousness through sensation, however rudimentary, of something upon which the instinctive action is directed. The consequence for its psychic life of the plant's lack of a nervous system is that a description of the plant's mode of existence — which is limited to passive nourishment, growth, reproduction and death — can be accomplished simply on the basis of this single psychic *Gefühlsdrang,* for example, toward the sun, the roots toward water and nitrates, whereas the psychic phenomena responsible for the behavior of a creature possessing instinct are much wider. These psychic and behavioral phenomena are carefully described by Scheler on the basis of the then most recent biological information.

In sum, he characterizes instinctive behavior as follows. It must first of all "make sense," in that it must be behavior directed toward the satisfaction of some need. Second, it must follow a certain pattern or rhythm in which various organs of the body are used. In this way, instinctive behavior is distinguished from mere reflex action, on the one hand, and from "learned" behavior (where the creature has tradition, practice, and memory at his disposal, such as the rat in the maze) on the other. A bird follows a certain pattern every winter, although this may be his first winter, and there are no other birds around to "show him what to do." Third, instinctive behavior always serves the species, not the individual; it is directed toward the accomplishment of tasks necessary to the preservation of the species, and not simply toward the satisfaction of a personal need. Finally, instinctive behavior is not produced through sensible experience, although it can be set in motion by an external stimulus. Scheler holds that, on the contrary, instinctual drives may determine *what* is given to consciousness from among the chaos of sense data to which the creature is constantly subject, but not the reverse. For this reason, instinctual behavior appears to be a *condition* of learned behavior, for a conscious apprehension of items in the physical environment is a presupposition of the "memory" and "association" that are involved in learning.

Scheler carefully argues these points with biologists and philosophers alike, and the wealth of detail and the experimental findings he presents are too great to receive treatment here. His central argument for the distinction between the faculty of "associative memory" (the third level of psychic behavior) and instinct is taken from physiology and not from the observation of animal behavior. This involves the discovery that behavior that depends upon the association of sensation (thus learned, and habitual, as opposed to instinctual behavior) is a function of nervous operations located higher in the brain than the operations upon which instinctive behavior is dependent, and thus represents a genetically later development than instinctive behavior. Still, it is by virtue of the instinct that the lower animals are released from their *passivity* toward their environment, while the plant is passively dependent upon its environment for its nourishment. Thus instinct is distinguished from still higher modes of psychic phenomena, such as that of the associative memory mentioned above, which is the condition of such animal behavior as that of the rat in the maze experiment or that of the dogs in the famous experiments performed by Pavlov. On a still higher level, Scheler distinguishes the faculty of "practical intelligence," as demonstrated by the experiments of Wolfgang Köhler, who observed that chimpanzees are capable of discovering that a stick can be used to draw a banana into their cages.

Now what of man? Does man possess a psychic characteristic that is found only in him, that is not prefigured in the animal world? Men certainly possess the faculty of practical intelligence, and they have developed it to an enormous degree; yet the rudiments of a practical intelligence are found in the ape. Now Scheler's answer is that only man possesses spirit. But what is spirit, and how is it different from intelligence? It is the capacity to contemplate essence and thus to "have meaning": only man is able to "step back" from the things of his immediate environment and to understand the things about him *apart from their significance to him as a biological organism.* Men *give names* to the things about them; in doing this, they objectify them and, as we might put it, "neutralize" them with respect to their biological significance. It is just this aspect of spirit that gives men their freedom from the biological structure and the psychic phenomena derived from it; *Gefühlsdrang,* instinct, associative memory, and practical intelligence all serve the life needs of the organism and do not allow the organism that possesses them to contemplate the world apart from these needs. For that reason, Scheler asserts that only men have a "world" in the true sense of the term; animals have simply an "environment" whose content is determined by what the animal "wants to see," that is, by a vitally directed attentiveness. Man, too, is "led" in his observations by vital interest, but not *exclusively,* as is an animal; men objectify, neutralize, "ideate," as Scheler coins the term. Both men and animals suffer hunger, and both know how to satisfy their hunger; but only men know what "hunger" is, only men can intuit the essence of hunger, for intuition is a function of spirit, and only men possess spirit. In addition, men alone are able to "collect together" the spiritual acts in which they intend objects of the world about them and reflect upon these acts as "their" mental acts; this is called "self-consciousness." "Animals hear and see," says Scheler, but without knowing *that* they hear and see. The psyche of the animal functions, but the animal is not a possible psychologist or physiologist."[12]

Now his central point in this analysis is that these phenomena are *primordial* phenomena of the spirit and cannot be "explained" either as extensions of the life impulse or as an expansion of the function of the practical intelligence such as is found in the higher animals. If there is an *essential* difference between man and animals, the species "man" can be said to have a *special place* in the cosmos, a place that he shares with no other species. Scheler describes this special place phenomenologically with the phrase "man is *Weltoffen,*" open to the world and not simply a *part* of the world.

The description is phenomenological, for it is purely descriptive of an essential relationship and does not involve a positing of existence or the attribution of a higher *value* to man. The scientific phenomena serving as evidence in Scheler's case are ingeniously collected and finely observed and described. But what of the "metaphysical uses" of this phenomenological distinction? What is man's "place" in the cosmos, where "place" is this time understood as his *role* in the cosmic drama?

Scheler begins his ascent by attacking the second central problem of *Die Stellung des Menschen im Kosmos,* that of the distinction between mind and body. Scheler's argument in this section is directed toward destroying the substantive distinction of Descartes and establishing the fundamental *unity* of body and soul; the phenomena of both body and soul will be shown to be not primordial but in fact reducible to *life* phenomena: "What we call 'psychological' and 'physiological' are only two ways of looking at *one and the same life process.* There is an 'internal biology' and an 'external biology.'"[13] Again, biological evidence is presented for this view. We will take only one brief example in order to indicate the nature of Scheler's analysis:

When a dog sees a piece of meat, and the corresponding stomach-fluids needed to digest it are secreted, this is for Descartes, who cast the entire emotional and impulsive life out of the soul and who at the same time insisted upon a purely chemical-physical explanation of life-phenomena even with respect to their structural laws, an absolute miracle. Why? Because on the side of the soul, he eliminated the appetite-drive, which is a condition of the occurrence of the visual perception of the food by the animal in the same way that the external stimulus [is a condition of that perception] ... and because on the other, physiological side, he does not hold the secretion of stomach fluids, which corresponds to the appetite, to be a true life-process ... but only a purely chemical process that takes place in the stomach independently of the central nervous system, just as soon as the food arrives there... One sees the error, Descartes' basic error: he completely overlooked the system of drives in man and animal that constitutes the *unity* and the means of *mediation* between every true life-process and the content of consciousness.[14]

Similar examples indicating the mutual interdependence of body and soul are brought in by Scheler as further illustrations of his point.

We see the point: Scheler (1) insists that the drives determine what *part* of what is given to the sensible field of both man and animal will become the object of explicit awareness; and he (2) intends to eliminate the element of *spirit* from the Cartesian "soul." But in this way he comes upon what he holds to be the true ontological duality: not of body and soul, as Descartes had taught, but of the unifying principle behind the merely apparent duality of body and soul, namely, the *life* principle, and the *spirit*. There is no "higher unity" behind these two principles, no higher phenomenon to which they may be "reduced" as body and soul to "life"; indeed, they are *in conflict*. From an anthropological point of view, man, the only animal to possess spirit, is a sick being, a *biologically disadvantaged* creature *because* he possesses spirit. Spirit, a principle that of itself has no power, operates only insofar as it can use the biological life power, whose element man also possesses. The principle by which the spirit uses the life force for its *own* ends is taken by Scheler from Freud; the spirit "sublimates" the life force by making spiritual instead of biological purposes the *objects* of *passion*. Yet in doing so, the spirit robs men of their vital energy; in general, the higher a living creature stands upon the scale of psychic capacity, the weaker it is as a biological organism. Even with lower creatures, Scheler claims, "the direction of life that is called animal signifies not only an advantage over plant life, but also a loss, for it no longer possesses the direct intercourse with the inorganic that the plant has by virtue of its kind of nourishment."[15] With this line of thought, Scheler not only has provided a basis for a system of values but is positing the categories of spirit and life as the warring forces whose conflict is responsible for the biological decadence of man. Where will this argument lead him with respect to the third problem of *Die Stellung des Menschen im Kosmos,* that of man's role in the universal process?

He tells us that "this train of thought cannot hold itself back from the highest being, from the Ground of the World."[16] His thought is that insofar as the Ground of the World is a personal Spirit, he must be powerless to realize in temporal existence the *Wesensreich* he has before his spiritual eye. Rather, the same tension of life force and spirit that exists in man must be attributed to the Ground of the World as the dynamic principle that constitutes the ground of the possibility of the world. God does not "create" the world; he sublimates the vital, world-creating *Drang* that lies within him, and in doing so, his ideas enter the temporal order. According to Scheler, "We express this when we say: the Ground of Things had to release from its bonds the world-creative urge, if it wished to *realize* itself in the temporal process."[17] What is the role of man in this process? He continues: "*For us the basic relationship of man to the Ground of the World* is found in the fact that in man — who, both as a spiritual and as a living creature, is a partial center of the Spirit and Urge of that which 'is-through-itself' — this Ground, I say, directly *grasps* and *realizes* itself."[18]

Man, as the only place known to us in which both elements in the cosmic dynamics come together, is thus a microcosmic version of the process in which God realizes Himself. Man has, in addition, a necessary role to play in the *further* self-development of God, which Scheler imagines will be a process in which Urge and Spirit interpenetrate one another, until — perhaps — the originally powerless Spirit attains the upper hand over the life force. Insofar as man reperforms the intentional act in which God knows the essences according to which the world is continuously created and maintained, he takes part in the world-creative act. This is an act that requires, as does the creation of the world itself, the same act of sublimation, the same attempt to let oneself become Spirit. The Deity (*Gottheit*) must *struggle to become God* (*Gott*). This reperformance has thus become for Scheler the paradigm of the *religious* act, and its performance requires the same "active commitment" of the center of our being to the further development of the universe as does the religious commitment to God. This is, as we noted earlier, a road open only to the few, a metaphysical commitment not meant for "weak men in need of support." As Scheler views it, "It presupposes a strong lofty sense in men. For that reason, it is easily understandable that a man first becomes conscious of the fact he is struggling and achieving along with the divinity only during the course of his development and after some self-knowledge."[19]

In this thought, Scheler's metaphysics, phenomenology, and theology attain their final synthesis: the "moral presuppositions of philosophy" are those required for this "active commitment," and the act of the phenomenological intuition of essence has become a religious act in which the phenomenologist takes part in, and even contributes to, the self-realization of the world and of God.

Thus, in the end, Scheler is out to give us a general metaphysical picture of the universe, and no longer to exhibit the intuitive foundation of our everyday experience. Yet is it not just at this point where the most profound difficulties with all of Scheler's efforts in metaphysics lie? Is there not throughout his entire work a constant *tension* between the slow, rigorous phenomenological method and the "spontaneous," inspiration-dependent method of metaphysics? Ultimately his earlier positive theology and his later metaphysics come to ruin on the thought that one can build a metaphysical system of the absolutely real using a phenomenological analysis of what is given from within the natural standpoint and scientific facts as one's evidence, as one's "criterion." Strange that the philosopher who realized that (1) metaphysics cannot flourish at a time when philosophy is concerned with the problem of discovering criteria of the true and the false; that (2) metaphysics is a spontaneous human activity and not a science; and that (3) as we have noted, phenomenology is, by virtue of its concept of evidence, not capable of building a system of positive knowledge of *any* kind, would yet attempt to build a metaphysical system upon a carefully laid scientific-phenomenological foundation! But when one finally comes to the insight that the two disciplines, metaphysics and phenomenology, cannot serve each other but are opposed in their essential natures and even in the temperaments of their ideal practitioners, then it is not startling to see Scheler, and us who have been trying to interpret him, struggling through all of his works with the problem of their relationship to each other, trying to keep them apart on the one hand and trying to perform a marriage between them on the other. His insistence upon rigorous method and his need for the transcendent are basic elements in the divisions so often noticeable in his work.

Notes and References

Preface

1. H. Spiegelberg, *The Phenomenological Movement*, p. 235.
2. J. R. Staude, *Max Scheler, 1874–1928*, p. 15.
3. *Ibid.*, p. 157.
4. Spiegelberg, *Phenomenological Movement*, p. 237.
5. One collection is published in English under the title *Philosophical Perspectives* (*Philosophische Weltanschauung*) by Beacon Press (1958), and another has been translated as *Man's Place in Nature* (*Die Stellung des Menschen im Kosmos*) by Noonday Press (1961, edited and translated by Hans Meynerhoff). There is also a long concluding section in "Erkenntnis und Arbeit" (1926) that has relevance for metaphysics, and a late essay entitled "Idealismus-Realismus" (1927) that deals with this traditional metaphysical problem. See the bibliography appended to this work.
6. In the introduction to *Die Wissensformen und die Gesellschaft* (1926).
7. They will not be available to the public until their publication, by Manfred Frings (who took over the editorship of the manuscripts from Scheler's widow after her death in 1969), in the final three volumes of the collected works.
8. Gustav René Hocke; in *Die Zeit,* no. 36 (August 30, 1974), p. 16.
9. Richard Bernheimer, *The Nature of Representation: A Phenomenological Study* (New York: New York University Press, 1961).
10. See *Man's Place in Nature,* final section; also, *Vom Ewigen im Menschen.*
11. Ninian Smart, *The Science of Religion and the Sociology of Knowledge: Some Methodological Questions* (Princeton: Princeton University Press, 1973).
12. Julius Kraft, *Von Husserl zu Heidegger: Kritik der phänomenologischen Philosophie*, 2nd ed. (Frankfurt: Verlag "Öffentliches Leben", 1957), especially pp. 78–80.

Chapter One

1. Scheler, *Vom Ewigen im Menschen* (*Gesammelte Werke,* vol. V), pp. 63–64.

185

2. Scheler, *Philosophische Weltanschauungen,* p. 5.
3. Scheler, *Wesen und Formen der Sympathie,* (Bonn: Verlag Cohen, 1926) p. 302.
4. Scheler, *Schriften aus dem Nachlass,* I (*Gesammelte Werke,* vol. X), 434.
5. In Scheler's language, "intuition" appears to refer to that part of the conscious act of perception directed upon the meaning content of the perception as opposed to the sensible content.
6. Scheler, *Der Formalismus in der Ethik und die materiale Wertethik* (*Gesammelte Werke,* vol. II), pp. 74 ff.
7. Husserl, *Ideen,* I, paragraph 1. "We observe the experience of others on the basis of their physical expression."
8. See Scheler, *Nachlass,* I, p. 435; further, the critique of pragmatism in "Erkenntnis und Arbeit," *Die Wissensformen und die Gesellschaft* (*Gesammelte Werke,* vol. VIII), pp. 212-282.
9. Scheler, *Nachlass,* I, 448.
10. Scheler is destroying "relativistic" doctrines of reductionism by exchanging the notion of a logical order among essences for that of a causal order between types of things. The force of his attacks upon contemporary "relativists," "pragmatists," and "positivists" must be judged in the light of this difference.
11. Scheler, *Nachlass,* I, p. 416.
12. *Ibid.,* p. 479.
13. *Ibid.,* p. 475.
14. Note a lingering parallel with Kant: Scheler's "meaning content of perception" is *a priori,* as he puts it; that is, it is prior to the given act of perception upon the natural standpoint, and serves as the ground of the possibility of that perception. The meaning content of the perception of, for example, this thing as a desk is the empirical concept of "deskness," whose constitution may contain nonempirical elements that are therefore said to be "pure." Important to remember is that for Scheler the *a priori* element in a given act of perception (oppose Kant's "judgment") is not merely formal, but has an intuitable content. Scheler, unlike Kant, was not trying to justify a system of knowledge by claiming that such knowledge contains a pure synthetic *a priori* element, that is, one not derived from experience, but rather was trying to describe both the empirical and formal meaning structures in terms of which the world is in fact thought — and he was willing to accept the possibility that the world is not thought of in terms of a single set of formal categories.
15. Scheler, *Nachlass,* I, 433.
16. *Ibid.*
17. Scheler, *Die Stellung des Menschen im Kosmos,* pp. 49–50.
18. Scheler, *Vom Ewigen im Menschen,* pp. 97–98.

Chapter Two

1. For example, in *Vom Ewigen im Menschen* (*Gesammelte Werke,* vol. V), pp. 195 ff.

2. Immanuel Kant, "Transcendental Analytic," *Critique of Pure Reason,* book II, ch. 1, translated by Norman Kemp Smith (New York: St. Martin's, 1965), pp. 180 ff.

3. Scheler, *Der Formalismus in der Ethik und die materiale Wertethik* (*Gesammelte Werke,* vol. II), p. 66.

4. See Scheler's discussions on this theme in *Die Stellung des Menschen im Kosmos* and in our final chapter. Does this view mean that efforts to teach chimpanzees to communicate through a human language are doomed to failure?

5. Scheler, *Vom Ewigen im Menschen,* p. 198. This entire passage is in italics in the text.

6. The fact that the intuition of specific essences may become clouded in given persons by nonrational elements does not rob essence of its *a priori* character. Knowledge of essence retains the characteristic of immutability even if it is a contingent fact whether a given essence is "known" by a given person or group of persons (i.e., whether primordial insight into that essence does or does not function upon the natural standpoint of that person, or whether it functions in a distorted manner.) We see here one of the principal theoretical points upon which Scheler attacked value relativism.

7. David Baumgart, "Some Merits and Defects of Contemporary German Ethics," *Philosophy,* XIII (April, 1938), 183–95.

8. We have in mind such psychological studies as those of Piaget in Switzerland, of Bruner's Center for Cognitive Studies at Harvard, and the philosophical investigation of language learning undertaken in Noam Chomsky's *Cartesian Linguistics.*

9. Scheler has in mind here not only the correspondence theory of truth but also such efforts as that of E. Mach to apply the principle of efficiency to the evaluation of theories, and that of pragmatists to develop a theory of meaning. See *Gesammelte Werke,* VIII, 219–21, 250–60.

10. These reductive acts, are, briefly, as follows. Science eliminates from consideration (1) questions of the relativity of its objects to a specifically constituted subject of knowledge (viz., Scheler's assertion that the objects of mechanistic physics are relative to a subject conceived merely as a corporeal living being, and not as a concrete human person); (2) all questions of the *value* of its objects; (3) questions concerning the origin of our understanding of the sphere of existence that science investigates (e.g., the biologist does not ask what is the *foundation* of our understanding of the phenomenon of "life"); (4) questions concerning the origin of acts of scientific knowledge and the levels of practical value assigned to each (by

this, Scheler is apparently referring to the question of how it is that science appears in certain cultures at certain times rather than in others; that is, in what other intuitions of essence is the possibility of grasping the meaning of the term "scientific knowledge" and all that this implies, *as* something possessing a specific value and founded upon specific act types). Further, (5) science "renounces evident, intuitive knowledge for the sake of approaching an essentially unattainable goal of "completion" of possible observations of infinite numbers of "contingent things and processes"; and finally (6) it renounces evident truth for the sake of the inductive knowledge of what can be only probabilities, that is, probable because they rest on a comparison of only a small part of the possible events relevant to the truth value of the scientific knowledge claim. *Nachlass,* I (*Gesammelte Werke,* vol. X), 209–10.

11. Scheler, *Der Formalismus,* p. 393.
12. Scheler, *Nachlass,* I, 460.
13. *Ibid.,* pp. 477–78.
14. *Ibid.,* p. 452.
15. *Ibid.,* p. 481.

Chapter Three

1. Scheler, *Vom Ewigen im Menschen* (*Gesammelte Werke,* vol. V), p. 80.
2. *Ibid.,* p. 68.
3. *Ibid.*
4. *Ibid.,* p. 89.
5. Scheler, "Erkenntnis und Arbeit," in *Gesammelte Werke,* VIII, 208n.
6. This is the claim of Julius Kraft, who asserts that Scheler was "doomed from the very start" to become no more than a "proselytizer for whatever belief he set his heart upon." *Von Husserl zu Heidegger: Kritik der phänomenologischen Philosophie,* 2nd ed. (Frankfurt: Verlag "Öffentliches Leben", 1957), pp. 78–80.
7. See Scheler, *Der Formalismus in der Ethik und die materiale Wertethik* (*Gesammelte Werke,* vol. II), and "Phänomenologie und Erkenntnistheorie," in *Nachlass,* I (*Gesammelte Werke,* vol. X).
8. Scheler, *Der Formalismus,* pp. 69–70.
9. Scheler, *Nachlass,* I, 382.
10. Scheler, "Erkenntnis und Arbeit," p. 228.
11. Scheler, *Der Formalismus,* p. 218.
12. *Ibid.,* p. 389.
13. Schopenhauer informs us of the following observation of an English officer in an Indian jungle: "A white squirrel is so affected by the

stare of a snake hanging from a tree, whose expression is that of a powerful appetite for his prey, that it gradually moves towards the snake and finally jumps into the open mouth awaiting it. The squirrel has identified itself with the snake." *Wessen und Formen der Sympathie,* 3rd ed. (Bonn: Cohen, 1926), p. 21.

Chapter Four

1. See Scheler, "Idealismus-Realismus," in *Philosophischer Anzeiger,* II: "Das Wissen ist ein letztes, eigenartiges und nicht weiter ableitbares Seinsverhältnis zweier Seienden."
2. Scheler, *Nachlass,* I (*Gesammelte Werke,* vol. X), 415.
3. Scheler, "Idealismus-Realismus," pp. 255-56: "So-sein kann *in mente* sein, Dasein niemals."
4. Scheler, *Die Stellung des Menschen im Kosmos,* p. 53. Scheler's word for "fortuitous" is *zufällig.* He is referring to what he considers to be the aspect of "brute fact" in what is given in sense knowledge. Only when we reflect on the meanings given with our everyday perceptions do we enter the realm of necessity, for only meanings possess necessary relationships; physical objects never do, as Hume pointed out.
5. Scheler, *Nachlass,* I, 483.
6. M. Dupuy, *La Philosophie de Max Scheler, son evolution et son unité* (Paris: Presses Universitaires de France, 1959), p. 263.
7. Scheler, "Weltanschauungslehre, Soziologie, und Weltanschauungssetzung," in *Gesammelte Werke,* VI, 13-26.
8. *Ibid.,* p. 15.
9. Scheler, *Gesammelte Werke,* VIII, 61.
10. Scheler, *Nachlass,* I, 400.
11. Scheler, *Der Formalismus in der Ethik und die materiale Wertethik* (*Gesammelte Werke,* vol. II), pp. 392-93.
12. *Ibid.,* p. 394.
13. The broadness of this mutual understanding will depend not upon a common understanding of the pure facts alone, of course, but also upon the fact of a common tradition and cultural *Weltanschauung,* a common language, etc., all of which are not original but derived phenomena, i.e., themselves functions of the primordial apprehension of essences. This "derived" intersubjectivity is possible despite the primordial individuality of the world of a person because, in addition to being an individual, each person is also universal, i.e., is a human being, a corporeal living being, etc., because men are capable of the sympathetic apprehension of the intellectual acts of other persons, and, of course, because all men have access to the unchanging realm of essence.
14. Scheler, *Der Formalismus,* p. 394.

15. Scheler, "Weltanschauungslehre, Soziologie, und Weltanschauungssetzung," pp. 15-16.
16. Scheler, *Nachlass*, I, 401.
17. Scheler, *Vom Ewigen im Menschen* (*Gesammelte Werke,* vol. V), pp. 68-71.
18. Scheler, *Nachlass*, I, 214-15.
19. Dupuy, *La Philosophie de Max Scheler*, p. 291.
20. Scheler, *Nachlass*, I, 513.
21. Scheler, *Philosophische Weltanschauung*, p. 11.
22. *Ibid.*, "Die Formen des Wissens und die Bildung," pp. 41-42.

Chapter Five

1. The word *Gefühl,* which we are translating here as "feeling state," is generally translated simply as "feeling" in English; however, we want to reserve this term for translating Scheler's *Fühlen.* He frequently uses the word *Gefühlzustand* for *Gefühl* in his writings.
2. Scheler, *Der Formalismus in der Ethik und die materiale Wertethik* (*Gesammelte Werke,* vol. II), pp. 261.
3. In general, the emotions intend the values higher than those of pleasure and pain, which are intended by feeling *per se,* although this is a semantical issue: the value of the pleasant is given in feeling, while the value of the just, the holy, etc., is given in that type of feeling Scheler calls "emotion."
4. Scheler points out that it is this very fact that led "eudaemonists," i.e., those who hold that happiness is the goal of practical human activity, to become hedonists, i.e., to direct their will toward increasing *sensual* pleasure; for only the causes of this kind of pleasure (which is only one constituent of happiness) are immediately and practically capable of manipulation.
5. Scheler, *Der Formalismus,* p. 260.
6. Scheler, "Ordo Amoris," in *Nachlass,* I, (*Gesammelte Werke,* vol. X), 362.
7. Scheler, *Wesen und Formen der Sympathie* (Bonn: Verlag Cohen, 1926) pp. 170-71.
8. *Ibid.,* p. 169.
9. *Ibid.,* p. 164.
10. Spinoza, *Ethics,* book III, prop. 13, note to corollary.
11. Scheler, *Wesen und Formen der Sympathie,* p. 169.
12. *Ibid.,* p. 160.
13. *Ibid.,* p. 172.
14. *Ibid.,* pp. 177, 187.
15. *Ibid.,* p. 177.

16. Scheler replies to the objection that we may in fact stop loving a person if he becomes miserable enough with the remark that this only proves that the love was not true. We refer the reader to the statements in *Der Formalismus* that the phenomenon of *duration* pertains to the essence of love: "Das *sub specie quadam aeterni* gehört zum *Wesen* des echten Liebesaktes."

17. Since for reasons of space we are confining our account of Scheler's *Aufweisen* of the phenomena of love and hate for the most part to that of love, we should note in what sense hate is the "correlative" of love. Hate, Scheler notes, is not simply love directed toward the *non*existence of the thing hated, but is a positive act in which a negative *value* is revealed.

18. Scheler says that "love is directed toward the *being* higher of a value; this is something quite different from 'towards a higher value'" (*Wesen und Formen der Sympathie*, p. 171). His meaning seems to be that love is not first a searching in the thing loved for a higher value than that value already given, but rather that the possibility of a "being higher" of that value is given in the movement of love.

19. Scheler, *Wesen und Formen der Sympathie*, p. 193.

20. A similar problem arose for Spinoza when he defined "joy" as the movement from one level of power of self-preservation to a higher: then the Blessed experience no joy in heaven? Note that in the work we are now considering (*Wesen und Formen der Sympathie*), Scheler considers love of God not as love "of" God thought of as a divine Person, but rather as a love that is a reproduction or imitation of the act in which God loves the world and Himself.

21. See *Die Stellung des Menschen im Kosmos,* final section; also the final chapter of this work.

22. Scheler, *Der Formalismus,* p. 267.

23. *Ibid.,* pp. 213, 245.

24. *Ibid.,* p. 360.

25. Naturally one can choose to live according to some established system of norms, i.e., to submit to an authority (tradition, Divine Will, one's own ego, etc.). But this is not the essence of virtue, if Scheler is right.

26. Scheler, *Der Formalismus,* p. 217.

27. *Ibid.,* p. 128.

28. Indeed, we can at times judge that a person has political aims similar to our own simply by sympathetically apprehending that his *Gesinnung,* his general "attunement" to life, is similar to our own, even before the subject of politics comes up for the first time!

29. Scheler, *Der Formalismus,* p. 129.

30. *Ibid.,* p. 117.

31. *Ibid.,* p. 122.

32. Soren Kierkegaard, *Either/Or* (Princeton: Princeton University Press, 1971), p. 280 (italics mine). In this doctrine Scheler enjoys the para-

dox of reversing the views of ethical empiricists: the "higher" values of the "beautiful," the "holy," are not "products" of sublimated biological urges (Scheler was well acquainted with the work of Freud); rather, we would not be cognitively aware of the lower "biological" values of pleasure and pain were we not *first* aware of the realms of the beautiful and the holy.

33. Scheler refers to the four modalities as the "last and highest division of the value-qualities" (*Der Formalismus,* p. 122).

34. *Ibid.,* pp. 327–28.

Chapter Six

1. See, for example, H. Becker, "Some Forms of Sympathy: A Phenomenological Analysis."

2. Sympathy is often written by Scheler in its German form, as *Mitgefühl* (the verb is *Mitfühlen*), literally, "feeling-with." It is generally used in this form to refer to the "true" act of sympathy while *Sympathie* denotes sympathy in all of its forms. *Mitleid,* or to "suffer-with," i.e., to pity, is one of the two primary forms of true sympathy; its correlative is *Mitfreude,* "rejoice-with." Both are forms of "taking part" in a foreign self.

3. The unspoken thought in these passages seems to be that I must first be open to this person as "possibly suffering," thus as possibly possessing a value I have not yet felt; thus the moment of love enters, which, Scheler says, is the *ultimate* foundation of *Mitgefühl.*

4. We translate *Leid* as the "emotion of suffering," which as a spiritual emotion is distinct from *Schmerzen,* the feeling state of pain. For this reason, apparently, Scheler puts quotes around "same"; two people can "feel" the identical emotion, but not the identical feeling state, insofar as the latter is the localizable, physical occurrence that may or may not accompany an emotion, and thus cannot be numerically identical with the pain of another person. *Wesen und Formen der Sympathie* (Bonn: Verlag Cohen, 1926), p. 7.

5. *Ibid.,* pp. 13–14n.

6. See *supra,* Chapter 3, note 13.

7. P. A. Schlipp, "The 'Formal Problems' of Scheler's Sociology of Knowledge." See also "Max Scheler, 1874–1928," *Philosophical Review,* 38 (1929).

8. Scheler, *Wesen und Formen der Sympathie,* p. 269 f; see also *Der Formalismus in der Ethik und die materiale Wertethik (Gesammelte Werke,* vol. II), pp. 510 ff.

9. Scheler, *Wesen und Formen der Sympathie,* p. 271.

10. *Masse, Lebensgemeinschaft,* and *Gesellschaft.*

11. Scheler is well known for his identification of this ideal form of

sociation with the type represented by early Christian societies.
  12. Scheler, *Die Wissensformen und die Gesellschaft (Gesammelte Werke,* vol. II), pp. 510 ff.
  13. *Ibid.,* p. 55.
  14. Scheler, *Vom Ewigen im Menschen (Gesammelte Werke,* vol. V), pp. 92–99.
  15. *Ibid.* "...dass 'nicht nichts sei.'"' We use the term "nothingness" for *nichts* to indicate not that the mere absence or nonexistence of something is intended by Scheler here but that rather the negation of *both* essence and existence, possibility *as well as* actuality, is meant.
  16. Scheler, *Die Wissensformen,* p. 55.
  17. Scheler, *Vom Ewigen im Menschen,* p. 96.
  18. Note as well that Scheler's doctrine of the "direct givenness" of others follows from the logic of the scale: one "knows" that there are other selves before one "knows" that there are foreign bodies.
  19. Scheler, *Die Wissensformen,* p. 57.
  20. There is a logical difficulty here: it is not clear why it should follow from the fact alone that the sphere of *Mitwelt* is prior to all other spheres except that of the Absolute, that knowledge is socially *conditioned.* According to the logic of the order, it simply follows that the *givenness* of the sphere of *Mitwelt* — which Scheler identifies with that of "community" in general — is logically prior to that of, say, of the dead, extended physical world, such that knowledge of the physical world presupposes knowledge of society, of other persons — but not that the former must "condition" the latter. Surely Scheler did not wish to imply that knowledge of the sphere of the Absolute is "above" social conditioning. In any case, it is clear that he holds — as against Marx's view — that knowledge can condition social and historical developments: he writes that there can be no knowledge without social phenomena, *and conversely,* no social phenomena without knowledge; knowledge of itself is implied in the essence of community. See *Die Wissensformen,* p. 52.
  21. Of course this conditioning of the content of knowledge by the material or "biological" interests of a people is the central process in which knowledge of essence is "functionalized." There is thus no hint of "relativism" here, nor of knowledge being socially "determined" in that it is impossible to "lift oneself above" the views and prejudices of one's class, epoch, nation, etc. Scheler's doctrine *does* mean, however — and, as we recall, this was Scheler's political hope — that if there is to be *total* knowledge, all nations and peoples of the world, leaning upon historical as well as current traditions belonging to each, must unite in the common pursuit of truth. And the doctrine *does* mean, as well, that a great deal of personal purification — as Scheler outlined in the essay on the "moral preconditions" of philosophy — is needed if not necessary for overcoming the "prejudices" of one's own historical and social standpoint.

Chapter Seven

1. Our discussion is taken from the section with that title in Scheler, *Der Formalismus in der Ethik und die materiale Wertethik (Gesammelte Werke,* vol. II), pp. 300 ff.

2. For example: what is the intuition of value that founds the notion of murder in a given culture? The value of human life? Of consciousness? Of life in general? Scheler claims that intuitive reflection upon the ethical life of the given culture may alone provide an answer.

3. Scheler, "Das Ressentiment im Aufbau der Moralen," in *Vom Umsturz der Werte (Gesammelte Werke,* vol. III), p. 65.

4. See Lewis A. Coser's introduction to his edition of *Ressentiment, by Max Scheler,* translated by W. W. Holdheim (New York: Free Press of Glencoe, 1961). There Scheler is accused of being "guilty of *ressentiment*" in his "attacks upon the bourgeois spirit."

5. "*Ressentiment* can make large and over-all processes in the history of moral views as comprehensible to us as it can do the same for the little developments which we see before us in our daily lives." Scheler, "Das Ressentiment im Aufbau der Moralen," p. 63.

6. Scheler, *Die Wissensformen und die Gesellschaft (Gesammelte Werke,* vol. VIII), pp. 74-75.

7. *Ibid.,* p. 69.

8. *Ibid.,* p. 70.

9. *Ibid.,* pp. 75-76.

10. *Ibid.,* p. 78.

11. Scheler, *Philosophische Weltanschauungen,* p. 118.

12. Cf. Habermas, Jürgen. *Technik und Wissenschaft als 'Ideologie.' (Suhrkamp Verlag (Edition Suhrkamp 287), Frankfurt am Main, 1968,)* pp. 146-147.

13. H. Becker, "Befuddled Germany: A Glimpse of Max Scheler," *American Sociological Review,* VIII (April, 1943), 209.

14. Spinoza on Descartes. *Ethics,* III, introduction.

Chapter Eight

1. Scheler, *Der Formalismus in der Ethik und die materiale Wertethik (Gesammelte Werke,* vol. II), p. 395.

2. We will be considering part two of the essay "Probleme der Religion," entitled "Die Wesensphänomenologie der Religion," from *Vom Ewigen im Menschen, (Gesammelte Werke,* vol. V), pp. 157 ff.

3. Scheler held at the time of the writing of *Vom Ewigen im Menschen* that the dogma of the Catholic Church (to which he adhered *as* dogma) was "separable" from Thomistic philosophy (which he rejected in favor of his own Augustinianism). He was forced later to abandon this position.

See *Die Wissensformen und die Gesellschaft (Gesammelte Werke,* vol. VIII), p. 81.
4. Scheler, *Vom Ewigen im Menschen,* pp. 167–68.
5. Scheler sometimes refers to only two, sometimes uses other descriptive terms vaguely equivalent to the ones I have chosen here. Is this just carelessness on Scheler's part, or does it represent a desire to avoid the appearance of a rigid categorical definition of God?
6. Scheler, *Vom Ewigen im Menschen,* p. 183.
7. *Ibid.,* pp. 184–85.
8. See *Philosophische Weltanschauung* (Franke, Bern), 1954.
9. Scheler, "Probleme einer Soziologie des Wissens," in *Die Wissensformen,* p. 87.
10. *Ibid.,* p. 84.
11. *Ibid.,* p. 87.
12. Scheler, *Die Stellung des Menschen im Kosmos,* p. 42.
13. *Ibid.,* p. 74.
14. *Ibid.,* pp. 75–76.
15. *Ibid.,* p. 65.
16. *Ibid.,* p. 70.
17. *Ibid.*
18. *Ibid.,* p. 91.
19. *Ibid.,* p. 92.

Bibliography

The following list of works by and about Max Scheler is intended to direct the reader to the basic literature in a growing field and to facilitate the finding of references made in this work. A complete Scheler bibliography was published in Germany in 1965:

Hartman, Willfred, *Max Scheler*. Stuttgart: Friedrich Frommann Verlag, 1965.

This work includes secondary literature and dissertations written up to the time of its publication. In addition, a complete bibliography of materials on Scheler in English was published in 1968:

"English-Language Literature on Max Scheler." *Philosophy Today*, XII (September, 1968), 38–41.

Further, an extensive bibliography of primary and secondary sources is to be found in Ranly's study (see below), and Frings' and Staude's books both contain solid bibliographical material.

PRIMARY SOURCES

For primary sources, we must turn to:

Scheler, Max. *Gesammelte Werke*. Edited by Maria Scheler and Manfred Frings. Munich: Franke Verlag, Bern University, 1954–.

Each volume contains introductory remarks concerning the manuscripts from which the texts were taken and the conditions under which they were written; corrections; and notes that often suggest interesting comparisons between Scheler's uses of terms, tell us where other passages relating to or clarifying a given passage may be found in the body of Scheler's work, and provide similar valuable pieces of information. These additions were prepared for the *Gesammelte Werke* by the philosopher's widow, Maria Scheler. Since her death in 1969, the work of editing Scheler's manuscripts has been continued by Manfred Frings. Of the planned thirteen volumes, eight have been published at the time of this writing:

I. *Frühe Schriften*. Edited by Frings (1970). Includes the dissertation and the habilitation.
II. *Der Formalismus in der Ethik und die materiale Werthethik*. Edited by Maria Scheler (5th edition, 1966). English edition: *Formalism in Ethics and Non-Formal Ethics of Values,* translated by M. S. Frings

197

and Roger L. Frank (Evanston, Ill.: Northwestern, 1973).
   III. *Vom Umsturz der Werte.* Edited by M. Scheler. Includes "Das
        Ressentiment im Aufbau der Moralen" (English edition: *Ressenti
        ment, by Max Scheler,* edited by Lewis Coser, translated by W.W.
        Holdheim [New York: Free Press, 1961]) and "Die Idole der
        Selbsterkenntnis."
    V. *Vom Ewigen im Menschen.* Edited by M. Scheler. English edition:
        On the Eternal in Man, translated by Bernard Noble (New York:
        (Harper & Row, 1960).
   VI. *Schriften zur Soziologie und Weltanschauungslehre.* Edited by M.
        Scheler. Includes the essay on Max Weber entitled "Weltan
        schauungslehre, Soziologie und Weltanschauungssetzung."
  VII. *Wesen und Formen der Sympathie.* Edited by Frings. English trans-
        lation by P. Heath, *The Nature of Sympathy;* with a general intro-
        duction to Max Scheler's work by W. Stark (London and New
        Haven: Yale University Press, 1954). All references in the text are
        taken from the edition of Cohen Verlag, Bonn, 1926.
 VIII. *Die Wissensformen und die Gesellschaft.* Edited by M. Scheler.
        Includes "Probleme einer Soziologie des Wissens" and "Erkenntnis
        und Arbeit."
    X. *Schriften aus dem Nachlass,* vol. 1. Edited by M. Scheler. Includes
        "Ordo Amoris," "Phänomenologie und Erkenntnistheorie," and
        "Die Lehre von den drei Tatsachen." Some of these essays appear
        in *Max Scheler: Selected Philosophical Essays,* translated by
        P. Lachterman (Evanston, Ill., Northwestern, 1973).

In addition to the *Gesammelte Werke,* the following editions of works
by Scheler were used in the preparation of this study:

Wesen und Formen der Sympathie. 3rd edition. Bonn: Cohen, 1926.
Die Stellung des Menschen im Kosmos. Bern: Francke, 1966. English
   edition: *Man's Place in Nature,* edited and translated by Hans
   Meyerhoff (New York: Noonday Press, 1961).
Philosophische Weltanschauung. Dalp Tschenbucher, vol. 301. Bern:
   Francke, 1954. Includes "Philosophische Weltanschauung," "Die
   Formen des Wissens und die Bilding," "Der Mensch im Weltalter des
   Ausgleichs." English edition: *Philosophical Perspectives,* translated
   by O.A. Haag (Boston, Beacon Press, 1958).
"Idealismus-Realismus." In *Philosophischer Anzeiger,* vol. II. Bonn:
   Cohen, 1927.

Two other English translations deserve mention:

"On the Tragic." Translated by B. Stamble. *Cross Currents,* IV (1954),
   178–91.
"Problems with a Sociology of Knowledge." Translated by E. Ranly.
   Philosophy Today, XII (Spring, 1968), 42–70.

SECONDARY SOURCES

IN ENGLISH

1. Books (Comprehensive through 1974)

DECKER, ALFONS. *Process and Permanence in Ethics: Max Scheler's Moral Philosophy.* Paramus, New Jersey: Paulist/Newman Press, 1974.

FRINGS, MANFRED S. *Max Scheler: A Concise Introduction into the World of a Great Thinker.* Pittsburgh: Duquesne University Press, 1965. The first Scheler study, by the present editor of the *Gesammelte Werke.* The book is oriented toward the later works and is expository.

LUTHER, A. R. *Persons in Love: A Study of Max Scheler's "Wesen und Formen der Sympathie."* Atlantic Highlands, N.J.: Humanities Press, 1972. A study of love as the highest form of openness toward others.

RANLY, ERNEST W. *Scheler's Phenomenology of Community.* The Hague: Nijhoff, 1965. Despite its specialized title, this work presents a good general introduction to Scheler's phenomenological philosophy.

STAUDE, JOHN RAPHAEL. *Max Scheler, 1874-1928: An Intellectual Portrait.* New York: Free Press, 1967. The author bases his portrait in part upon conversations with those who knew Scheler personally. The book is also valuable as a description of life and thought in the early Weimar Republic.

2. Selected Journal Articles

BECKER, HOWARD. "Some Forms of Sympathy: A Phenomenological Analysis." *Journal of Abnormal Psychology,* XXVI (April, 1931), 58-68. An attempt to apply the typology of *Wesen und Formen der Sympathie* to empirical studies in psychology.

BUBER, MARTIN. "The Philosophical Anthropology of Max Scheler." Translated by R. G. Smith. *Philosophy and Phenomenological Research,* VI (1946), 207-11. Reflections by an outstanding contemporary on Scheler's later attempts toward a philosophy of man.

CLARKE, MARY EVELYN. "A Phenomenological System of Ethics." *Philosophy,* VII (1932), 414-30; VIII (1934), 52-65.

_____. "The Contribution of Max Scheler to the Philosophy of Religion." *Philosophical Review,* XLIII (1934), 577-97. Two lucidly written articles that were pioneers in the introduction of Scheler to English-speaking readers.

EMAD, PARVIS. "Max Scheler's Notion of the Process of Philosophy." *Southern Journal of Philosophy,* X (Spring, 1972), 7-16. The first critical appraisal of Scheler's concept of phenomenological method to appear in English.

200   MAX SCHELER

FARBER, MARVIN. "Max Scheler on the Place of Man in the Cosmos."
Philosophy and Phenomenological Research, 1953/54, pp. 393–99. A
study of one of Scheler's late essays by a man who is often a trenchant
critic of his thought.
FRINGS, MANFRED, "Max Scheler: Rarely Seen Complexities in Phenom-
enology." In *Phenomenology in Perspective,* ed. F. J. Smith, Kent
State University Press, 1961.
GUTHRIE, HUNTER. "Max Scheler's Epistemology of the Emotions."
Modern Schoolman, XVI (1939), 51–54. An early Catholic study in
English on Scheler's ethics.
HARTMAN, W. "Scheler's Theory of the Person." *Philosophy Today,*
(Winter, 1968), 246–61. Deals with Scheler's theme of the indefin-
ability of the person.
LAUER, QUENTIN. "The Phenomenological Ethics of Max Scheler." *Inter-
national Philosophical Quarterly,* I (1961). Excellent study of the
phenomenological foundations of Scheler's ethics by one of the lead-
ing American students of the phenomenological movement.
LEISS, WILLIAM. "Max Scheler's Concept of *Herrschaftswissen.*" *Philo-
sophical Forum,* II (Spring, 1971), 316–31. A critical study of
Scheler's concept of scientific and technological knowledge, a type of
knowledge that he contrasts with phenomenological knowledge and
religious knowledge.
LUTHER, A. R. "Scheler's Interpretation of Being as Loving." *Philosophy
Today,* XIV (Fall, 1970), 217–27. How Scheler's concept of love
illuminates the existential analysis of the human situation.
RANLY, ERNEST W. "Ethics in the Community." *Proceedings of the
Catholic Philosophical Association,* XLII (1968), 152–58. Traces the
role of Scheler's analysis of the person in his ethics.
SCHLIPP, PAUL ARTHUR. "The 'Formal Problems' of Scheler's Sociology
of Knowledge." *Philosophical Review,* XXXVI (1927), 101–20. One
of the first attempts in English at a genuinely critical appraisal of
Scheler's thought.
SPIEGELBERG, H. "The Phenomenology of Essences: Max Scheler
(1874–1928)." In Herbert Spiegelberg, *The Phenomenological Movement: A Historical Introduction.* (The Hague: Martinus Nijhoff
1960), I, 220–70. A useful brief introduction to Scheler's world.

Index

201

DATE DUE